Newspapers, Politics, and Public Opinion in Late Eighteenth-Century England

HANNAH BARKER

CLARENDON PRESS · OXFORD

1998

Oxford University Press, Great Clarendon Street, Oxford OX2 6DP

Oxford New York

Athens Auckland Bangkok Bogota Bombay Buenos Aires
Calcutta Cape Town Dar es Salaam Delhi Florence Hong Kong Istanbul
Karachi Kuala Lumpur Madras Madrid Melbourne Mexico City
Nairobi Paris Singapore Taipei Tokyo Toronto Warsaw
and associated companies in
Berlin Ibadan

Oxford is a registered trade mark of Oxford University Press

Published in the United States
by Oxford University Press Inc., New York

British Library Cataloguing in Publication Data

Data available

Library of Congress Cataloging in Publication Data

Barker, Hannah.

Newspapers, politics, and public opinion in late eighteenth-century
England / Hannah Barker.
p.   cm.—(Oxford historical monographs)
Includes bibliographical references and index.

1. Press and politics—Great Britain—History—18th century. 2. English
newspapers—History—18th century. 3. Public opinion—Great Britain—
History—18th century. 4. Press—Great Britain—Influence—History—18th
century. 5. Great Britain—Politics and government—1714–1837.
I. Title. II. Series.

PN5116.B37 1998
072'.09'033—dc21   98-5243

ISBN 0–19–820741–7

1 3 5 7 9 10 8 6 4 2

Typeset by Best-set Typesetter Ltd., Hong Kong
Printed in Great Britain
on acid-free paper by
Bookcraft Ltd., Midsomer-Norton
Nr. Bath, Somerset

*In memory of Greta Barker
and Bob and Vera Leonard*

ACKNOWLEDGEMENTS

I owe much to my fellow research students in eighteenth-century history at Oxford between 1990 and 1995 for their advice and friendship. I would like to thank Chris Brown, Simon Burrows, Philip Carter, Cindy McCreery, and Marius Quint, and reserve particular gratitude for Elaine Chalus and Roey Sweet, who have read and commented upon my work in its various stages. I am also grateful to Martyn Atkins, Polly Barker, and Neil Townsend, who, though eighteenth-century history was not their field, still gave important help. Others who were especially helpful in writing both the thesis and the book are Colin Brooks, David Eastwood, Joanna Innes, Frank O'Gorman, and John Stevenson, all of whom gave me valuable advice and criticism. My biggest debt, though, is to my supervisor, Paul Langford. His great knowledge, careful guidance, and cheerful encouragement have been invaluable.

Since moving to the Department of History at Keele, I have been blessed with the support of my new colleagues, who have not only offered a stimulating intellectual environment in which to work, but also allowed me a semester free from teaching in order to complete this book. I am particularly grateful to Ann Hughes and David Vincent, for reading and commenting upon my work. Others who deserve thanks are Tony Claydon and Stephen Taylor, both of whom have given me important advice, Julian Hoppit, who enlightened me concerning some of the mysteries of eighteenth-century accounting practice, and my long-suffering father, Rodney Barker, who has read practically everything I have ever written.

Vital financial support came from various sources. I would particularly like to thank Lincoln College, Oxford, for making me a Lord Crewe's Scholar between 1991 and 1993, St Cross College, Oxford, where I was Junior Research Fellow from 1994 to 1995, and the Scouloudi Foundation in association with the Institute of Historical Research, for a grant which enabled me to travel to various record offices in the summer of 1994. I am grateful to *Historical Research* for permission to reproduce 'Catering for provincial taste? Newspapers, readers and profit in late eighteenth-century England' which forms the basis of Chp. 4.

I am also grateful to Olive, Countess Fitzwilliam's Wentworth Settlement Trustees and the Director of Libraries in Sheffield for permission to quote from the Rockingham and Fitzwilliam papers held in Sheffield

Archives, and to the British Museum for allowing me to reproduce prints from their collection. I was also greatly assisted by staff from the following institutions: Berkshire Record Office, Birmingham Archives, the Bodleian Library, the Borthwick Institute of Historical Research, Bradford Record Office, the British Library, the British Museum, the Brotherton Library, the Brynmor Jones Library, Castle Howard Archives, the Centre for Kentish Studies, Essex Record Office, Gloucester Record Office, Hampshire Record Office, Humberside Record Office, Leeds Record Office, the National Register of Archives, North Yorkshire Record Office, Northamptonshire Record Office, Northumberland Record Office, Norwich Record Office, Nottinghamshire Record Office, the Public Record Office, Sheffield Archives, Shropshire Record Office, Staffordshire Record Office, Warwick County Record Office, and York City Archives.

CONTENTS

LIST OF PLATES

LIST OF FIGURES

ABBREVIATIONS

BL	British Library
BM	British Museum
DNB	*Dictionary of National Biography*, ed. Sir Leslie Stephen and Sir Sidney Lee, 22 vols. (Oxford, 1917 onwards)
EHR	*English Historical Review*
ERO	Essex Record Office
Foljambe	Nottinghamshire Record Office, Foljambe of Osberton MS
NRO	Nottinghamshire Record Office
NYRO	North Yorkshire Record Office
PCC	Public Record Office, Prerogative Court of Canterbury
Pratt	Centre for Kentish Studies, Pratt MS
PRO	Public Record Office
SRRU	Shropshire Records and Research Unit
WWM	Sheffield Archives, Wentworth Woodhouse Muniments
YCA	York City Archives

INTRODUCTION

On 21 January 1780, a London newspaper published an anonymous letter which proclaimed 'the freedom of the press is the palladium of English liberty; it is the prop and foundation of it; and when that is, by open violence, or treacherous undermining, destroyed, it will most assuredly involve in its ruin the general liberty of the subject'.[1] Such claims for the constitutional importance of newspapers were made frequently in late eighteenth-century England, where many believed that the press could act as a public tribunal in which the behaviour of the country's rulers could be judged, criticized, and ultimately kept in check. However, as the letter suggests, it was a degree of influence which was not always welcomed unconditionally by contemporaries. The political commentator Vicesimus Knox wrote of his fears concerning the potential misuse of the press, warning that although this 'grand battery' had been 'erected by the people to defend the citadel of liberty', it could, in the hands of a corrupt regime, become 'a powerful engine of oppression'.[2]

Given the power which contemporaries attributed to newspapers, the well-established historical interest in the role of the press in eighteenth-century British society is not surprising. For the last two decades, studies focusing on the growth of consumerism and the middling sorts, the rise of national sentiment and polite culture, or the vibrancy and increasing importance of popular politics, have stressed—in varying degrees—the significance of the newspaper press. In his radical reinterpretation of politics in the early years of George III's reign, John Brewer depicted newspapers as a vital component of the 'alternative structure of politics' which developed outside the narrow circle of the country's parliamentary classes.[3] More recently, H. T. Dickinson's discussion of popular politics in the eighteenth century describes the 'crucial role' played by the press

---

[1] *Gazetteer*, 21 Jan. 1780. Throughout this book 'the press' is used to refer to the newspaper press, whilst ignoring other forms of print, such as pamphlets, periodicals, ballads, and broadsides, which formed an important part of contemporary print culture, and might reasonably be presumed to come under the broad title of 'the press'. The omission of such material was dictated by limitations of time, rather than a lack of recognition of their significance to the wider picture of politics and print in eighteenth-century England.

[2] Vicesimus Knox, 'The Spirit of Despotism' [1795], in *The Works of Vicesimus Knox*, 7 vols. (London, 1824), v. 174.

[3] John Brewer, *Party, Ideology and Popular Politics at the Accession of George III* (Cambridge, 1976), 139–60. See also John Money, *Experience and Identity: Birmingham and the West Midlands, 1760–1800* (Manchester, 1977), ch. 3.

both in keeping the British people informed about political matters and in acting as 'the principal medium for the articulation and distribution of popular protests against the government'.[4] Yet although historians increasingly view the newspaper as a potent force in eighteenth-century society, accounts of its role remain sketchy and generalized. Though some important detailed work on newspapers has been done in recent years, it tends to concentrate on the earlier half of the century, or is limited in terms of geography.[5]

This book attempts to fill some of the gaps in our knowledge of newspapers in the later part of the eighteenth century. In particular, it aims to form a clearer understanding of the press's relationship with politics and with its readers, and to explore the ways in which newspapers both represented and helped shape 'public opinion'. In doing so, it will examine the changing nature of popular political debate, the role of 'the people' in politics, and the manner in which the political nation—that cornerstone of eighteenth-century political legitimacy—was thought to be composed.

By the late 1770s newspapers had assumed a powerful position in English society. They were read by a significant proportion of the population, which although socially diverse, nevertheless appears to have been linked to the wider political nation: that section of the population outside the ruling elite, which was variously thought to constitute 'the public' or 'the people', and which, despite its exclusion from government, nevertheless exercised a growing level of political influence through the medium of organized 'public opinion'. However, such terms were not applied with much rigour in the eighteenth century. 'The people' and 'the public' were often interchangeable, and to contemporaries these expressions could mean different things: Edmund Burke's estimate of the size of the political nation in the 1790s was 400,000. 'This', he claimed, 'is the British

---

[4] H. T. Dickinson, *The Politics of the People in Eighteenth-Century Britain* (Basingstoke, 1995), 204–5. See also Frank O'Gorman, *Voters, Patrons, and Parties: The Unreformed Electoral System of Hanoverian England 1734–1832* (Oxford, 1989), 286–9; Kathleen Wilson, *The Sense of the People: Politics, Culture and Imperialism in England, 1715–1785* (Cambridge, 1995), 37; Linda Colley, *Britons: Forging the Nation 1707–1827* (New Haven and London, 1992), 40–1.

[5] G. A. Cranfield, *The Development of the Provincial Newspaper, 1700–1760* (Cambridge, 1962); Money, *Experience and Identity*; Michael Harris, *London Newspapers in the Age of Walpole: A Study in the Origins of the Modern English Press* (London, 1987); Bob Harris, *A Patriot Press: National Politics and the London Press in the 1740s* (Oxford, 1993). More general studies include Jeremy Black, *The English Press in the Eighteenth Century* (Beckenham, 1987) and Bob Harris, *Politics and the Rise of the Press: Britain and France, 1620–1800* (London, 1996).

publick'.[6] The radical politician John Jebb's interpretation, on the other hand, encompassed all adult males.[7] For many in the eighteenth century, 'the people' described those whose constitutional standing, education, or wealth gave them a legitimate say in the nation's affairs; for others, the term was synonymous with the mob. Such varieties of meaning often arose from political expediency. Few political activists, in or out of power, would not have claimed to represent, or to aim to protect, the public interest, although many might have wished to limit the numbers, or more importantly, the social status, of those whom they supposedly served. Contemporaries were vague and divided, and it is equally difficult to pin down definitions for 'the people', 'the public', and 'public opinion' within existing historiography. However, despite such ambiguities, it seems evident that eighteenth-century Britain witnessed the emergence of a dynamic extra-parliamentary political culture, and that many contemporaries believed that beyond the world of the political elite, opinion was being formed and expressed which was at once powerful, coherent, and legitimate.[8]

In this context, and for the purposes of this book, public opinion can be perhaps best described as a body of argument or discussion about (amongst other things) government, but not conducted within the limits of governing institutions nor confined to a governing class. It involved a kind or level of activity wider than the private, the domestic, or the narrowly economic, and at the same time broader than the private or semi-private communications of government. Its existence depended on the belief that those who participated in and constituted it—'the people' or 'the public'—were more than simply subjects, and were in some sense citizens. These individuals were thought to have a legitimate interest in the public affairs of their nation which they could pursue and express without either challenging the broad constitutional structures within which they lived, or aspiring to take part in the direct management of

---

[6] Edmund Burke, 'First Letter on a Regicide Peace' [1796], in *The Works of the Right Honourable Edmund Burke*, 8 vols. (London, 1854–71), viii. 140.

[7] John Jebb, *The Works Theological, Medical, Political, and Miscellaneous of John Jebb . . . With Memoirs of the Life of the Author*, ed. John Disney, 3 vols. (London, 1787), i. 147.

[8] In particular see Brewer, *Party Ideology and Popular Politics*; E. P. Thompson, 'Eighteenth-Century English Society: Class Struggle without Class?', *Social History*, 3 (1978), 123–65; Nicholas Rogers, *Whigs and Cities: Popular Politics in the Age of Walpole and Pitt* (Oxford, 1989); O'Gorman, *Voters, Patrons, and Parties*; Colley, *Britons*; Wilson, *Sense of the People*.

those structures. For although 'the public', and 'the people' in particular, were often conceived of as having interests in opposition to those in power, 'public opinion' in England was not revolutionary. It was instead a tribunal based outside the political structures of the state where state power could be judged and criticized by those who deemed themselves fit to be included within the boundaries of the political nation.

Newspaper editors who presumed to represent the 'voice of the people' in their publications were not alone in identifying the newspaper-reading public with the wider political nation. Those who wrote in and about the press, and those who sought to manipulate it for political ends, also acknowledged its power to influence public opinion. Hence the belief that newspapers had a significant constitutional role, acting to check government corruption and defend Englishmen's liberties. The importance attributed to the press is hardly surprising, since newspaper contents were highly political. For most of the population it was information and ideas gleaned from newspapers which made possible any kind of informed political debate: the essential prerequisite for the formation of opinion.

Because of the perceived influence of the press, politicians actively sought to determine its political contents. However, it will be argued that despite their endeavours, politically motivated individuals and groups exercised only limited influence, and were rarely able to dictate the political stance of newspapers, which were profitable businesses reliant upon the money raised from sales and advertising rather than political subsidies. The need to maintain extensive distributions meant that newspapers were dependent not upon political patronage, but upon their appeal to readers. The political debate which took place in the capital's press was thus far more open and less dependent upon Westminster than would have been the case if newspapers had been mere party organs. Instead newspapers represented a genuinely wide body of opinion which engaged in a vigorous and frequently polarized debate. Outside London, and in the face of competition from the capital's press, provincial papers provided a uniquely local view of politics and events, for readerships which were—on the whole—more homogeneous than in the capital. In both cases, newspaper politics appear to have been shaped less by politicians than by a desire on the part of editors to engage with public opinion.

Newspapers produced both in London and the provinces presented the nation's political life as something in which their readers could and should participate. In so doing they remind us that the separation by historians of 'high' and 'low', or popular, politics is often an artificial one. Although both possessed their own dynamic, elite and popular political worlds in eighteenth-century England interacted with each other, and indeed, frequently overlapped, in ways which render many historically imposed boundaries meaningless. In newspapers, letters to the editor offered the public the opportunity to contribute to public debate. Individuals were encouraged by the press to exercise their constitutional rights, and the familiarity with which those in government were described assumed that the well-informed reader had a degree of political knowledge which made her or him more than just a passive observer. Yet this inclusive approach was not all-embracing. Provincial newspapers could be particularly restrictive in the ways in which they represented the political nation—according to property ownership, political independence, and 'respectability'—in contrast to much of the London press, where a more radical interpretation of 'the people' was frequently employed. Since the newspaper press as a whole sought to appeal to its readers and to instil in them a belief that they were members of a rational, concerned, and influential public, this suggests geographical differences in newspaper readership, with the audience in the capital being more socially diverse than elsewhere. By implication, provincial public opinion may have been formed by a narrower cross-section of the population. However, this dichotomy is by no means clear, since the ways in which newspapers defined the political nation were often intentionally vague and were subject to change. This was apparent during the 1780s, when debates about reform prompted a shift in focus amongst both London and provincial newspapers. During this period, the affairs of 'high' politics made room for discussions of popular sovereignty, and the political nation became less rigidly defined.

The reform debate, promoted largely by members of the Association movement, constitutes an important component of this book. As a broad-based political organization, linked to both 'high' and 'low' politics on a nationwide basis, the Association, or reform, movement of 1779–85 provides a useful focus for an examination of newspapers, politics, and public opinion in this period. The first reform agitation began in Yorkshire in December 1779, when several members of the local gentry, led by Christopher Wyvill, called a county meeting to discuss 'economical reform'. The resulting parliamentary petition, signed by over 8,000 freeholders, alleged that government squandering of public money had allowed the Crown to gain undue political influence over the House of Commons, and that traditional liberties were being threatened as a result. In the hopes of ending corruption in Parliament, the Yorkshire petitioners demanded a number of reforming measures from the government, including the abolition of sinecures and unmerited pensions and the reduction of exorbitant emoluments.

Such moderate proposals were soon overtaken by the more ambitious plans for parliamentary reform put forward by more radical groups in London and elsewhere, and by the Yorkshire reformers themselves. In 1780, Wyvill and his followers began to campaign for triennial parliaments and additional seats in the Commons for one hundred 'knights of the shire': county MPs who were believed to be particularly immune to Crown-inspired corruption. Lord Rockingham, a powerful player in Yorkshire politics and leader of the Rockingham Whigs in Parliament, had initially encouraged the movement as an irritant to the government, but by early 1780, he was already alarmed at the direction being taken, and unsuccessfully attempted to rein it in.[9] Until Rockingham's death in 1782, Wyvill continued attempts to conciliate him and win parliamentary backing for his reforms. His efforts proved as unsuccessful with Rockingham as subsequently with politicians such as William Pitt. Despite proclaiming their support for a change in the representative system, most MPs lacked the political will to produce modifications of any substance. Even Charles James Fox, whose hold over the radical Westminster committee was to become increasingly tight between 1780 and 1782, seems to have lacked any real conviction to enact reform, as was demonstrated once he attained office.

Radical reformers, most influential in the capital, dismissed the piecemeal alterations proposed by those in Yorkshire in favour of far more sweeping plans for changes in parliamentary representation, such as annual parliaments, universal male suffrage, and a more 'equal representation' of the people (to be achieved by redistributing parliamentary seats according to the size of the electorate and abolishing the notorious rotten boroughs). John Jebb, a leading light in the radical London reform movement, argued that a popular association could dictate to Parliament and even supersede it if the Commons failed to represent the people: 'the members of the House of Commons sit, not in their own right, (like the king and nobles) but as proxies for others; and the proxy ought, in all reason, to be regarded as annihilated when the voice of the principal shall be thus distinctly heard'. Furthermore, he maintained that the people had

---

[9] Herbert Butterfield, *George III, Lord North and the People: 1779–1780* (London, 1949), 278; Ian R. Christie, *Wilkes, Wyvill and Reform: The Parliamentary Reform Movement in British Politics 1760–1785* (London, 1962), pp. 102–3; Eugene Charlton Black, *The Association: British Extra-parliamentary Political Organization, 1769–1793* (Cambridge, Mass., 1963), 52.

the right to dictate new terms for electing members and convening Parliament with which they could force the other branches of the legislature to comply by withholding taxes, in order to ensure 'the blessing of an equal, annual, and universal representation of the commons'.[10]

Just as Wyvill had attempted to win the support of parliamentary politicians by a process of persuasion and conciliation, so he tried to prevent divisions within the reform movement as a whole by appealing to the radicals to moderate their proposals. However, here also Wyvill met with little success, and as early as January 1780, he began to dissociate the Yorkshire reformers publicly from the radicals' 'extreme' principles, stressing that county associations set up to promote reform should use only 'legal and constitutional' means.[11] Wyvill's failure to unite the movement did not augur well for its prospects of success. Despite meetings of representatives from various county associations being held in 1780 and 1781, and a renewed petitioning campaign in 1783, only minor reforms were enacted by Parliament in 1782, whilst there were just fleeting prospects of legislative change in 1780, 1783, and 1785, when Burke and then Pitt introduced half-hearted and inadequately supported reform bills.

Yet although the reform movement ultimately failed to achieve its aims, it had substantial political impact at most levels of political life. Moreover, reformers and their organizations could be found throughout the country, influencing events and political debate at both local and national levels. This, and attempts by both reformers and their enemies to influence the press, meant that the reform issue was given extensive coverage in newspapers throughout England. The debate over reform which took place in the press reflected popular politics which were both vigorous and dynamic as well as complex and often factional. Newspaper evidence suggests that the provinces witnessed variations in political opinion according to region, as well as sharp divisions within localities, whilst in the capital public debate was even more prone to rifts. Across the country, the discussion of reform appears to have had profound implications for the way Englishmen and women thought about the constitution, about individual rights and liberties, and about their representation in government.

This book is divided into two parts: the first devoted to an examination of the capital's press and the second to provincial newspapers. Chapter 1

---

[10] *Works of John Jebb*, ii. 475–81.
[11] See the letter by 'A Yorkshire Freeholder' in the *London Courant*, 8 Jan. 1780; *London Evening Post*, 8 Jan. 1780; also *York Chronicle*, 14 Jan. 1780; *York Courant*, 18 and 25 Jan. 1780.

looks at the influence and readership of London newspapers, and together with Chapter 2, explores the ways in which the press was run and considers the degree to which its contents were politically manipulated. By studying, amongst other things, newspaper finances, it argues that attracting readers was of more importance to editors than receiving political bribes, and that the contents of the capital's newspapers were shaped accordingly. Chapter 3 examines the debate over reform which took place in London papers and the way in which 'the public' was defined.

Opening the discussion of the provincial press, Chapter 4 describes the proliferation of newspapers outside the capital in the eighteenth century and questions the assumption that provincial papers were small-scale, amateurish, and merely regurgitated versions of their London counterparts. Instead, as was the case in the capital, newspapers in the provinces relied on attracting significant numbers of readers, and did this by exploiting, through their contents, a peculiarly local appeal. Chapter 5 assesses the influence that provincial newspapers wielded in the areas they served, and explores the degree to which politicians could determine newspaper politics. Finally, Chapter 6 uses contemporary correspondence to examine the relationship between public opinion and newspaper contents in the provinces, as well as studying the ways in which definitions of 'the public' contrasted with those found in London.

I

NEWSPAPERS AND NEWSPAPER READERS IN LONDON

The serious study of eighteenth-century newspaper history began in 1850 with F. Knight Hunt's *The Fourth Estate: Contributions towards a History of Newspapers, and the Liberty of the Press*.[1] As its title suggests, *The Fourth Estate* depicted the emergence of press freedom in England and the eventual establishment of newspapers as the bulwark of British democracy: the 'fourth estate' of the constitution. Hunt's rather Whiggish interpretation of newspaper history—which presents the heroic struggle of the newspaper to wrest itself from the corruption of eighteenth-century politics—was soon followed by other studies in a similar vein.[2] In one work, James Grant claimed that the press had a mission 'to enlighten, to civilize, and to morally transform the world.'[3] As an ex-newspaper editor, Grant's sentiments about the press in contemporary society necessarily coloured his view of its past history (as did the dependency of his and other such works on uncritical readings of eighteenth-century memoirs).[4] Yet the research of many press historians of this century continues to be dominated by the original Whig thesis mapping the rise of English newspapers from the mire of eighteenth-century corruption to the glorious independence of

---

[1] F. Knight Hunt, *The Fourth Estate: Contributions towards a History of Newspapers, and of the Liberty of the Press* (London, 1850). James Savage's *An Account of the London Daily Newspapers, and the Manner in Which They Are Conducted* (London, 1811) did appear in the early 19th cent., but it was largely a study of contemporary newspapers, and the historical information which was included was sketchy at best.

[2] Alexander Andrews, *The History of British Journalism, from the Foundation of the Newspaper Press in England, to the Repeal of the Stamp Act in 1855, with Sketches of Press Celebrities*, 2 vols. (London, 1859); Charles Pebody, *English Journalism, and the Men Who Have Made It* (London, 1882); H. R. Fox Bourne, *English Newspapers: Chapters in the History of Journalism*, 2 vols. (London, 1887); James Grant, *The Newspaper Press: Its Origin, Progress, and Present Position* (London, 1871).

[3] Grant, *The Newspaper Press*, p. vi.

[4] Prominent amongst these were John Almon, *Memoirs of a Late Eminent Bookseller* (London, 1790); John Benjafield, *Statement of Facts* (Bury St Edmunds, [1813]); John Taylor, *Records of My Life*, 2 vols. (London, 1832); and William Jerdan, *The Autobiography of William Jerdan*, 4 vols. (London, 1832).

the Victorian age.[5] This model of newspaper history has profound and misleading implications for the portrayal of the eighteenth-century press. The underlying assumption that newspapers in eighteenth-century England had been rendered impotent by political corruption and manipulation is in need of extensive revision.

The Power of the Press

Although some historians of eighteenth-century England are cautious not to attribute too much importance to newspapers in Hanoverian society, contemporaries appeared to be in no doubt that the press was influential at most levels of political life. By the later part of the century, the debate concerning the liberty of the press, and the argument linking it to Englishmen's freedom, was well rehearsed (particularly by the newspapers themselves). So too was the condemnation of newspapers which overstepped their bounds as 'guardians of the constitution' and became absorbed with gossip and invective. This remained a constant cause of complaint, not just because it was seen as disrespectful, but more importantly, because it was viewed as a misuse of power.[6]

In March 1782, Dennis O'Bryen made clear his belief in the importance of newspapers when he wrote to Edmund Burke hoping to secure a place for himself under the new Rockingham administration. In exchange for this act of patronage, O'Bryen offered his services 'to secure the press in the interest of the new ministry', for which, he claimed, Sheridan had already hinted an attempt might be made. O'Bryen was in no doubt as to the wisdom of such a measure:

Whether the effort shall, or shall not be made, I know not, but perfectly confident I am, the effort ought to be made and he who should urge against it, that as this administration was constituted by the Leaders of the people and fully possessed

---

[5] Examples include: William Wickwar, *The Struggle for the Freedom of the Press* (London, 1928); Laurence Hanson, *Government and the Press, 1695–1763* (Oxford, 1936); A. Aspinall, *Politics and the Press: c. 1780–1850* (London, 1949); Harold Herd, *The March of Journalism: The Story of the British Press from 1622 to the Present Day* (London, 1952); Frederick Siebert, *Freedom of the Press in England, 1476–1776: The Rise and Fall of Government Control* (Urbana, Ill., 1965).

[6] For an examination of how these issues were dealt with in the preceding two decades, see Eckhart Hellmuth, ' "The Palladium of All Other English Liberties": Reflections on the Liberty of the Press in England during the 1760s and 1770s', in Eckhart Hellmuth (ed.), *The Transformation of Political Culture: England and Germany in the Late Eighteenth Century* (Oxford, 1990), 467–501. For discussions of press freedom earlier in the century, see J. A. W. Gunn, *Beyond Liberty and Property: The Process of Self-Recognition in Eighteenth-Century Political Thought* (Kingston, Ont., 1983), 88–9; Bob Harris, *A Patriot Press: National Politics and the London Press in the 1740s* (Oxford, 1993), 31–3.

the hearts of the people, to the people only it should trust for support, and not to the miserable aid of the press, I am sure would argue with more spirit than wisdom, and with more candor than discernment—he should reflect that this very people, with collective sense, is a giddy monster, very transitive, very uncertain, and although capable of great public virtue, that is just as capable of great public baseness, and public folly. Human nature is suseaptive [*sic*], and no animal of the creation is so facile of fluctuation as man himself, and the effect of the press proves this changeable quality beyond dispute.—Let newspapers be held ever so contemptible, and they cannot be held more contemptible than they deserve, that they have a most important influence upon the multitude is demonstrable—I am sure they made no trifling part of that place, which rendered your talents, and those of men like you, of so little efficiency, for seventeen years.[7]

O'Bryen had vested interests in making such a statement, but he was not alone in believing newspapers to be highly influential. Philip Yorke wrote in December 1784 that 'the publication of the debates and opposition speeches have lost America'.[8] The writer 'D W', in a letter found amongst the Pelham papers, asserted that 'the Press is a power seldom much inferior;—sometimes superior to the Government'. 'D W' claimed that Shelburne had been forced out of office in 1783 when 'the Literary hounds, well packed & well fed, opened on the Premier, and worried him out of his Place, his Reputation, & even his private Character'.[9] The Whig writer, Vicesimus Knox, was equally convinced of the influence which newspapers could wield:

Perhaps there is nothing which contributes so much to diffuse the spirit of despotism as venal newspapers, hired by the possessors of power, for the purpose of defending and prolonging their possession. The more ignorant classes have a wonderful propensity to be credulous in all that they see in print, and will obstinately continue to believe a newspaper, to which they have been accustomed, even when notorious facts give it the lie.[10]

Knox's arguments were echoed by the Marquis of Buckingham in 1789, who warned Grenville that Fox had bought up all the newspapers except one, so that 'the cry of the mob will be turned against you'.[11]

---

[7] O'Bryen to Burke, Mar. 1782, WWM, BK 1/1557.

[8] Cited by Jeremy Black, in 'Flying a Kite: The Political Impact of the Eighteenth-Century British Press', *Journal of Newspaper and Periodical History*, 1 (1984), 12–19, p. 13.

[9] MS letter, signed 'D W' and entitled 'Observations on ye Press' [1803?], BL, Add. MS 33124, fos. 79–81.

[10] Knox, *Works of Vicesimus Knox*, v. 174.

[11] Marquis of Buckingham to William Grenville, 15 Jan. 1789, in Historical Manuscripts Commission, *The Manuscripts of J. B. Fortescue, Esq, Preserved at Dropmore*, 9 vols. (London, 1892), i. 400.

Despite their rather mixed reputation, newspapers themselves were confident about their right to comment upon, and to criticize, the way the nation's political affairs were conducted. During the 1780s the press assumed a traditionally strong defence of its role as protector of the constitution and champion of the people's freedom: 'the palladium of English liberty'. A letter to the Duke of Portland published in the *London Courant* in August 1781 commented that 'of all the blessings incident to our happy constitution, that of the liberty of the press is undoubtedly the greatest. The dread Ministers discover at it, and the many years they have laboured to destroy it, is the best criterion by which its value can be estimated'.[12] A few months later, the *Courant* described itself as a 'watchful guardian over the rights of the people, and the interests of the state'.[13] In 1784, the *Public Advertiser* claimed that 'where the press is free, the people may be sometimes misled, but can never be enslaved. It is the Sun which illuminates the Human Mind, and dispels the dark clouds of ignorance and error'.[14]

However, 'Alfred', in the *Public Advertiser*, was one of many who defended the liberty of the press, but attacked its 'licentiousness'.[15] 'Frankly', in the *Morning Post*, stated that 'the freedom of the press is justly deemed the bulwark of English liberty, and, in my opinion, the licentiousness of the press ought equally to be dreaded as the bane of the English constitution'.[16] In the same paper, on 7 November, 'The Examiner' asserted that

It must be granted that many of our public miseries and dissensions may be ascribed to the abuse of the daily vehicles of intelligence, which are too often employed in the service of faction, to circulate false alarms, ill-grounded invectives against Government, misrepresentations of the Legislature, and indecent calumnies against Majesty itself. By this means, the minds of the people, who draw their information, and form their political creeds in a great measure from these sources, are poisoned traitors, and in the mask of patriotism, make good men unhappy under the most excellent government. But these inconveniences should not lead the lovers of their country to condemn the Liberty of the Press, but to guard against the perversions of this inestimable blessing.

This sentiment was echoed by 'Candor' in the *London Courant*:

I am a warm friend to the Liberty of the Press, but, in order to make that liberty beneficial instead of hurtful to the state, I think it ought to be exercised with a due

---

[12] *London Courant*, 3 Aug. 1781. See also ibid. 25 Nov. 1780 and 10 Dec. 1781.
[13] Ibid. 14 Nov. 1781.   [14] *Public Advertiser*, 21 Jan. 1784.
[15] Ibid. 28 Jan. 1780.   [16] *Morning Post*, 21 July 1780.

regard to decency, and that it ought not to swallow up every other liberty. I object not to your news-paper correspondents, when they attempt to answer the arguments used in the House of Commons, and they state these arguments fairly; but when they discover a disposition to intimidate gentlemen from delivering their sentiments freely in that House, by recurring to personalities and abuse, I own I disapprove highly of that exercise of the Liberty of the Press.[17]

Another attack on such behaviour in the *Town and Country Magazine* charged John Almon, editor of the *Courant*, with inserting false scandals and other lies merely to increase his paper's sales.[18]

However, foreign visitors were more likely to write in praise of the way England's press conducted itself than to censure it. The Swiss writer Jean Louis de Lolme described the liberty of the press as being the 'extreme security' of the English constitution:

it is the public notoriety of all things, that constitutes the supplemental power, or check, which . . . is so useful to remedy the unavoidable insufficiency of the laws, and keep within their respective bounds all those persons who enjoy any share of public authority. As they are thereby sensible that all their actions are exposed to public view, they dare not venture upon those acts of partiality, those secret connivances at the iniquities of particular persons, or those vexatious practices, which the Man in office is but too apt to be guilty of, when, exercising his office at a distance from the public eye, and as it were in a corner, he is satisfied that provided he be cautious, he may dispense with being just.[19]

Another foreigner, although writing at a later date, expressed similar views. Christian Goede described the liberty of the press as 'an invaluable palladium' which the English people held 'by the right of prescription', and in which 'public characters, public bodies, or objects comprehending the national welfare, are all liable to be called before the tribunal of the public'.[20] Indeed, such arguments were also adopted by politicians themselves. In a speech to the House of Commons on 3 July 1789, concerning Pitt's plan to raise the duty on newspapers, Sheridan proclaimed that 'he was a friend to newspapers not merely because they blazoned forth the virtues of the present administration, but because they proclaimed its deeds'.[21]

One way in which newspapers proclaimed the deeds of government was

[17] *London Courant*, 15 Nov. 1780.

[18] *Town and Country Magazine*, Dec. 1780, 127–9.

[19] Jean Louis de Lolme, *The Constitution of England, or an Account of the English Government* (London, 1784), 299–300.

[20] Christian August Gottlieb Goede, *The Stranger in England: or, Travels in Great Britain*, 3 vols. (London, 1807), i. 216.

[21] Cited in Walter Sichel, *Sheridan*, 2 vols. (London, 1909), ii. 198.

by publishing accounts of parliamentary debates. In doing so, newspapers made the official business of both houses publicly accessible, and encouraged wider notions of accountability and openness in government. The publication of division lists on certain controversial issues, another practice of some standing, meant that the newspaper audience could also discover not only what was said, but also how individual MPs voted. This tactic was particularly popular amongst those papers which campaigned for parliamentary reform. The *London Evening Post* published the division on Burke's Bill on 14 March 1780, as did the *London Courant*, which later attacked individual MPs who had voted for Dunning's motion criticizing the influence of the Crown on 6 April, only to side subsequently with the government. The *Courant* referred to these men as the 'duck and drake members . . . who one moment, with seeming manliness, hold up their heads in defence of the public, and the next sink under the flood of corruption'.[22] The same pro-reform papers which printed the division lists also supported the demand that MPs should represent directly the wishes of their constituents and advocated the 'testing' of MPs.

It was only newspaper coverage of parliamentary affairs that allowed 'Honestus', writing in the *London Courant*, to urge electors to 'keep a watchful eye' over their parliamentary representatives.[23] In the same paper, 'Alfred',[24] a regular campaigner for the restoration of Britain's 'ancient constitution', suggested that

opposite to the name of every member, whose character we would exhibit to his constituents, let us not only mark the vote he gave in every constitutional question of importance, but also place portions of the speeches, fairly quoted, which he has made in Parliament . . . and then let every man, on reading them, be left to draw his own inference, and form his own idea of the faithfulness of the representative, in discharge of his duty.[25]

On 1 April 1785, the *Morning Post*, by now firmly in the pro-reform camp, asserted that

---

[22] *London Courant*, 18 Apr. 1780.

[23] Ibid. 6 Oct. 1780.

[24] This, and other letters by 'Alfred', were probably the work of the radical reformer John Jebb. His collected works include addresses 'to the People of England' from 'Alfred', which appeared in the newspapers. He also used the pseudonyms 'Hampden', 'Mentor', and 'Lælius': *Works of John Jebb, passim*.

[25] *London Courant*, 9 Mar. 1781. The publication of division lists had taken place from the early part of the century. Sometimes called 'black lists', they were intended as propaganda: Aubrey Newman, 'Introduction', and P. D. G. Thomas, 'Division Lists, 1760–74', in Aubrey Newman (ed.), *The Parliamentary Lists of the Early Eighteenth Century: Their Compilation and Use* (Leicester, 1973), 14 and 43–4.

the public prints, with a spirit that does honour to the independence of the press, have frequently proclaimed the names of those Members who on any great question have been inimical to the sense of the people; the same line of conduct should be now pursued, and the same provision held out *in terrorem* of marking the delinquents on that great national business, a Parliamentary Reform, which will certainly be brought before Parliament in the course of next week.

Newspapers were not alone in assuming that the press had an important constitutional role as a facilitator of accountable, responsible government. In May 1780, the *General Evening Post* reported that a complaint had been made in the commons on 18 May by David Hartley because the Strangers' Gallery had been closed. Hartley is quoted as saying that

the people of England were at this time peculiarly interested in the conduct of their representatives, and . . . it was neither fair, nor decent, to shut them out, and prevent them from hearing the reasons given both for and against the measures proposed by gentlemen on either side of the house. Mr Hartley, argued this point in a very handsome way on the part of the people, and put the impression, which shutting the doors made upon the minds of their constituents, in various points of view, each tending to shew, that the measure was likely to produce a bad effect without doors, without answering one good purpose within.

He was supported by another MP, who argued that 'the public should know what was done within those walls'.[26] For most Englishmen and women not connected to the political elite, newspapers were the main source of parliamentary information. As one writer to the *St. James's Chronicle* noted, 'out Doors people' were dependent upon newspapers 'to deliver with accuracy the debates of our representatives.'[27] It was for this reason, and in spite of a professed dislike in both houses of the practice, that some MPs actively encouraged the publication of parliamentary debates by providing newspapers with reports of the proceedings. This must have been the case during February 1778, when the Gallery was closed to strangers and yet the *Gazetteer* continued to carry brief abstracts of the debates,[28] and also when division lists were published, as the Gallery was also closed during votes.[29]

When MPs sent texts of their speeches to the papers, their motivation appears to have been for personal or for 'party' propaganda purposes, rather than an altruistic desire to keep the public informed of events. The

[26] *General Evening Post*, 18 May 1780.
[27] *St. James's Chronicle*, 12 Dec. 1780.
[28] Robert L. Haig, *The Gazetteer, 1735–1797: A Study in the Eighteenth-Century English Newspaper* (Carbondale, Ill., 1960), 167.
[29] Thomas, 'Division Lists', 45.

younger Pitt visited the House of Commons in 1780, and noted the differences between the original and the newspaper versions of speeches. On one occasion he wrote that 'Burkes Extempores have both Times exceeded his corrected Publication, which (entre nous) is in my opinion much the worse for revision'.[30] Horace Walpole accused both John Wilkes and Temple Luttrell of having their speeches printed.[31] John Taylor, the editor of the *Morning Post* from 1788 until 1790, recorded an incident when Wilkes begged permission to make a speech in the House of Commons because, he said, 'I have sent a copy to the "Public Advertiser", and how ridiculous should I appear if it were published without having been delivered'.[32] Few MPs were as brazen about sending their speeches to the papers, a practice which seems to have left them open to ridicule. In January 1782, for example, the *General Advertiser* mocked 'a young Member of Parliament, who has made two or three speeches which nobody understood even after he had sent them to the newspaper.'[33] The same paper attacked John Luttrell on 12 May 1783, asking:

what can possibly induce him to send his long speeches to a certain morning paper, thereby occupying never less than three columns, and depriving the public of reading a great deal of much better sense.—It is really grown quite a tax on the Morning Chronicle, for when expectation is on tip-toe, for an account of Mr. Fox's, Mr. Pitt's, and the speeches of other able men, we find a most interesting debate either mutilated, or lost by the absurd vanity of the hon. gentleman alluded to.

Similar ridicule was heaped upon Lord Mahon in a paragraph published in the *Morning Chronicle* in February 1784. 'The publick may be assured', it noted, 'that not twenty words of *the rhapsody* which has appeared in the

[30] Pitt to Edward James Eliot, 14 Mar. [1780], cited in John Ehrman, *The Younger Pitt: The Years of Acclaim* (London, 1969), 21. Burke's speech on American taxation in 1774, and that on Conciliation the following year, can be seen as landmarks in terms of MPs consciously appealing to the public via their Commons speeches. At a time when the publication of parliamentary speeches and debates was becoming increasingly common, Burke deliberately set out to exploit the new medium of the press: see *The Writings and Speeches of Edmund Burke. Vol. II. Party, Parliament, and the American Crisis, 1766–1774*, ed. Paul Langford (Oxford, 1981), 24 and 406–62; *The Parliamentary History of England, From the Earliest Period to the Year 1803*, 36 vols. (London, 1806–20), xvii. 1215–69 and xviii. 478–538. See also Christopher Reid, *Edmund Burke and the Practice of Political Writing* (Dublin, 1985), 118–36. However, Burke was also amongst those MPs who complained that their parliamentary speeches were reported incorrectly by newspapers: see *Party, Parliament, and the American Crisis*, 32–5; Dror Wahrman, 'Virtual Representation: Parliamentary Reporting and Languages of Class in the 1790s', *Past and Present*, 136 (1992), 83–113, pp. 88–9.

[31] Horace Walpole, *Horace Walpole's Correspondence*, ed. W. S. Lewis, 48 vols. (London, 1937–83), xxxiii. 147.

[32] Taylor, *Records of My Life*, i. 114.

[33] *General Advertiser*, 7 Jan. 1782.

papers as Lord Mahon's speech in the House of Commons, were in fact uttered by the noble bawler'.[34]

As some of these comments make clear, speeches given in Parliament may have been altered significantly by the time they appeared in print. Many politicians were concerned not just to have their views made public, but that these views should be properly and eloquently expressed. An advertisement for the *New Parliamentary Register* attacked misleading reports of parliamentary proceedings,

which has excited the complaints of some of the most distinguished Members of either House, who (virtuously supposing themselves accountable, in their legislative character, to the Public) have seen, with indignation and concern, that pretended copies of their speeches, wilfully misrepresented to serve the views of party, ascribed to them, ideas which they never could have given utterence, as they were incapable of entertaining them.[35]

The *London Courant* of 17 December 1781 contained a letter from the MP John Webb, contradicting the report of his speech on the Navy which had appeared in the *Morning Herald*. In December 1784, Lord Camden complained to his daughter that his recent speech had been 'better than the papers have represented it'.[36] However, on an earlier occasion, Camden had written to his son-in-law and noted rather proudly that 'I am apt to think what I s[ai]d was material, because I find this morning the whole substance of my argument is industriously supplied in all the daily papers'.[37]

Examining the papers of newspaper editors provides further proof of politicians' desire to influence reports of their own speeches. John Almon's correspondence contains letters from several politicians, some of whom ask him to publish their parliamentary speeches in his paper, the *London Courant*. Two undated letters, which appear to have been written in 1765 and 1779, are from the MPs Nicholson Calvert and Lord Bristol respectively. Calvert appeared very concerned that the wording of his speech should remain unaltered.[38] He claims his written version to have been 'literally the same as spoken in the House, w[i]thout the least

---

[34] *Morning Chronicle*, 25 Feb. 1784.

[35] *London Courant*, 19 May 1781.

[36] Sir Charles Pratt, 1st Earl of Camden to Fanny Stewart, 4 Dec. 1784, Pratt, C173/90.

[37] Camden to Robert Stewart, 2 June 1780, Pratt, C173/63.

[38] BL, Add. MS 20733, fo. 28. *Parliamentary History*, xvi. 40–5 and 108–10, records that Calvert spoke in the Commons on 4 Mar. 1765, in a debate respecting the dismissal of General Conway, and on the Stamp Act on 14 Jan. 1766, in a debate concerning an address of thanks for the King's speech. His attack on the Stamp Act in 1766 represented a complete change of heart on Calvert's part, since the year before he had voted in favour of it, and this might explain some of his anxiousness in his letter to Almon.

addition or diminution', and promises Almon further speeches in the following month. Lord Bristol wrote to Almon that,

as last night's debate was a very [essential?] one, and one I should not wish Ld. Sandwich's Morning Post, to misrepresent me in to the Public: I beg you to publish this in yr paper tomorrow—& to put it in any of the Ev'ning papers you please; with[ou]t saying you had it from me—I have sat down this morning to recollect all that [passed?] as near as I can, & believe is really almost word for word what I said—as my memory seldom fails me;—I send you also the motion least you s[houl]d not have an authentick copy, & will ever be glad to contribute to yr useful paper by any thing I learn that may be proper to convey to the Public.[39]

More complicated arrangements emerge from the correspondence of William Woodfall, the printer and editor of the *Morning Chronicle*, with the politician William Adam.[40] On 9 December 1780, Woodfall wrote complaining that he had been promised a copy of Sir Hugh Palliser's speech on Admiral Keppel's court-martial by 'a friend of Sir Hugh' who 'called upon me on Monday evening while I was scribbling'.[41] This speech had not been sent, despite the receipt of three notes confirming that its arrival was imminent. It seems Woodfall's badgering was rewarded, for a four and a half column version of the speech finally appeared in the *Chronicle* four days later. In another letter, dated 24 February 1784, Woodfall wrote to Adam concerning an important debate on the removal of the coalition by the King:

I intended in to-morrow's paper to have given an account of Mr. Fox's most admirable speech of Friday last, accompanied with Mr. Pitt's. The later [*sic*] has been sent me from their party; but when I went down to the House this day, I had not written more than a column of the former, and from the effect of the extreme fatigue of the past week, find myself wholly incapable of doing that justice to Mr. Fox that I had wished, and the speech so well deserved. Can you help me by loosely throwing upon paper any points you recollect to be strongly put which have not appeared or have not been given in the papers already? I will readily and thankfully take the trouble of weaving them into my manufacture. I wrote to

[39] BL, Add. MS 20733, fo. 16. In Apr. 1779, Bristol was involved in a series of debates concerning the Admiralty. On the 23rd, he put forward a motion to have the Earl of Sandwich removed as First Lord of the Admiralty, which was defeated by 78 votes to 39: *Parliamentary History*, xx. 426–7.

[40] Blair Adam MS, letters from which are printed in an appendix to Aspinall, *Politics and the Press*, 433–44. Adam was appointed Treasurer of the Ordinance by North in Sept. 1780, and became North's 'intimate friend and defender'. He was later involved in the alliance of the North party with the Foxites, and 'bore a major responsibility' for the Coalition's formation: *The History of Parliament: the House of Commons, 1754–1790*, ed. Sir Lewis Namier and John Brooke, 3 vols. (London, 1964) ii. 8–10.

[41] Aspinall, *Politics and the Press*, 433.

Sheridan for this purpose on Saturday, and he said I should have some assistance, but I have not hitherto received any.[42]

In this letter, Woodfall appears keen to contrast in Adam's mind the lack of action taken by Sheridan with the efficiency of Pitt's party, who sent a copy of the Premier's speech, without, it seems, having to be asked. Woodfall's plea had its desired effect, since sketches of both Pitt's and Fox's speeches were published in the *Chronicle* on the 27th, with Fox given more than double the space allotted to his rival.

Politicians were often eager to have other types of material appear in newspapers, and to demand more favours of their editors. Indeed, it is evident that editors often dictated the terms of publication to politicians, rather than vice versa. A letter to John Almon from Sir James Caldwell in 1779 asked him to help publicize Sir James's pamphlet on Ireland, and noted that 'this will be Acting in a very liberal manner towards the Publick & an instance of friendship to me w[hi]ch I shall never forget.'[43] In February 1773, the Earl of Sandwich wrote to Henry Woodfall, William's brother and publisher of the *Public Advertiser*: 'I shall be obliged if you without mentioning my name or giving any hint where this comes from, you would, if possible, insert the underwritten paragraph in your paper of tomorrow, otherwise in that of Thursday; but I wish to have it to morrow; the fact with regard to the action is true'.[44] On 5 July 1779, a letter to Woodfall written on behalf of Lord George Gordon requested that he 'oblige him by allowing the enclosed to appear in the Public Advertiser when he finds a spare column'.[45] In an undated letter, Charles James Fox asked Woodfall to tell him the identity of 'Ulysses', who had mentioned Fox in a letter published in the paper. He added, stressing either the familiarity of their relationship or the importance of the request, 'I beg you will understand that I do not write this to be printed in your paper but merely because I have not found you at home'.[46]

Although Fox was particularly interested in what the papers printed, other politicians were less concerned. On 9 December 1779, William Woodfall wrote to Charles Jenkinson, the Secretary-at-War, and requested 'a correct statement of the several estimates voted in the House of Commons yesterday'. Woodfall was worried that John Almon had already advertised that 'an exact account shall be laid before the Publick tomorrow in his *London Courant*', and although Woodfall's request to Jenkinson was

---

[42] Ibid. 444.
[43] Caldwell to Almon, 17 Dec. 1779, BL, Add. MS 20733, fos. 21–4.
[44] BL, Add. MS 27780, fo. 21.   [45] Ibid. fo. 44.   [46] Ibid. fo. 56.

a polite one, it did include the pointed comment that 'Mr. Jenkinson will perhaps be in accord with W.W. in thinking that it is better to give the Publick a correct than an incorrect account of a matter of figures, which by the mistake of a single figure might be grossly perverted'.[47] But no such figures—accurate or not—ever appeared in the *Chronicle*, and it seems that, for whatever reason, Jenkinson did not comply with Woodfall's request.

Whilst some politicians took a personal part in attempts to direct newspaper coverage, as Dennis O'Bryen's letter demonstrated, MPs also had the option of engaging someone else to undertake such onerous tasks for them, and conduct a more general campaign for positive publicity. Indeed, Tobias Smollett claimed that 'a late Nobleman who had been a member of several Administrations, owned to me that one good Writer was of more Importance to the Government, than twenty placemen in the House of Commons'.[48] In his letter to Burke, O'Bryen argued for the political expediency of shaping one's public image: 'it is not enough that the measures of an administration are *right*, but they must *appear* so. Ministers cannot spend their time in explanations, and the newspapers can create a grumbling at any hour'.[49] Despite the fact that his initial request for preferment was rejected,[50] O'Bryen eventually undertook such duties on behalf of Fox.[51]

On 19 February 1784, a J. W. Holford offered William Pitt similar services:

the calumnies & misrepresentations with which some of the Public Prints daily abound, are not altogether unworthy [of] your Lordship's notice for I am inclined to think, you will not differ with me in opinion, that the major part of the people of this kingdom, form their ideas of Public Man & their measures from what they

---

[47] Woodfall to Jenkinson, 9 Dec. 1779, BL, Add. MS 38212, fo. 274.

[48] Tobias Smollett to Caleb Whitefoord, 18 May 1770, *The Whitefoord Papers: Being the Correspondence of Colonel Charles Whitefoord and Caleb Whitefoord from 1739 to 1810*, ed. W. A. S. Hewins (Oxford, 1898), 148–9.

[49] O'Bryen to Burke, Mar. 1782, WWM, BK 1/1557.

[50] Burke replied to O'Bryen that 'the pains you have taken, and the variety of arguments you have used' inclined him to comply with O'Bryen's wishes, but that he was powerless to grant any places under the new administration: Edmund Burke to [Dennis O'Bryen], 25 Mar. 1782, *The Correspondence of Edmund Burke*, ed. T. W. Copeland *et al.*, 10 vols. (Cambridge, 1958–78), iv. 425–6.

[51] O'Bryen became Fox's agent at Westminster: L. G. Mitchell, *Charles James Fox* (Oxford, 1992), 104. In 1803, Fox wrote to O'Bryen to congratulate him on a piece of political propaganda which he had just written: letter dated 22 June 1803, BL, Add. MS 34079, fo. 81; and in 1806 Fox appointed O'Bryen to the patent office of Marshal of the Admiralty at the Cape of Good Hope, said to be worth £4,000: *DNB*, xiv. 785. However, there is little evidence for a close connection between O'Bryen and Fox prior to 1796.

find recorded in the Newspapers: if so, your Lordship will admit the propriety of refuting the malevolent attacks of Party-spirits & disappointed ambition. Under this idea, I have anonymously sent to the Editor of the Morning Post, the paragraphs of which the enclosed are copies; & which have appeared agreeable to the dates annexed to them. I should have submitted them to your Lordships inspection immediately after their insertion had I not thought I should have intruded upon your more important concerns, just upon the eve of the Parliamentary adjournment.—I send them now, by way of sample, & if upon a perusal, they should engage your Lordships approbation, I shall be extremely happy to dedicate my whole time, to a daily examination of all the Public Papers; from which I am inclined to think such observations may be drawn, as shall be neither improper, or unpleasing to your Lordship to countenance.[52]

Since no further correspondence with Holford can be found, it appears that his offer was declined. However, William Woodfall's letter to Adam, quoted above, and written just five days later, suggests that Pitt had already taken steps to ensure a favourable press.

But despite some open acknowledgement of the important role played by newspapers in influencing public opinion, politicians were wary of admitting direct involvement with the press. Public denial of such activities could lead to misunderstandings amongst those excluded from the privileged circle of Westminster and the capital's newspaper offices. In a letter to the writer Caleb Whitefoord in 1770, Tobias Smollett noted that

I hope you will not discontinue your Endeavours to represent Faction and False patriotism in their true colours, tho' I believe the Ministry little deserves that any man of genius should draw his pen in their defence. They seem to inherit the absurd stoicism of Lord Bute, who set himself up as a Pillory to be pelted by all the Blackguards of England, upon the supposition that they would grow tired and leave off. I don't find that your Ministers take any pains even to vindicate their moral Characters from the foulest Imputation; and I would never desire a stronger proof of a bad heart, than a total Disregard of Reputation.[53]

Smollett was clearly unaware that, as John Brewer has shown, Bute's press activities contrasted very forcibly with his traditional image as a Court politician.[54]

The newspaper press's lack of respectability was important in discouraging politicians from dealing publicly with the press.[55] Even Dennis

[52] Holford to Pitt, 19 Feb. 1784, PRO, 30/8, 140/2.

[53] Smollett to Whitefoord, 18 May 1770, *Whitefoord Papers*, 148–9.

[54] Brewer, *Party Ideology and Popular Politics*, ch. 11.

[55] See A. Aspinall, 'The Social Status of Journalists at the Beginning of the Nineteenth Century', *The Review of English Studies*, 21 (1945), 216–32.

O'Bryen, who proposed working directly with newspaper editors for the government, described the profession as not being 'a clean one'.[56] At a Middlesex meeting of electors on 5 March 1783, John Wilkes is reported to have said that

> he had been called upon by an anonimous writer in a newspaper, he said, to answer some queries, under the signature of a Freeholder, but he did not think it proper to answer them in the same channel; yet, if that Freeholder was present, he begged he would stand forward, and he would give him a full answer . . . for it was his wish that he might have an opportunity of clearing himself from an imputation of blame in his public conduct.[57]

Christopher Wyvill, leader of the Yorkshire reformers, was also advised to steer clear of direct involvement in the press. The *General Advertiser* of 20 January 1785 commented:

> We hear the friends of the Rev. Mr. Wyvill have advised that gentleman to decline entering into any discussion with anonymous writers in Newspapers, on the subject of Mr. Pitt's Declaration of his intention to support the question of Parliamentary Reform in the next session, as a minister, by fair and honest means, to the utmost of his power. This is good advice, and we hope it will be followed; for Mr. Wyvill ought not to think so meanly of the Public, or of himself, as to suppose the assertion which he has made can be discredited in the smallest degree, by any unauthenticated contradiction.

Yet despite their reputation, newspapers were clearly thought to be extremely important by many politicians. For members of the political elite, the press proved to be a major weapon in the fight to influence public opinion.

Newspapers and their Readers

The weight attached by contemporaries to the public and to the opinion it produced in late eighteenth-century England is much easier to establish than it is to discover the constitution of this powerful body. But from the discussion so far, it has become clear that 'the public' was often implicitly equated, at least in part, with those who read newspapers. However, the identity of this body can appear almost as elusive as that of the public itself. Even the circulation figures of the capital's newspapers are difficult to determine. Newspaper publishers had to pay a stamp tax on every paper they produced, but because the relevant Stamp Office records no longer exist, it is very hard to gauge levels of sales with any certainty.

---

[56] O'Bryen to Burke, Mar. 1782, WWM, BK 1/1557.
[57] *General Advertiser*, 6 Mar. 1783.

Surviving Audit Office records concerning advertising tax, coupled with John Trusler's *London Adviser and Guide* of 1786, do reveal that there were at least nine daily newspapers (appearing six times a week), eight tri-weekly, and approximately nine weekly papers in London at any time during the 1780s.[58] Of these, the daily newspapers probably achieved the highest sales. The account book of one such paper, the *Gazetteer*, shows that circulation figures of over 1,500 copies per day were needed in order for the paper to stay solvent.[59] But most daily newspapers would have fared much better than this. Henry Bate, editor of the *Morning Post*, claimed to have achieved sales of 5,000 copies a day in 1778.[60] In the following year, Johann Wilhelm von Archenholz, a visiting Prussian soldier, estimated that the *Public Advertiser* sold between 3,000 and 4,500 papers per day, and that the *Daily Advertiser* reached sales of 5,000 copies.[61] These figures must be treated with caution, since Bate would have gained much by exaggeration, and Archenholz's accuracy is also questionable. A more conservative estimate would place total sales of daily newspapers at between about 15,000 and 20,000 copies per day.

Jeremy Black's estimate that 25,000 papers were produced each day in 1782 seems a reasonable figure if we include tri-weekly and weekly papers. He also claims that each paper may have been read by twenty or more people: a level of readership duplication which equals Addison's estimation for the *Spectator* some seventy years earlier.[62] But the resultant figure of 500,000 readers is an overestimate according to at least one contemporary account. In O'Bryen's letter to Burke in 1782, he stated that 'there are 25 thousand papers published every day in London', but allowed for only ten readers to each paper.[63] Since O'Bryen was trying hard to convince Burke of how powerful the press was, it is unlikely that he would have underestimated his figures knowingly. Relying on O'Bryen's version gives us a readership of 250,000. This constitutes a sizeable proportion of the London population, which was some 750,000 in 1780.[64] Recent historical

---

[58] AO 3/950 et seqq.: these records have been collated by A. Aspinall in 'Statistical Accounts of the London Newspapers in the Eighteenth Century', *EHR* 62 (1948), 210–32; John Trusler, *The London Advisor and Guide* (London, 1786), 124–6.

[59] PRO, C104/67.

[60] Cited in Solomon Lutnick, *The American Revolution and the British Press: 1775–1783* (New York, 1967), 28.

[61] Johann Wilhelm von Archenholz, *A Picture of England* (Dublin, 1791), 42.

[62] Black, *The English Press*, 104; Joseph Addison, 'Essay No. 10', in *The Spectator*, ed. Donald F. Bond, 5 vols. (Oxford, 1965), i. 44.

[63] O'Bryen to Burke, Mar. 1782, WWM, BK 1/1557.

[64] C. M. Law, 'Some Notes on the Urban Population in the Eighteenth Century', *Local Historian*, 10 (1972), 13–26. The population of England as a whole was over 7 million: E. A. Wrigley and R. S. Schofield, *The Population of England, 1541–1871* (London, 1981), 207.

work concerning the social structure of London society in the eighteenth century has suggested that the size of the 'middling classes' was about the same as O'Bryen's figure for newspaper readership.[65] Indeed, O'Bryen claimed that 'these 250 thousand, include by much the Majority of the reading class of the community'.[66] Conflating the capital's newspaper readers and its middling sort, however, is almost certainly an oversimplification. As will be argued, it is unlikely that those who read newspapers in the capital were members of any distinct social group.

O'Bryen's estimate of 250,000 must be tempered by the knowledge that some people would almost certainly have read more than one paper. In addition, the circulation, and therefore the possible influence, of London newspapers was not restricted to the capital. The tri-weekly newspapers in particular were dispatched to the provinces (John Trusler referred to them as 'country' papers[67]) and most, in recognition of this fact, contained a 'country news' section in addition to the larger space allocated to 'London'. The owners of the tri-weekly London paper, the *General Evening Post*, regarded provincial circulation as an important factor in their financial arrangements. The *Post*'s records from the 1770s and 1780s show that its publication was co-ordinated with the departure of Post Office coaches to the provinces, and that Clerks of the Road were paid to hold up the coaches if the publication of the paper was delayed.[68] The provincial appeal of the tri-weeklies was reflected in the *St. James's Chronicle* in February 1781, when a local dispute over property sales and local political influence caused a flurry of letters to the newspaper from Truro. However, a daily paper like the *London Courant* also felt able to claim that

Besides being taken by all the people of fashion at the West End of the Town; by almost every capital family in the cities of London and Westminster; it is to be seen in all the coffee-houses in Town; in many of the principal inns in the country; at Bath, Bristol, Liverpool, York, Scarborough, Southampton, Oxford, Cambridge, Portsmouth, Plymouth, Brightelmstone, and many other cities and towns; and all other places of genteel resort.[69]

[65] L. D. Schwarz estimates that the 'middling classes' constituted 20–30% of the adult male population in late eighteenth-century London: *London Life in the Age of Industrialisation: Entrepreneurs, Labour Force and Living Conditions, 1700–1850* (Cambridge, 1992), 167. Rudé was more conservative in his study of London society, and put the number of the 'middle sort' at only 1 in 7: George Rudé, *Hanoverian London, 1714–1808* (London, 1971), 56–8.

[66] O'Bryen to Burke, Mar. 1782, WWM, BK 1/1557.

[67] Trusler, *London Advisor and Guide*, 126.

[68] John Feather, *The Provincial Book Trade in Eighteenth-Century England* (Cambridge, 1985), 48.

[69] *London Courant*, 1 June 1780.

London newspapers did not constitute a national press in a modern sense. It is true that they were widely read outside the capital, and used extensively by the provincial press as a major source of information,[70] but it should be noted that this arrangement was reciprocal. The *Gazetteer*'s records reveal that payment was made for newspapers published in Liverpool, Exeter, Ipswich, Newcastle, Oxford, Salisbury, Gloucester, Lewes, Birmingham, York, Bath, Bristol, Glasgow, Canterbury, and Derby,[71] from which material was extracted. Similarly, news from abroad—from Ireland, Holland, France, the West Indies, and America—was gleaned largely from native papers.

This discussion of geographical circulation and production figures tells us something about the numbers who could have read London newspapers in the late eighteenth century, but very little about what sort of people they were. John Brewer has shown that the accounts of the *Public Advertiser* between 1765 and 1771 demonstrate changes in circulation within the calendar year which correspond with the London season: sales reached a peak in February and March, just before Parliament ended its business for the year, and did not pick up again until October or November with the new parliamentary session.[72] Brewer concludes that these fluctuations are a sign that most newspaper readers came from amongst the elite classes, whose members followed the fashionable rules of the social season concerning London residence.

A similar examination of the sales of the *Gazetteer* between 1784 and 1795 is less indicative of an elite readership. Comparing the two newspapers by plotting the average percentage change in circulation figures from one month to the next (Figs. 1 and 2) reveals that whilst sales of the *Public Advertiser* could vary by almost 30 per cent, this was not the case for the *Gazetteer*. Here, although the troughs and peaks of the annual cycle are similar to those of the *Advertiser*, the variation is never more than 10 per cent between months, revealing that the *Gazetteer*'s sales remained far more constant than those of the *Advertiser*. Since the London season still operated in broadly the same manner towards the end of the eighteenth century as it had done twenty years earlier, the graphs suggest differences in the readership of the two papers: those of the *Public Advertiser* being predominantly from amongst the more wealthy upper and middle classes, and those of the *Gazetteer* drawn largely from lower down the social scale. Although it is possible that each paper appealed to different social groups

[70] G. A. Cranfield, *The Development of the Provincial Newspaper 1700–1760* (Oxford, 1962); see also Chs. 4 and 5 below.
[71] PRO, C104/67, Book M. [72] Brewer, *Party Ideology and Popular Politics*, 143.

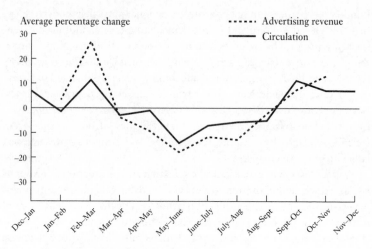

FIG. 1. Circulation of the *Public Advertiser*, 1765–1771

Note: As figures for Dec. advertising are missing for all years except 1766, this month is not included in the advertising revenue curve.
Source: BL, Add. MS 38169.

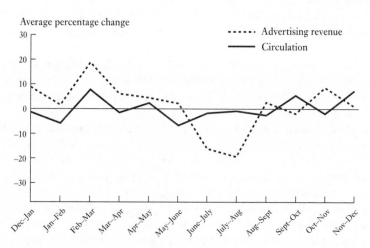

FIG. 2. Circulation of the *Gazetteer*, 1784–1795
Source: PRO, C104/67.

as part of a commercial tactic to target different audiences, the similarities in the make-up and stance of both papers, and of others published at the same time, make such readership divisions unlikely. Rather, the figures suggest that newspaper readership as a whole had altered between the two periods. If this is true, then the declining importance of the London season to newspaper sales indicates a broadening of the newspaper-reading public. Although actual monthly sales figures do not differ greatly between the two papers, the *Public Advertiser* was one of about five dailies in London in the late 1760s, whereas the *Gazetteer* had to contend with at least twice the number of rivals.[73] This suggests that total newspaper sales had increased dramatically, certainly far more so than the growth of the middling sorts, and by implication, the findings indicate that sales were being made to a larger, and more socially mixed, proportion of the London population.

Some indication of the identity of this new readership can be found in studies of literacy. David Cressy's work demonstrates high levels amongst craftsmen and traders in London. He claims that by the early eighteenth century almost all of those who constituted the commercial classes in the capital were literate.[74] This is helpful up to a point, since the capital's newspaper readership, in its strictest sense, would have come from amongst the literate population. But judging literacy levels is notoriously difficult, since, for example, the ability to read might not have been dependent upon the ability to write. In her study of late seventeenth-century spiritual autobiography, Margaret Spufford claimed that reading was a more socially diffused skill than writing.[75] Moreover, the audience for newspapers was not limited to those who could read, since papers could be, and often were, read aloud. Naomi Tadmor's study of household reading in the eighteenth century demonstrates how the practice of reading was frequently sociable, rather than solitary, and involved individuals reading to family members and guests.[76] Reading newspapers aloud was a common theme in eighteenth-century prints. Here the

[73] These figures are estimated from Audit Office records: AO 3/950 et seqq.

[74] D. Cressy, *Literacy and the Social Order* (London, 1975), 154.

[75] Margaret Spufford, 'First Steps in Literacy: The Reading and Writing Experiences of the Humblest Seventeenth-Century Spiritual Autobiographies', *Social History*, 4 (1979), 407–35.

[76] Naomi Tadmor, 'In the Even My Wife Read to Me: Women, Reading and Household Life in the Eighteenth Century', in James Raven, Helen Small, and Naomi Tadmor (eds.), *The Practice and Representation of Reading in England* (Cambridge, 1996), 162–74. See also John Brewer, 'Reconstructing the Reader: Prescriptives, Texts and Strategies in Anna Larpent's Reading', in ibid. 226–45.

The Parson, Barber & the Squire,
Three Social Souls who News admire.

PLATE 1. *The Country Politicians*, Jan. 1784 [first appeared Mar. 1777]

PLATE 2. *The Morning News*, Dec. 1772 '*The Rabble gather round the Man of News/And listen with their mouths/Some tell, some hear, some judge of news, some make it/And he that lyes most loud is most beleive'd*'

practice of reading was often more 'public' than in the type of familial settings described by Tadmor. In 'The Country Politicians' (Plate 1), Gillray depicted three country gentlemen reading a newspaper together indoors. However, 'The Morning News' (Plate 2) is a street scene, in which 'the rabble' are read to by 'the man of news'. In 'A Meeting of City Politicians' (Plate 3), a large group of men sit around the table of a public house. Some read newspapers to themselves, at least one reads aloud to his companions, and several look over others' shoulders.[77] Here newspaper reading is presented as a form of communal activity which

[77] 'The Country Politicians', Jan. 1784 [first appeared Mar. 1777], BM, DG 6730; 'The Morning News', Dec. 1772; 'A Meeting of City Politicians', July 1779, BM, DG 5613. I am grateful to John Stevenson for the generous gift of the print entitled 'The Morning News'.

PLATE 3. *A Meeting of City Politician's*, July 1779 'With staring Eye & open Ear / Each cobling, Horned City seer / Swallow's down Politics with Beer / Neglects his Family & Calling / To enter into Party Brawling / Gets Drunk & Swears — the Nation's falling'

could extend far beyond the limits of the literate, or indeed, the purchasers of newspapers.

Jeremy Black has argued that the price of newspapers kept them out of range of the lower classes.[78] But high circulation figures, coupled with accounts of both the role of coffee-houses in providing access to newspapers and the practices of lending, hiring, and public reading, suggest that poorer individuals were not necessarily excluded from contact with newspapers.[79] Indeed, contemporary reports concerning the social composition of the capital's newspaper readership usually emphasized its diversity. As early as 1726, César de Saussure remarked that 'all Englishmen are great newsmongers. Workmen habitually begin the day by going to coffee-rooms in order to read the latest news. I have often seen shoeblacks and men of that class club together to purchase a farthing paper'.[80] An article in the *Monthly Miscellany* of March 1774 described newspapers as vehicles of general information for all types of person (both male and female), including 'the city miss', sportsmen, merchants, farmers, and tradesmen.[81] In the satirical prints already discussed, newspaper readers range from gentlemen to artisans: both 'The Morning News' and 'A Meeting of City Politicians' include men wearing work aprons, and in the former, one man also carries a hammer to indicate his profession.[82] 'A news-reader' noted in the *London Courant* that

There are few people, of whatever sex, age, or condition, that are prepared for the conversation of the day, until they have had an opportunity of perusing the public prints. When those vehicles of information have set the reader a-going, he comes abroad a man of the world; knows every thing that is passing in it, and spends the day most agreeably, in retailing out the news that he has taken in wholesale in the morning.[83]

Commentators were often critical of the effect that printed material in general, and newspapers in particular, could have on the lower orders. Vicesimus Knox spoke of newspapers deceiving 'the more ignorant classes',[84] and an anonymous pamphlet of 1764, claiming to describe a typical day of the capital's 'low-life', reported: 'the Newspapers in every

---

[78] Black, *The English Press*, 106.

[79] On coffee-houses see: Aytoun Ellis, *The Penny Universities* (London, 1956); Bryant Lillywhite, *London Coffee Houses* (London, 1963).

[80] César de Saussure, *A Foreign View of England in the Reigns of George I and George II* (London, 1902), 162.

[81] 'The Rise and Utility of News-Papers', *Monthly Miscellany*, Mar. 1774, 121–2.

[82] 'The Country Politicians'; 'The Morning News'; 'A Meeting of City Politicians'.

[83] *London Courant*, 18 Dec. 1780.

[84] Knox, *Works of Vicesimus Knox*, v. 176.

little Ale-house, the Subject of much low Conversation, more especially by Persons who neither understand Religion, Geography, Trade or Politicks'.[85] Lolme commented on the wide circulation of newspapers, and wrote that 'every man, down to the labourer, peruses them with a sort of eagerness'.[86] Archenholz echoed his sentiments. He described reading the daily papers to be 'actually an epidemical passion among the English', and that 'sometimes a politician will insert an essay on a subject which concerns the welfare of the whole nation, and every body, even a fish-woman, is able to comprehend it. It is not at all uncommon to observe such persons reading and commentating on the public prints'.[87]

This sort of anecdotal evidence is suggestive, but as proof of the social make-up of newspaper readers, it is, of course, limited. Another way to try to identify readership is to examine the content of the papers themselves. Such a text-based approach assumes that what appears as a paper's targeted audience corresponds to the actual readership. Schweizer and Klein have used this method in a study of London newspaper advertisements in the early 1790s. From this they have concluded that newspapers were 'a vehicle for the expression of the sentiments of the new moneyed class who comprised a vital segment of the reading public'.[88] The types of goods and services advertised by most London newspapers in the 1780s appear to support the thesis linking newspapers to a growing commercial, consumerist 'middle class'. Thus one finds advertisements for books, magazines, medicines, wines and spirits, perfume, dentistry, hair-styling products, fashionable clothing, stabling services, horse medicines, race meetings, and ecclesiastical livings. But whilst an examination of newspaper advertisements does suggest a certain type of reader, it is an approach which places great weight upon the ability of advertisers to gauge the effectiveness of advertising, and, more importantly, it assumes that advertisers catered for the bulk of newspaper readers.

The fact that advertisers continued to advertise suggests that this method of attracting business was successful. Indeed, this was no doubt one of the reasons why many businessmen invested in newspapers, since

---

[85] *Low-Life: or One Half of the World Knows Not How the Other Half Live, Being a Critical Account of What is Transacted by People of Almost All Religions, Nations, Circumstances, and Sizes of Understanding, in the Twenty-Four Hours Between Saturday-Night and Monday-Morning. In a true description of a Sunday. As it is usually spent within the Bills of Mortality. Calculated for the twenty-first of June*, 3rd edn. (London, 1764), 85.

[86] Lolme, *The Constitution of England*, 300.

[87] Archenholz, *A Picture of England*, 44 and 39.

[88] K. Schweizer and R. Klein, 'The French Revolution and the Developments in the London Daily Press to 1793', *Publishing History*, 18 (1985), 85–97.

they could then place advertisements at reduced rates.[89] But there is evidence that advertisers may have targeted only a section of the capital's newspaper readership. The graph plotting the average percentage changes from one month to the next in the *Gazetteer*'s circulation and advertising revenue between 1784 and 1795 (Fig. 2) shows that unlike the *Public Advertiser*, the *Gazetteer*'s advertisers appeared to be out of step with its circulation levels during the summer: in other words, advertising revenue dropped even though sales remained steady. This suggests that advertisers intended to appeal to a select and richer proportion of the readership; that is, those whose residence in London continued to be determined by the social season. In this case, advertisements largely indicate the identity of only a section of the newspaper readership, which suggests that historians should be wary of equating this group with the wider audience for newspapers.

However, there appears to be a difference in this respect between advertisements for goods and sales, and other types of advertising. For example, the *Morning Herald* seems to have specialized both in advertising for servants wanted and in carrying advertisements placed by servants seeking employment. The latter tended to be from those at the top end of their profession: ladies' maids, manservants, upper maids, and housekeepers, but servants' advertisements add weight to the notion that newspaper readership was not confined to one end of the social scale. Newspapers also carried notices placed by hopeful candidates for parliamentary election, addressed to their prospective constituents. Indeed, it is important to note (see Fig. 3 below) how markedly newspaper advertising revenue increased during the 1784 and 1790 general elections and the impact of the political advertisement upon the income of eighteenth-century papers. Assuming that these advertisements reached the right audience, this suggests that those who could vote comprised at least a section of the newspaper-reading public, which in places like Middlesex and the City could mean a very broad constituency. However, since the Opposition press was a forceful proponent of electoral reform, and carried many advertisements placed by reform committees and associations, it also seems likely that papers were read by those who could not vote, but might be persuaded they had a right to do so. As the discussion in Chapter 3 will reveal, this could indicate an extremely large proportion of the capital's male population.

---

[89] This was the case with the *London Packet*. The paper's minutes, dated 6 Jan. 1770, show that any of its 14 partners could insert advertisements at less than the rate normally charged: BL, Add. MS 38729, Fos. 165–6.

As an alternative means of identifying their readership, it would prove helpful to determine why people read newspapers in the eighteenth century. Again, one is reliant upon the assumption that newspaper content was closely related to the preoccupations and preferences of a paper's readership; but in many cases this might be a safer bet than concentrating on advertising. Given the importance of sales to newspaper revenue (discussed below), it might safely be assumed that newspapers which did not satisfy their audience would have gone out of business. A circular dated 6 November 1779, advertising the launch of the *London Courant*, suggests one of the main tactics which editors used to attract readers:

The principal design of this undertaking is, to furnish the Public with early and authentic Intelligence of every public transaction, both at home & abroad; for which every known channel of communication has been opened, nor will any pains or expence be spared to discover others, as well as to preserve every source of information. At the same time no attention will be wanting, to prevent the insertion of any articles of falsehood, malignancy & private scandal.[90]

In attempting to promote sales, John Almon, the *Courant*'s publisher, stressed the inclusion of accurate news above all other factors. A similar claim was made by the *Morning Post*, which boasted of containing 'the most authentic parliamentary intelligence'.[91] In all the London newspapers of the 1780s, 'news' was allocated most space and given greater prominence than any other type of material, with the possible exception of advertisements. However, when particular items of news were considered to be of great importance, even the space allocated to advertising could be greatly reduced. This was the case when the *Morning Herald* covered Lord George Gordon's trial in great detail on 6 February 1781, which prompted an apology to its advertisers the following day.

Readers appear to have valued newspapers primarily as a means of keeping informed of current events and political affairs. 'The Examiner', writing in the *Morning Post* in November 1780, was critical of the press's tendency to mislead the public, and claimed that they 'draw their information, and form their political creeds in a great measure from these sources'.[92] 'Legion' wrote to the *St. James's Chronicle* that 'as I live in a retired village, [I] am obliged, in general, to gather my knowledge of publick matters from your paper, and other resources of the like nature'.[93] Much surviving private correspondence from this period is full of references to newspapers, and to information obtained from them. For

---

[90] BL, Add. MS 20733, fo. 1. [91] *Morning Post*, 28 Oct. 1780.
[92] Ibid. 7 Nov. 1780. [93] *St. James's Chronicle*, 30 Nov. 1780.

example, the Earl of Buckinghamshire wrote to Lady Suffolk from Petersburg in 1763 that

Were it not for the information which I occasionally receive from that chaos of truth and falsehood, which composes the English newspapers, I should return to London as much a stranger to the manners, ideas, and passions of my countrymen as well as to the names, merits, and qualifications of those eminent personages, who are distinguished by the applause of their fellow subjects upon the great theater of London, as if I had never seen my Lord mayor, Nelly O'Brien, the Lions, Mr. Wilkes, or the Monument.[94]

Lady Sarah Lennox, writing in December 1778 to her sister the Duchess of Leinster in France, asked: 'Pray, what newspapers do you get? Not the *Morning Post*, I hope, for it's full of lies and no news. The *General Advertiser* has the best intelligence & gives, as I am told, a very correct account of the speeches in the debates, which entertains me vastly'.[95] Due to the increasing politicization of the wider political nation—for which newspapers were partly responsible—the desire to keep up with current events was not restricted to a narrow social group. 'WC', in a letter to the *St. James's Chronicle*, described the newspaper as 'a bill of fare, containing all the luxuries, as well as the necessaries of life. *Politicks* are now the *roast-beef* of the times, and a dish equally sumptuous to the king and the cobbler.'[96]

Allied to the growth in political awareness amongst the English public, the growth of parliamentary reporting was one of the most striking developments in newspaper content in the late eighteenth century. Coverage of the debates of both houses seems to have become increasingly popular, with one contemporary asserting that William Woodfall's detailed reports were the reason for the *Morning Chronicle*'s popularity.[97] Indeed, the seasonal fluctuation of newspaper sales may have had more to do with the lack of parliamentary news, resulting in a general loss of readers' interest, than with a specific decline amongst an elite readership. In his memoirs, John Almon claimed that parliamentary debate reporting began in earnest in the late 1760s due to the emergence of popular radicalism: 'When the spirit of the nation was raised high by the massacre in St. George's-fields, the unjust decision upon the Middlesex election, &c. . . . [I] resolved to

[94] Earl of Buckinghamshire to Lady Suffolk, 11 Nov. 1763, in Historical Manuscripts Commission, *Report on the Manuscripts of the Marquess of Lothian Preserved at Blickling Hall, Norfolk* (London, 1905), 179.
[95] Irish Manuscripts Commission, *Correspondence of Emily, Duchess of Leinster*, ed. Brian Fitzgerald, 3 vols. (Dublin, 1953), ii. 264.
[96] *St. James's Chronicle*, 22 July 1780.   [97] Taylor, *Records of My Life*, ii. 245.

make the nation acquainted with the proceedings of Parliament'.[98] It was the increase in newspaper coverage of parliamentary debates that led to the clash between Parliament and the City in 1771. One of the results of this battle was that Parliament unofficially gave up its right to prosecute the press for publishing its proceedings. This was a decision which was to result in the proliferation and lengthening of reports. However, during the 1770s, both houses still regularly made use of their power to exclude strangers from the Galleries during 'sensitive' debates, and note-taking was not allowed until after 1783.[99] By the 1780s, debate reporting held a prominent place in the hierarchy of newspaper contents. The competition between individual newspapers over parliamentary coverage intensified, which along with the amount of space allocated to them, indicated how important they were considered to be. Indeed, James Stephen, a one-time debate reporter for the *Morning Post*, recorded how a late sitting of the House caused by an important debate would often hold up the publication of the next day's paper.[100]

A growing awareness of events outside one's own locality in the eighteenth century, has, of course, been linked to the development of a British 'national consciousness',[101] and newspapers were a crucial element in this change. In consequence, of almost equal, and sometimes greater, importance in newspapers than the proceedings of Parliament was the coverage of foreign affairs. This is perhaps not surprising, considering that Britain was almost constantly at war with one of its continental neighbours during the 1770s and 1780s. By far the greatest source of such information came from the official government paper, the *London Gazette*. The commercial press's reliance on this government publication can give the appearance of mere space-filling and of a 'scissors and paste' approach. However, the extensive use of the *Gazette*, coupled with other sources such as 'private' letters from abroad, and the foreign press, shows how important the coverage of foreign news was perceived to be, often taking precedence over other, usually more prominent, types of news. Despite the love of London gossip and local crime stories shown by newspapers, the large part played by foreign affairs reveals the absence of a narrow provincialism amongst the newspaper readership.

---

[98] Almon, *Memoirs*, 119.

[99] P. D. G. Thomas, 'The Beginning of Parliamentary Reporting in Newspapers, 1768–1774', *EHR* 74 (1959), 623–36.

[100] James Stephen, *The Memoirs of James Stephen. Written by Himself For the Use of His Children*, ed. Merle M. Bevington (London, 1954), 219.

[101] Brewer, *Party Ideology and Popular Politics*.

John Brewer, in his examination of the creation of a fiscal-military state in seventeenth- and eighteenth-century England, suggests that the British public followed the progress of hostilities during wartime 'with an assiduity worthy of Tristram Shandy's Uncle Toby', because of their interest in its economic repercussions.[102] Brewer stresses the importance of narrowly defined commercial and trading interests in the public's interest in 'world' events. There is some evidence of this in the London press. For a start, there was usually a debate running about the general economic state of the nation, particularly in relation to the effects of war. The *Gazetteer* of 14 May 1780 noted that 'The encrease of taxes, the fall of rents, and the general bankruptcy among the small farmers, are the chief topics of complaint. Every person, from the gentlemen of landed property down to the day-labourer, feels the effects of the ruinous and destructive war we have been engaged in for some years.' 'A Manufacturer' wrote to the *St. James's Chronicle* from Norwich in January 1781, and complained of the decline of the woollen industry, whilst in the same month 'Norvicensis' in the *London Courant* bemoaned the state of the weaving industry in Lincoln, Norfolk, and Suffolk.[103] The preoccupation with the nation's economic and commercial life was also reflected in the wide coverage given to shipping news, East India Company business, and issues related to trade, particularly concerning the West Indies and Ireland, the regular reporting of the prices of stocks and shares, and the listing of bankrupts.

But once again, we should be wary of assuming that newspaper interests solely reflected the concerns of the growing commercial classes, since foreign news had occupied a prominent place in English newspapers throughout the eighteenth century. De Saussure, writing about newspaper readership in 1726, remarked with surprise that 'you often see an Englishman taking a treaty of peace more to heart than he does his own affairs'.[104] In addition, foreign news would have appealed to more than just those interested in the economic repercussions of war. In the case of Anglo–American relations in the 1770s, for example, the capital's radicals would have had political, rather than commercial, motives for their interest in the progress of events, and indeed, in the case of many London merchants, the 'commercial' and the 'political' are not easy to disentangle.

Politics and political debate loomed just as large in the capital's papers as did purely commercial concerns. One of the major sources of debate

---

[102] John Brewer, *Sinews of Power: War, Money and the English State, 1688–1783* (London, 1989), p. xxi.
[103] *St. James's Chronicle*, 16 Jan. 1781; *London Courant*, 18 Jan. 1781.
[104] Saussure, *A Foreign View of England*, 162.

was letters, which typically occupied between one and three columns of a paper's space of sixteen columns (around half of which were usually advertisements). As these were almost always anonymous, there is little way of knowing what proportion of letters were, as their format suggested, sent in by readers, and which were 'manufactured' by the editor and his staff.[105] However, the authenticity of such letters does not necessarily determine their significance. Apart from the types of opinion they portray, their value lies in the implicit assumption that anyone had a right to contribute to the debates of the day, and as such letters stressed the importance and authority of the wider political nation, as well as enhancing the immediacy felt between a paper and its readership.

In his study of John Reeves and his correspondents in the 1790s, Colin Brooks argued that not only did the anonymity of letters serve to shield their authors, but this anonymity allowed for the contribution of those either so lowly they ought not to presume to rise, or so high that they should not have sunk, to involve themselves in public debate.[106] In this sense, the newspaper allowed for greater involvement in political discussion, by removing social barriers. In the case of those normally thought too inferior to contribute, anonymity, rather than association with the socially obscure, would have been seen as preferable for the promotion of a particular cause. Indeed, greater weight was attached by the choice of some pseudonyms: historical figures such as Cato, Brutus, and Alfred were typical choices, whose names were used to add authority to a cause in a society which used historical precedent as an ultimate sanction.

In the undated draft of a letter attacking 'Junius' and addressed to the *Public Advertiser*, Caleb Whitefoord stressed the importance of anonymity:

when a writer takes upon him to counsel Kings & Ministers, to censure the measures of Government & to lead the Public Opinion, such a writer should be particularly cautious to keep himself totally concealed; For whilst the source is unknown from whence his lubrications flow, we are apt to suppose that (like some Heroes & foundlings of old) they spring from a very high origin; But no sooner does a vain author step forth from his concealment, or is detected by the prying eye of criticism, in short no sooner do we discover who the person *is* that presumes to dictate to us so dogmatically & magisterially, then his writings lose all their

[105] For example, John Almon claimed to have written letters as an 'Independent Whig' and as 'Lucius' which appeared in the *Gazetteer* in 1760 in support of Pitt: Almon, *Memoirs*, 14.

[106] Colin Brooks, 'John Reeves and his Correspondents: A Contribution to the Study of British Loyalism, 1792–1793', in L. Domergue and G. Lamoine (eds.), *Après 89: La Révolution modèle ou repoussoir* (Toulouse, 1991), 49–76, p. 57.

effect; His scurrility and abuse recoil upon himself, and we can only wonder at his extreme impudence and presumption.[107]

Archenholz noted how highly the public prized the ability to write anonymously for newspapers. He described the method by which articles and letters could be delivered secretly to printers by means of a special post-box, and claimed that 'if you chose to make yourself known to the printer, he is obliged to observe secrecy. Nothing can force him to violate this, for were he to do so, he would not only lose his business, but also have his house exposed to the fury of the populace'.[108]

Many letters consisted of attacks on individual public figures. Newspapers offered the unique opportunity to utter a tirade against, or to appeal to, those individuals—like politicians, ministers, bishops, or even the King—who would normally have been at too great a social distance. 'Philo-Georgius', writing in the *London Evening Post*, addressed George III as 'a loving subject, who, from the obscurity of his station, is precluded the benefit of a private audience with your Majesty', but who hoped to relate his views on the American war, 'in a series of letters, thus publicly addressed to you (the only mode he can adopt of communicating his political sentiments to his Sovereign).'[109] Similarly, 'An Independent Freeholder of Yorkshire' was able to remonstrate with the Archbishop of York over his comments concerning the York committee of association.[110] As 'John Bull' noted in a letter addressed to the King, 'it is the Birth-right of all free Britons to study public affairs, it is their duty to lay the result of their enquiries with candour and impartiality before your Majesty, and even the Public, when their views are laudable to your Royal interest, and the Good of their Fellow Citizens'.[111] In addition, letters could be written by women, whose involvement in the 'public sphere' was often more circumscribed than that of men.[112]

However, such involvement, although anonymous in terms of individual identity, was frequently not 'classless'. Like the 'Independent Freeholder of Yorkshire', many chose to sign their letters with a description of their social standing and local identity, such as 'A Country Gentleman' who wrote to the *Morning Herald* in April 1781, complaining of 'the state of landed interest', and 'A London Merchant' who protested at the publication of news 'relative to what may affect the credit of the

[107] BL, Add. MS 36595, fo. 316.   [108] Archenholz, *A Picture of England*, 39–40.
[109] *London Evening Post*, 27 June 1780.   [110] *London Courant*, 27 July 1781.
[111] *Public Advertiser*, 14 July 1781.
[112] For example, the letters from 'a female constitutionalist' which appeared in the *London Courant* on 18 Feb. and 3 Mar. 1780.

Merchant'.[113] Even more common than such occupational descriptions were those relating to one's constitutional standing, involving terms such as 'freeholder' and 'elector'. In all these cases, writers concealed their individual identity, but still chose to identify themselves with a much larger group, thus stating quite clearly their authority as members of the political nation to comment upon affairs. The 'Herefordshire Freeholder', whose letter was published in the *London Courant* on 15 January 1780, remonstrated against aristocratic opposition to proposed resolutions for a forthcoming county meeting and asserted that 'the voice of the few, who derived advantage from the sufferings of the many, can have *no weight* in this matter.' His position as a freeholder was represented as one of great authority, and his provenance the proof of justifiable interest. More radically, many writers chose not to address members of the political elite at all, and directed their letters of grievance 'to the people'. Such immediate appeals to those out of doors, from one of their number, bypassed traditional political authority altogether. A letter in the *London Courant* in June 1781, addressed to 'the deputies of the associated and petitioning counties, cities, and towns', complained about an address from the York committee specifically addressed to electors: 'if you think you can depend upon the crown for relief, resort you to parliament, where that power moves every spring. But if the power of the people be your choice, why then apply to the people. The electors are not the people. They are not the representatives of the people. They are nothing more than a faint shadow of their ancient majesty'.[114] The writer of this letter clearly believed that he could appeal to 'the people' in this way. In common with those politicians who sought to influence the public by using newspapers, it was assumed that the press formed a direct channel to the wider political nation.

But more than providing a means of access to the public, newspapers encouraged their readers to believe that this process worked both ways, and that the world of politics was something in which they could participate. The sense of immediacy with this world which newspapers encouraged their readers to feel was never more evident than during elections. London newspapers would carry detailed reports of candidates' speeches and audience reaction at hustings, and when an election was contested, papers would provide their readers with a daily report of the poll based on the state of play at its close on the previous day. The assumption that readers would engage in the electoral process, and not simply witness it

---

[113] *Morning Herald*, 7 Apr. and 1 Aug. 1781.   [114] *London Courant*, 28 June 1781.

second hand, was clear. Politicians used the press to address voters directly, and election time saw newspapers full of entreaties from parliamentary candidates to 'independent electors' and 'worthy liverymen'. Those with the franchise were left in no doubt that they mattered in terms of the capital's and the nation's political life. Aside from the advertisements soliciting votes, letters addressed to electors increased this sense of importance. 'A Conscientious Elector' urged Westminster voters to refuse bribes from candidates in 1780,[115] and a paragraph which appeared in the *Morning Herald* in April 1784 encouraged them to 'come forth . . . like BRITONS and give your suffrages in defence of your own FREEDOM.'[116]

Indeed, such was the degree to which the newspaper audience was presumed to be able to involve itself in the nation's political affairs that the modern separation of 'high' and 'low' politics appears artificial and inadequate to describe the complexities of political life in the capital. Newspapers encouraged their readers to believe that they could participate in political life in a variety of ways: most clearly, in the letters which appeared to allow individuals to address important figures, or the public en masse, and which also gave the opportunity to contribute to public debate in its truest sense. In addition, the familiarity with which those in 'high' politics were described was flattering in its assumption that the well-informed newspaper reader was politically 'in the know', rather than just a passive observer of political life. Moreover, readers were constantly reminded of their constitutional rights and encouraged to exercise them whenever possible, particularly during elections.

Perhaps most importantly, in terms of their relationship with their readers, newspapers presumed to speak on behalf of the people. The *Gazetteer*, for example, described itself as 'the *Paper* of the *People*. Uninfluenced by the countenance of Ministers, or the promises of Opposition.'[117] Other papers made the same implicit claim through their presentation of political argument, use of popular appeals, and treatment of 'the people' and 'the public'.[118] One writer in the *Morning Post* made even bolder, if sarcastic, claims:

The standard by which the complexion of the great body of the people of England can be known is, without one doubt to the contrary, allowed by all true Patriots, to be the sentiments of a newspaper. There, Sir, whatever one typographical director choses to set down under the head of WE hear, or WE can with justice

---

[115] *London Courant*, 15 Sept. 1780.   [116] *Morning Herald*, 7 Apr. 1784.
[117] *Gazetteer*, 11 Nov. 1783.   [118] See Chap. 3 below.

assert, is considered as the unanimous opinion of the AGGREGATE BODY OF
THE KINGDOM. The word WE is monarchical in the mouth of a King, but
when a printer uses it, the signification is vox populi. Thus, Sir, a newspaper; I
must add the word patriotic,—and then it will thus stand, a patriotic newspaper,
becomes the delegated voice of England.[119]

Despite this attempt to prove the social diversity of the London newspaper audience, the results of this examination are far from conclusive. It
is clear that great numbers of Londoners read newspapers, and likely that
they spanned the social spectrum. But in terms of assessing the influence
of newspapers, it is important to know not just who read them, but *how*
they were read. In other words, it must be remembered that readers'
response to newspapers and the cultural and political meanings they
ascribed to newspaper contents were dependent upon the conditions in
which they were read. There is a great deal of difference between the
solitary and leisurely perusal of a paper, and hearing excerpts read aloud
as part of a group, when what was read was decided by others and the text
was almost certainly accompanied by the comments and discussion of
one's fellow listeners. No doubt the success of the newspaper press owed
much to the flexibility with which newspapers could be read—either alone
or accompanied, and from start to finish or in part (a practice to which the
provision of news in short-paragraph form lent itself). This, coupled with
the sense of immediacy and reader interaction which newspapers offered
by way of their letter pages and their frequent publication, and because
they appeared to represent their readers, seems to have fuelled their
popularity. However, for historians, the very foundations of newspapers'
success in the eighteenth century must serve to complicate the contemporary meanings of their contents.

[119] *Morning Post*, 11 Aug. 1780.

2
NEWSPAPER POLITICS
IN THE CAPITAL

London newspapers in the 1780s were overtly political and seemed obsessed with 'high' politics. Newspapers filled their pages with parliamentary proceedings, the behaviour of ministers, and the real or supposed
activity which took place behind the scenes at Buckingham House or St
Stephen's. Individual papers often had their own clear political stance
which was readily identifiable with that of a particular 'party' or politician,
so that the political divisions which existed between newspapers often
mirrored those of particular political groups in Parliament. Political allegiance was expressed in various ways; most importantly, in what could be
called the 'editorial' sections, often headed 'London', and in the letters
published. These sections tended to consist of numerous short paragraphs
providing comment on current political debates, individual politicians,
and general 'society news' or gossip. The format of the editorial sections,
in which an argument or commentary had to be expressed in a very few
lines, lent itself to a style of writing which was direct, unequivocal, and
dramatic. Where politics were concerned, such paragraphs were rarely
unbiased, but involved the blunt statement of a particular point of view.
Because of this lack of complexity and real substance, one contemporary
described paragraphs as 'fleeting arrows'.[1] Whilst individual newspapers
might sometimes appear ambivalent on certain issues by printing contradictory paragraphs, a consistency of opinion was usually apparent, and
made more obvious by the forceful nature of the journalistic style used.

Since, in theory at least, letters were not written by newspaper employees, they could appear less indicative of a paper's avowed political stance.
Nevertheless, the letters which appeared in newspapers often reinforced
the ideological beliefs and party-political allegiances expressed elsewhere
in a paper. Letter-writers had more time to argue their point, and usually
did so in a less hard-hitting and immediate fashion than the writers of
paragraphs. However, their relatively verbose nature did not preclude a
partisan appearance, and contributed to a newspaper's overall politics.

---

[1] MS letter, signed 'D W' and entitled 'Observations on ye Press' [1803?], BL, Add. MS
33124, fo. 79.

Indeed, since letters allowed for more detailed discussion on a given topic, they might well have had more impact than the much shorter, and perhaps less persuasive, paragraphs. In a letter to Richard Fitzpatrick in 1785, Charles James Fox outlined his views on the differences between letters, pamphlets, and paragraphs for propaganda purposes:

I can not think as you do of the Insignificancy of Newspapers though I think that others over rate their importance. I am clear too that Paragraphs alone will not do. Subjects of Importance should be first treated gravely in letters or pamphlets or best of all perhaps in a series of letters, and afterwards the Paragraphs do very well as an accompaniment. It is not till a subject has been so much discussed as to become almost threadbare that Paragraphs which consist principally in allusions can be generally understood. Secret Influence, Indian Government and now Irish propositions are all fit subjects therefore for paragraphs; but foreign Politics must first be treated in some serious & plain way, and must be much explained to the Public before any Paragraphs alluding to them can be understood by one in a thousand.[2]

The more partisan newspapers tended to publish largely letters which supported their own established political stance. More 'moderate' newspapers would reproduce a variety of letters containing various and opposing views. William Woodfall, who edited the *Morning Chronicle*, stated in a letter to William Adam that 'to ensure a publication of any matter in the *Morng. Chronicle*, the writer has only to begin with arraigning its veracity, or attacking its conductor—my high, but I trust, proper notions of impartiality impel me to an instant publication of the charge as its best refutation'.[3] The contents of the *Morning Chronicle* appear to support Woodfall's claim. The result of such a policy was a newspaper which could appear politically uncommitted, or at least less committed compared with many of its rivals. This does not seem to have been unintentional, and could be regarded as an asset. 'A Moderate Man' wrote in the *Morning Chronicle* that 'it is the principle of the MORNING CHRONICLE, in contradiction to almost every other newspaper in town, to steer a middle course, and by equally avoiding the fulls[o]me servility of the Ministerialists, and [t]he factious fury of Opposition, to govern all it gives the public by a scrupulous attention to candour and impartiality, and a strict regard to the general good'.[4]

The *Gazetteer*, another less partisan newspaper, was also self-

---

[2] Fox to Fitzpatrick [Nov./Dec. 1785], BL, Add. MS 47580, fo. 129-d.

[3] Woodfall to Adam, 14 Dec. 1780, Blair Adam MS, printed in Aspinall, *Politics and the Press*, 343.

[4] *Morning Chronicle*, 29 Dec. 1779.

consciously politically non-allied. It proclaimed itself as 'the Paper of the People. Uninfluenced by the countenance of Ministers, or the promises of Opposition',[5] and attempted to win advertising revenue by asserting that its 'extensive circulation' was far superior 'to a confined sale, within the narrow limits of a party'.[6] In contrast, the *London Courant* dismissed ideas of political non-alliance. On 11 August 1781, it announced that

the idea of an *impartial* print, and of an *impartial* individual in politics, are equally mean and contemptible. They are both alike avoided and execrated by honest men, because they are both alike destitute of principle. In this hour of ministerial turpitude, it cannot but be competent to every one to discern the ruinous tendency of the measures of Administration. Every honest man cries out shame upon them, and shuns them as they would a pestilence. Those creatures, and those prints, however, that *affect* an impartiality, observe another kind of conduct. They are base enough to fawn upon Ministry while in power, for what they can get by them, and when justice overtakes them, will be the *first* to cut their throats.

Despite the *Gazetteer*'s claims for the commercial value of impartiality, the most successful papers in this period were almost certainly John Almon's *London Courant* and Henry Bate's *Morning Post* and *Morning Herald*, both of which were aggressively partisan.

The political stance of individual newspapers was emphasized by their mutual relationships as well as by their commentary on political matters. The *General Advertiser* singled out the editor of the *Morning Post* in December 1779 for attacking 'those gentlemen who will not comply with the wicked designs of the Ministry'.[7] The *Morning Post* took great delight in 1784 in mocking the 'coalition writers'. On 1 July it commented that 'If Mr. Pitt does not speedily do something which may "appear disgracious in the country's eye," the coalition writers must inevitably starve. They have raised every farthing they can on his youth; and if he does not get older by winter, they will never be able to weather it through!' The *Public Advertiser* of 24 February 1784 asserted that 'the dull and base scurrility of the writers in support of the present unconstitutional Administration has compleatly disgusted the Public', whilst claiming on 12 March that 'the weakness of real virtue and honour in the present Opposition, is in nothing more conspicuous than in their filling the Newspapers with squibs, pasquinades, and illiberal reflections on the ministry'. For its part, the *Morning Post* claimed that 'Great pains have been taken by the writers for the Opposition, though in vain, to blind the eyes of the people, and to

[5] *Gazetteer*, 11 Nov. 1783. [6] Ibid. 30 May 1780.
[7] *General Advertiser*, 14 Dec. 1779.

persuade them that their interests are involved with that of the late majority', and that coalition supporters had been involved in a plot against the paper, by removing it from coffee-houses.[8] The *General Advertiser* attacked the ministerial press throughout 1782, and on 9 February referred to 'A Morning print, manifestly in the pay of Administration', whilst the *London Courant* of 23 March 1781 claimed that 'the money of the public is lavished on the purchase of hireling writers and speakers, who applaud every measure of the Ministry; cry up their victories on every little success . . . and brand every man, however distinguished by his abilities or property, who attempts to detect their weakness, with the odious imputations of faction and treachery'.

Such accusations of political corruption were common. In February 1780, the *London Evening Post* accused Bate, the editor of the *Morning Post*, of being patronized by the Ministry, and 'a prostituted hireling and betrayer of his country'.[9] The *Morning Post* hit back on 12 June 1780, claiming that 'there has been more French gold distributed among certain newspapers than the fee simple of their proprietors was ever worth', and on 28 July, that after the start of the American War, 'public newspapers were hired by Opposition to inflame the vulgar, and scandalise Government'. During March 1780, the *London Courant* claimed that Lord Sandwich was paying writers to attack Admiral Rodney and Lord Shelburne in print,[10] and in the following month, that ministers had given £25,000 during the last six months to pay for 'political and abusive writings'.[11] The same paper was to claim subsequently that 'the low malignant abuse poured fourth daily from ministerial hirelings against the best and wisest men in the kingdom, is a part of that infamous system began by Lord Bute at the beginning of the present reign, and pursued since by his pupils'.[12] In a comparison of newspapers which appeared in the *General Advertiser* on 9 January 1782, the *Daily Advertiser, Public Advertiser, Public Ledger, Morning Chronicle, Morning Post, Morning Herald, General Evening Post, London Courant, St. James's Chronicle, Lloyd's Evening Post*, and *London Packet* all received scores of nought for 'independencey'. The *General Advertiser* also printed a letter from 'Old England', which accused William Woodfall of receiving a pension of £400 a year from the government in exchange for altering the reports of the parliamentary debates carried in the *Morning Chronicle*, and giving 'the nation such an account as Ministers chuse they should have of those public proceedings'.[13]

---

[8] *Morning Post*, 6 and 16 Apr. 1784. [9] *London Evening Post*, 24 Feb. 1780.
[10] *London Courant*, 16 and 23 Mar. 1780. [11] Ibid. 11 Apr. 1780.
[12] *London Courant*, 27 Nov. 1780. [13] *General Advertiser*, 16 Jan. 1782.

Newspaper attacks on other newspapers and their writers reflected political and commercial rivalries, and, by identifying political enemies, helped to define further the politics of the paper making the allegations. However, as proof of high political manipulation, they must be read with extreme caution. Although some of those involved in newspapers no doubt did receive political bribes, the constant barrage of accusation and counter-accusation concerning press corruption which appeared in London papers was almost certainly based upon rumour and attempts to discredit rivals rather than being a fair representation of the degree of high political control. Yet this picture of political corruption is one which historians have perpetuated. Perhaps the most influential of these was Arthur Aspinall, whose work depicts eighteenth-century newspapers as victims of the rampant and pervasive corruption of the period:

During the last decades of the eighteenth century when newspapers were beginning to play an important part in politics, they were not independent and responsible organs of public opinion. There were Gatton and Old Sarum newspapers as well as Gatton and Old Sarum boroughs. The great majority of the London newspapers accepted subsidies either from the Government or from the Opposition, and were tied in various ways to the Party organizations.[14]

Lucyle Werkmeister supports this view. She describes the 1770s and 1780s as the 'age of the scandal sheet' which 'was characterized by such unprecedented corruption that during these two decades the number of daily newspapers increased from five to as many as fifteen'.[15] Werkmeister cites the *Morning Post* as an example, and claims that by 1780, there was 'hardly a paragraph . . . that was not paid for by someone'.[16] Further, she asserts that 'the support which the *Morning Post* had always given the Ministry was owing to expedience rather than principle, for . . . the Ministry [could] pay more than the Opposition, the Treasury being more opulent than any individual or group of individuals'.[17] The *Morning Post*'s method of obtaining money from bribes, for puffs, or for the suppression of pieces was, according to P. M. Handover, so successful that by 1780 other papers began to copy this 'lucrative corruption'.[18] But this type of 'corrupt' practice is not indicative of party-political control, as seems to have been assumed. There is an important difference between the acceptance of political bribes by newspapers to increase profits or the personal

---

[14] Aspinall, *Politics and the Press*, p. v.
[15] Lucyle Werkmeister, *The London Daily Press: 1772–1792* (Lincoln, Nebr., 1963), 4.
[16] Ibid. 7.
[17] Ibid. 61.
[18] P. M. Handover, *A History of the London Gazette* (London, 1965), 58.

income of those who ran them, and a level of political subsidy which determined a paper's survival. Whilst it would be naive not to assume that many newspaper pieces were inserted for payment, the levels of press manipulation which Aspinall, Werkmeister, and Handover allege remain unproven.

Many of the conclusions Aspinall drew in relation to the eighteenth-century press fail to stand up to close scrutiny. This is particularly true of his claim that a newspaper's politics were controlled by the payment of subsidies. Aspinall asserted that the sale of newspapers was too restricted to make them self-supporting, and that they were therefore dependent for their survival on party organizations, the government, or syndicates of 'City men'. The economic weakness of eighteenth-century newspapers is also accepted in later scholarship, as too is another of Aspinall's claims, that newspapers in the late eighteenth century were primarily advertising vehicles in which the dissemination of news was a secondary priority. Aspinall backed his argument on the role of subsidy by pointing to the government's Secret Service accounts which list the sums of money channelled to various newspaper interests. Between July 1782 and April 1783, for example, £1,084 10s. 6d. was given by the Shelburne Ministry to a Thomas Orde to distribute amongst unspecified newspaper editors, whilst an extra £800 was put aside as 'reservation to be made for sundry articles particularly writers and to complete engagements with editors of newspapers'.[19] An undated Secret Service account, evidently for the year 1784, suggests that during the first year of Pitt's ministry, he 'bought' the support of the press with subsidies paid via Thomas Harris, a printer and proprietor of the Covent Garden Theatre.[20] The account shows that the *Public Ledger*, *London Evening Post*, *Whitehall Evening Post*, and *St. James's Chronicle* all received £100 (which Aspinall suggests was not intended to cover the whole year). In addition, Henry Bate, editor of the *Morning Herald*, was also given £100, and John Benjafield received a total of £310 to reimburse his purchase of a share in the *Morning Post*.

Aspinall's model of political manipulation is particularly problematic in terms of the sums of money with which the Treasury supposedly secured press loyalty (whilst any amounts paid by the Opposition were presumably even smaller). According to Aspinall, such payments were crucial to a newspaper's financial stability, which was why they could command

[19] *The Correspondence of King George the Third*, ed. Sir John Fortescue, 6 vols. (London, 1927–8), vi. 342–3.
[20] *The Later Correspondence of George III*, ed. A. Aspinall, 5 vols. (Cambridge, 1962), i. 116–18.

newspaper compliance on matters of content. However, other evidence concerning newspaper economics contradicts Aspinall's claims. In the case of one moderately successful paper, the *Gazetteer*, its account books record monthly turnovers of between £700 and over £1,000.[21] Archenholz described the newspaper business in the 1780s as 'extremely lucrative, and maintains, in the city of London alone, a prodigious multitude of persons'.[22] More concrete evidence can also be given: for example, a thirty-second share of the *Gazetteer* was, according to the paper's records, sold in 1785 for £100,[23] which values the whole paper at over £3,000. John Benjafield records that he purchased two twenty-fourth shares of the *Morning Post* in 1783 for between 400 and 500 guineas.[24] In this case, the paper's value was somewhere between 4,800 and 6,000 guineas. In addition, the dividend for the *Post* was recorded in 1784 as £1,500.[25] Daniel Stuart, who published the paper after 1788 with his brother, referred to its situation in 1783 as 'not flourishing so much as in Mr. Bates's time, though a great and profitable property'.[26] In 1786, the *Morning Post*'s lease was sold to Tattersall for £1,400 per annum.[27]

Few ledgers of eighteenth-century newspapers survive, and those of the *Gazetteer* are an exception.[28] Werkmeister discounts the importance of such documents since they were subject to periodic inspections by the Stamp Office, and therefore likely to have been falsified and not to have included 'illegitimate' transactions.[29] However, it seems likely that she has overestimated the importance to a paper's finances of such sources of income as bribes and 'puffs', and the *Gazetteer*'s records still offer valuable insights into the internal workings of a newspaper and its finances. The surviving Treasurer's accounts, cash books, and Treasurer's petty expenses book cover the period from October 1783 to March 1796. Between October 1783 and the end of 1785, the average monthly circulation recorded was 56,389, or approximately 2,169 copies per day. These were sold at £10 per thousand to the vendors, thereby bringing in a monthly sum of about £560. In the same period, advertising revenue, although it could vary considerably from one month to the next, averaged £362 per month.[30]

[21] PRO, C104/67.   [22] Archenholz, *A Picture of England*, 42.

[23] PRO, C104/67, Book H.

[24] Benjafield, *Statement of Facts*, p. iv.

[25] Wilfrid Hindle, *The Morning Post, 1772–1937: Portrait of a Newspaper* (London, 1937), 44. The account book in which Hindle discovered the information has been lost.

[26] Letter quoted in Benjafield, *Statement of the Facts*, p. iv.

[27] Benjafield, *Statement of the Facts*, p. v.   [28] PRO, C104/67–8.

[29] Werkmeister, *The London Daily Press*, 5.   [30] PRO, C104/67.

When the expenses of printing, paper, the editor's pay, petty expenses, and stamp duty on both the newspapers and the advertisements they contained were subtracted from sales and advertising revenue, the clear profit was divided amongst the shareholders at twice-yearly intervals after the accounts were agreed at a general meeting. Although the profits tended to fluctuate, between October 1783 and December 1785 they averaged about £744 per annum.[31] Since the paper's ownership was divided into sixteen full shares,[32] this meant a yearly return per share of approximately £46. The report of the general meeting of September 1785 records the sale of a half share to John Debrett and a full share to Thomas and John Egerton for £100 and £200 respectively.[33] Even if newspapers were considered by their proprietors to have been risky investments,[34] an annual return of over 20 per cent was a very good one.[35] Of course, this is a figure which has been calculated according to the *Gazetteer*'s 'official' books. However, as the sums received by the paper for the sale of newspapers and advertising are unlikely to have been exaggerated, since tax was payable on both, and any illegitimate income from the selling of puffs and paragraphs and from political subsidy would only have increased the paper's income (if such sums did not go straight into the editor's pocket), it is clear that the *Gazetteer* was a commercially sound enterprise.[36] Certainly it does not appear that political subsidy would have been essential to the paper's survival.

A decade later this was not the case. The *Gazetteer* was in serious financial difficulties, which came to a head in 1796 after the paper had made a loss over ten consecutive months.[37] Comparing the *Gazetteer*'s main sources of income, from advertising and sales, with the paper's profits covering the whole period for which records exist (October 1783 to March 1796) reveals several important points about the economics of the

[31] PRO, C104/67, Book H.   [32] Ibid. Book M.   [33] Ibid. Book H.

[34] Hoppit's examination of bankruptcy shows the importance of risk avoidance and the 'security motive' amongst 18th-cent. businessmen, since failure carried with it considerable social stigma on top of possible legal ramifications: Julian Hoppit, *Risk and Failure in English Business 1700–1800* (Cambridge, 1987).

[35] Although it is difficult to know what levels of profits 18th-cent. businessmen would have considered acceptable, this figure compares well with Peter Earle's estimate of profits of 15–30% that successful merchants would have expected in the late 17th cent.: *The Making of the English Middle Class: Business, Society and Family Life in London, 1660–1730* (London, 1989), 138–40.

[36] There is evidence to show that it was not as prosperous as it had once been. On 20 July 1778, a 32nd share of the paper had been sold to William Owen for £200, which is double the 1784 price: PRO, C104/68, loose papers.

[37] PRO, C104/67.

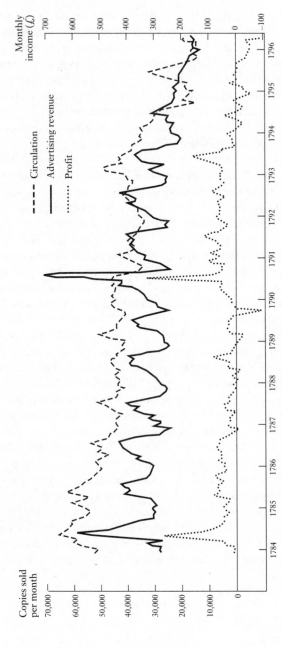

FIG. 3. Sources of income for the *Gazetteer*, October 1783–March 1796

Source: PRO, C104/67.

newspaper (Fig. 3). What is most noticeable is the marked link between advertising revenue, sales, and profit. Having already established the commercial viability of the paper, this correlation confirms that the *Gazetteer*'s success was dependent on its legitimate income. When these sources declined below a certain level in the 1790s, the paper was naturally forced out of business. Given the basis of newspaper profitability, it seems likely that the eighteenth-century newspaperman would have concentrated on increasing his paper's readership and advertising revenue, rather than chasing relatively small sums of political subsidy.

In his book, *The Stranger in England: or, Travels in Great Britain*, published in 1807, Goede maintained that 'editors are not a set of hungry scribblers, ready to barter their reputation for a mess of porridge, but mostly men of considerable fortune'.[38] It is an assertion which also carried some weight twenty years earlier. O'Bryen claimed he was offered £300 a year to edit 'the most fashionable paper in London' in 1779.[39] Both Almon and Bate appeared to have prospered during their time as newspapermen, in common with others. John Taylor saw the 'public press' as 'a shorter and more probable path, than my profession [as an oculist] afforded, to that independence which, from a very early period of my life I was always anxious to attain'.[40] Henry Sampson Woodfall, who edited, printed, and owned the *Public Advertiser* from 1758 until 1793, willed his two sons and daughter 'all sum or sums of money in the Government funds or India Companys [sic] funds and all my furniture plate silver china and all the rest and residue of my personal estate'.[41] His brother, William Woodfall, the editor, printer, and proprietor of the *Morning Chronicle* between 1769 and 1789, left £650 to his wife and, in common with his brother, possessions which indicated a comfortable middle-class lifestyle: sets of prints, china, plate, books, and mahogany furniture.[42] William Parker, a newspaper printer for many years and owner of the *General Advertiser* from 1781 until his death in 1784, left £600 to his daughter and numerous small gifts of money to his family and friends amounting to more than £1,600.[43] Alexander Chalmers, who edited the *Public Ledger* and *London Packet* in the 1770s, and contributed to newspapers as a political writer, left generous sums to his housemaid and housekeeper when he died.[44] Most spectacular in his success was James Perry, who in the 1780s founded and

---

[38] Goede, *The Stranger in England*, 222.
[39] O'Bryen to Burke, Mar. 1782, WWM, BK 1/1557.
[40] Taylor, *Records of My Life*, 23.
[41] PCC, PROB. 11/879.
[42] PCC, PROB. 11/744.   [43] PCC, PROB. 11/567.   [44] PCC, PROB. 11/676.

edited the *European Magazine*, edited the *Gazetteer* and *Debrett's Parliamentary Debates*, and finally took over the *Morning Chronicle* from Woodfall. He was careful to provide for his children, and in 1821 he left £7,000 to each of his four daughters, and the *Morning Chronicle*, an obviously valuable commodity, to his two sons.[45]

It was the profitability of newspapers which led to an increase in titles as the century progressed. This development was not limited to the capital, and the provincial press also grew prolifically (with little question here of political subsidy). However, the fact that newspapers were not dependent on political subsidy does not render such payments entirely insignificant, although in order to understand their importance and implication, each case needs to be examined individually. Unusually, the monies given to John Benjafield in order to help him buy a share in the *Morning Post* were part of a Treasury-inspired plan to change the paper's previously Foxite stance to a pro-ministerial one. A total of £310 was given to Benjafield in 1784 from government Secret Service funds 'to reimburse him for a share in the *Morning Post*' and 'for expenses of various sorts'.[46] In his autobiography, Benjafield claims he bought the shares 'on the persuasion of an high political friend . . . the Morning Post being at that period somewhat indecisive in its politics'.[47] This friend may well have been George Rose, the Secretary to the Treasury, in whose hand the Secret Service account is written. In any case, it seems clear that this was a direct act of party-political involvement in newspaper affairs, with Benjafield buying into the paper and then manoeuvring William Jackson into the editor's position.

Two established proprietors of the paper in 1784 were Joseph Richardson and his patron, Thomas Skinner. James Stephen, who was hired in 1781 as a parliamentary reporter on the *Post*, claimed that Richardson had probably been advanced money by Skinner to buy a share in the paper 'in order to obtain support by his talents in the committee of Proprietors, against the despotism and insolence of Bate', then editor.[48] Skinner's actions demonstrate that planting proprietors for political reasons was not unheard of, even though it does seem to have been rare. Both Skinner and Richardson were staunchly Foxite. Skinner, an alderman,

---

[45] PCC, PROB. 11/683. For a detailed picture of Perry's newspaper career after 1790, see Ivon Asquith, 'James Perry and the Morning Chronicle, 1790–1821' (University of London Ph.D. thesis, 1973).

[46] *Later Correspondence of George III*, vi. 118.

[47] Benjafield, *Statement of Facts*, p. iv.

[48] Stephen, *The Memoirs of James Stephen*, 289.

was involved in radical City politics, whilst Richardson's circle of friends included Fox, Sheridan, Townshend, and the Dukes of Portland and Northumberland.[49] Benjafield was evidently a match for the two however, for by March 1784, William Jackson was installed as editor, and Benjafield's assistant, William Augustus Miles, was also writing for the paper. On 22 March 1784, the *Post* announced that

the Proprietors of the Morning Post think it necessary to acquaint the Public, that they have changed their Editor, and are determined that this paper shall henceforward be conducted on the most liberal principles. They have come to a resolution, that the impartiality hitherto observed in the Parliamentary Reports, shall be extended to every other department; and that the Morning Post shall neither be prostituted to the corrupt support of a Minister nor devoted to the purposes of Faction.

The *Post*'s claim to a new impartiality was, however, a hollow one. It was to become far more partisan in support of the ministerial cause than it had ever been for Fox. Indeed, Jackson was particularly keen to attack the paper's old hero. He wrote the pamphlet *Thoughts on the Causes of the Delay in the Westminster Scrutiny*,[50] and seems likely to have been the author of letters signed 'Scrutineer' in the *Post*, which repeated the pamphlet's attacks on Fox over claimed irregularities in the Westminster election.

Jackson appears to have passed through a number of political conversions during his career. Originally hostile to Wilkes, Hindle claims he 'caught the flame of freedom' during the American Revolution, which led him to publish two works in its defence: a reply to Dr Johnson's *Taxation No Tyranny*, and *A Collection of the Constitutions of the Thirteen United States of North America*.[51] The latter was dedicated to the Duke of Portland, and should be seen as a failed attempt at securing patronage rather than the literary outpourings of a republican convert.[52] A year later, Jackson was supporting the Ministry against Fox. After his dismissal from the *Post*, he worked as a secret emissary between Paris, London, and Dublin, in the pay of both the French government and Pitt,[53] and ended by committing suicide in a Dublin prison after having been accused of

[49] Taylor, *Records of My Life*, ii. 165.
[50] William Jackson, *Thoughts on the Causes of the Delay in the Westminster Scrutiny* (London, 1784).
[51] Hindle, *The Morning Post*, 49.
[52] William Jackson, *A Collection of the Constitutions of the Thirteen United States of North America* (London, 1783).
[53] Hindle, *The Morning Post*, 50.

treason.[54] Jackson's lack of political consistency throughout his life was indicative of his opportunism when it came to obtaining a living. Unlike others involved in political writing, even those who could properly be described as hired propagandists (some of whom are discussed below in greater detail), Jackson was quite ready to change sides, and to do so more than once. This may only have been due to his successive failures in securing lasting patronage, but considering his end, he seems to have been more disreputable and mercenary than most.

William Augustus Miles worked with Jackson in the anti-Foxite campaign on the *Morning Post*, writing as 'Gracchus' and 'Neptune'.[55] According to his biographer, he had been working as a pamphleteer and political writer in the capital since the 1770s, and had had Earl Temple and Shelburne as patrons in the early 1780s.[56] His involvement with Jackson on the *Morning Post* almost certainly put him in the pay of the Treasury, and by the autumn of 1785 he was in direct correspondence with Pitt concerning his activities on behalf of the British government in the Principality of Liège. Despite being out of the country, Miles still felt obliged to contribute to the anti-Foxite cause in the press. In a letter to the second Earl Temple, which accompanied material for publication, Miles commented: 'You will perceive that at this distance, and without facts to go upon, I am restricted in my information on home politics. Like the spider, I spin from myself: would to Heaven I could resemble it farther, and entangle the factious fly in my patriotic web'.[57] By the time he wrote to Pitt in November 1785, Miles probably had some justification in claiming that 'my pen has been indefatigable in your service',[58] and this no doubt prompted Pitt's agreement to give him money.[59] This makes rather a mockery of the *Post*'s assertion on 27 April 1784: 'What a striking contrast between Mr. Pitt and Mr. Fox! Mr. Pitt *unfeelingly* leaves the *newspapers* to their fate, and cares neither for their praise or their censure; but Mr. Fox, when Secretary of State, takes care, by a good pension, to secure them from *insolvency*'.

Although the political stance of the *Morning Post* was altered as part of

---

[54] Lucyle Werkmeister, 'Notes for a Revised Life of William Jackson', *Notes and Queries*, 206/8 (1961), 43–7, p. 46.

[55] William Augustus Miles, *The Correspondence of William Augustus Miles on the French Revolution 1789–1817*, ed. Charles Popham Miles, 2 vols. (London, 1890), i. 14–17.

[56] Ibid. i. 4.

[57] Cited in Miles, *Correspondence*, i. 18.

[58] Miles to Pitt, 30 Nov. 1785, PRO, 30/8, 159.

[59] See Pitt's letter to Miles, 11 Sept. 1785, cited in Miles, *Correspondence*, i. 19; and Miles to Pitt, 9 Jan. 1786, PRO, 30/8, 159.

a Treasury-inspired plan, it should be stressed that in order to ensure that the paper's political transformation was successful, the Treasury had to buy into it, and then effect a change in its staff. It was simply not enough to offer an existing editor bribes. This level of 'high' political involvement with the press seems to have been rare, and does not provide a model of typical newspaper relations with politicians in this period. The political struggle which no doubt took place between Benjafield, Skinner, and Richardson was probably similar to the one which had resulted in Bate's departure from the *Post* four years earlier. Perhaps not surprisingly, considering Bate's reputation as the 'fighting parson', the battle in 1780 had ended in a duel between Bate and Richardson.[60] The often uneasy alliance of individual proprietors and those who staffed newspapers in the late eighteenth century suggests how unreliable a single payment to one person could be in determining a paper's political allegiance. In the case of Benjafield it was a gamble that paid off for the government, but this was not always the case.

Aspinall suggested that newspapers which were not subsidized by the government or party organizations were supported by syndicates of 'City men'.[61] It was certainly true that the proprietors of several London newspapers were groups of businessmen, based in the City of London. In the case of the *Morning Post*, the original proprietors of 1772, most of whom were still shareholders in the 1780s, included John Bell, a bookseller; James Christie and William Skinner, both auctioneers; Richard Tattersall, a horse dealer; and Joseph Richardson, a minor playwright.[62] The article of agreement in 1775 between Mrs Say, the printer of the *Gazetteer*, and the proprietors lists eleven booksellers, a ship broker, a stationer, and a merchant.[63] However, as events concerning the *Morning Post* demonstrate, such men were not necessarily politically unified, and in any case, they were unlikely to have supported a newspaper solely out of a desire to promote a particular political cause or ideological point of view. The motives of these men in owning newspapers were almost certainly commercially linked. Newspaper advertisements show how frequently proprietors advertised their other businesses in their papers. In addition, and perhaps more importantly, since newspapers were good financial investments regardless of political connections and subsidy, it is hardly surprising that enterprising businessmen should choose to diversify into this area.

---

[60] Hindle, *The Morning Post*, 15 and 52.   [61] Aspinall, *Politics and the Press*, 66.
[62] Hindle, *The Morning Post*, 9.   [63] PRO, C104/68.

The other payments to newspapers which the Secret Service accounts record are less conclusive than those made to Benjafield. In 1784, several newspapers were given at least £100 by the Treasury.[64] At the time of the election, one of these, the *Whitehall Evening Post*, did appear to support Pitt's administration and was hostile towards the Fox–North coalition. The *St. James's Chronicle* usually demonstrated similar beliefs, but its support of Pitt was not constant.[65] The *Morning Herald*, on the other hand, backed Fox rather than Pitt. Although its editor, Henry Bate, was given £100 by the government, the *Herald* remained militantly Foxite and defended the Prince of Wales. These payments can only be explained if it is accepted that they could not secure a paper's loyalty. It seems more likely that such sums were for coverage of (or silence concerning) particular issues at certain times, or conversely, merely rewards, as was the nature of eighteenth-century patronage, for a political loyalty which was already established and demonstrated.

But once we accept that subsidies from the Treasury or from political groups did not necessarily dictate newspaper politics, it is then unclear why individual papers professed certain, usually very consistent, views, and espoused the cause of particular politicians or parties. The role of readership here cannot be ignored. It seems unlikely that individual newspapers were able to prosper without eliciting a favourable response from at least a section of the capital's newspaper readership. Moreover, newspapers could not have operated successfully if unaware of the tastes, preoccupations, and concerns of the readers they hoped to appeal to. Even though the exact nature of readership response to newspapers is impossible to discern, it seems likely to have been connected in some way to political content. With so many titles being produced in the capital at one time, readers were faced with a choice which would probably have been made upon this basis, since it was politics which appear to have divided papers amongst themselves more than any other factor: thus John Trusler, in his guide to London, described daily newspapers according to their political allegiances.[66] The notion that political stance could attract readers was certainly behind the *General Advertiser*'s belief that it could claim the *London Courant*'s old readership when that paper folded in 1783.

---

[64] These included the *London Evening Post*, the *Ledger*, *St. James's Chronicle*, the *Morning Post*, and the *Whitehall Evening Post*: *The Later Correspondence of George III*, vi. 118. Of these, only the latter 3 are extant.

[65] See for example the letter from 'A True Whig' which appeared in the paper on 16 Mar. 1784.

[66] Trusler, *The London Advisor*.

The *Advertiser* assumed for itself the position of the capital's leading radical paper, as a supporter of Whig administrations, the reform of parliamentary representation, the rights of the people, and the 'glorious cause of liberty'.[67]

The use of such editorial strategies to attract readers did not necessarily mean that newspapers were consciously targeted towards particularly narrow groups. Indeed, a letter from 'Impartial' in the *St. James's Chronicle* remarked: 'As I think it fair to hear both sides in every dispute, I take in a news-paper which professes to be an advocate of the Court, and one which stands up a Champion for the People'.[68] But since political contents were clearly so crucial to securing readers, it was important that the London press displayed a diversity of political stances and a varying intensity of party-political loyalty in order to satisfy its audience. Various factors determined the politics of individual newspapers, and these differed from paper to paper. The role that Aspinall and others have attributed to political subsidy stresses only one form of external pressure. But it was the internal processes of newspaper production, and in particular the role of the editor, that was crucial in forming the political opinions which a paper expressed.

Late eighteenth-century newspapers were small-scale affairs. Although they were often owned by consortiums of ten or more people, day-to-day operations did not involve such numbers. The actual production of newspapers was the job of a printer, who would usually have been paid a fixed fee.[69] Such jobbing printers were usually responsible for the production of more than one paper, and although most printers were not involved in deciding the content of newspapers, there does seem to be some correlation between certain printers and the politics of the papers they printed. John Miller, for example, printed the *London Evening Post*, *General Advertiser*, and *London Courant* in the 1780s,[70] all of which were 'City' or Opposition papers. Elsewhere the definitions of 'printer', 'editor', and 'proprietor' can appear more blurred. The Woodfall brothers assumed all three roles in both the papers which they ran in the 1780s, and Henry Bate was proprietor and editor of the *Morning Herald*, having previously been only the editor of the *Morning Post*. All of the most successful papers appear to have been under the ultimate control of a single editor. Despite the fact that legally, it was the printer who was responsible for what

---

[67] *General Advertiser*, 12 May 1783.   [68] *St. James's Chronicle*, 17 Aug. 1780.
[69] For example, the records of the *Gazetteer* show its printer, Mary Say, received a fixed payment according to the number of papers printed: PRO, C104/67.
[70] Ian Maxted, *The London Book Trades 1775–1800* (Folkestone, 1977), 154.

appeared in print, it is clear that the editor dictated contents almost exclusively.

Editorial control was not foolproof though, and occasionally references were made to material which was published without the editor's knowledge. John Taylor said that as editor of the *Morning Post* from 1788 to 1790, he used to stay in his office until three in the morning to 'guard against the accidental insertion of any improper article, moral or political'.[71] The *Post* reported that at Bate's trial for a libel on the Duke of Richmond in 1781, Robert Haswell, the paper's printer, claimed that paragraphs often appeared without Bate seeing them, since 'the Editor's office was a common room, dedicated to the business of the Morning Post' and 'a great variety of persons came into it occasionally'.[72] John Almon maintained that a letter by 'Junius' was placed in the *London Museum* in 1770 whilst he was out of town,[73] and that in 1788, a paragraph which attacked the King was inserted in the *General Advertiser*, also without his knowledge.[74] However, since both Bate's and Almon's claims followed the onset of libel actions against them, some doubt must be cast upon their version of events.

On the whole the editor's role in forming a paper's politics appears to have been of prime importance. William Jerdan, who worked on the short-lived daily newspaper, the *Aurora*, which appeared for only a few months in 1781, blamed its failure on management by committee, rather than by one editor, or as he put it, a 'despotic power'.[75] The *Aurora* had been set up as a business venture by a group of hoteliers and inn landlords from the West End. Jerdan commented that

our rulers of the hotel dynasties, though intelligent and sensible men, were neither literary nor conversant with journalism; thus under any circumstances their interference would have been injurious, but it was rendered still more fatal by their differences in political opinion, and two or three of the number setting up to write 'Leaders' themselves. The clashing and want of *ensemble* was speedily obvious and detrimental; our readers became perfect weathercocks, and could not reconcile themselves to themselves from day to day. They wished, of course, to be led, as all well-informed citizens are, by their newspaper; and they would not blow hot and cold in the manner prescribed for all the coffee-room politicians in London.[76]

Although newspapers were primarily business ventures, some were run by men who showed an active interest in politics. The memoirs of William

---

[71] Taylor, *Records of My Life*, ii. 270.   [72] *Morning Post*, 24 June 1780.
[73] Almon, *Memoirs*, 62.
[74] Ibid. 136.   [75] Jerdan, *Autobiography*, i. 89.   [76] Ibid. i. 89–90.

West, a bookseller in late eighteenth-century London, describe a John Huddlestone, who was 'for a considerable time Editor of the Gazetteer, and was a well known speaker at the Robin Hood and Coach Maker Hall debating societies'.[77] John Almon's paper, the *London Courant*, certainly did not suffer in the same way as the *Aurora*. Under his editorship it remained staunchly anti-ministerial throughout the early 1780s, reserving particular venom for the Prime Minister. On 10 April 1780, a typical attack on Lord North asked: 'is it your characteristic insolence and somnolency to brave the effects of their [the public's] determined resentment; they smart and bleed under all the fatal consequences of your Administration; to bear your head aloft, tho' branded, as I have already observed, with the mark of universal reprobation?' The *Courant*'s themes remained consistent. It attacked the threat to the constitution posed by a growth of Crown influence and the corruption of Parliament, and bemoaned the people's loss of the 'ancient rights' of annual parliaments and equal representation.

John Almon was arguably one of the most politically active newspaper editors in London at the time. In his *Memoirs of a Late Eminent Bookseller*, Almon described his early employment by the *Gazetteer* in the 1760s, and his efforts to promote the cause of Pitt the Elder.[78] Almon was also keen to discuss later friendships with Earl Temple, Edmund Burke, the Dukes of Newcastle and Devonshire, the Marquis of Rockingham, and Lords Townshend and Camden. His involvement in such circles, if only partial, is apparent in his surviving correspondence,[79] and it is clear that he had gained particularly by Earl Temple's patronage in the 1760s.[80] In addition to his friendships with members of the Whig elite, Almon also had strong links with John Wilkes. During Wilkes's period of exile in France, he and Almon maintained a regular correspondence, in which Almon kept his exiled friend informed of domestic events.[81] Almon also claims to have supported Wilkes in elections,[82] and in 1763 he wrote and published a pamphlet in his defence.[83] Almon's political pedigree and subsequent

---

[77] [W. West], *Fifty Years' Recollections of an Old Bookseller* (Cork, 1835), 72–5.
[78] Almon, *Memoirs*, 15.
[79] BL, MS 20733.
[80] Deborah D. Rogers, *Bookseller as Rogue: John Almon and the Politics of Eighteenth-Century Publishing* (New York, 1986), 7.
[81] John Wilkes, *Correspondence of the Late John Wilkes, With His Friends, Printed from the Original Manuscripts, In Which Are Introduced Memoirs of His Life*, ed. John Almon, 5 vols. (London, 1805).
[82] Almon, *Memoirs*, 51.
[83] [John Almon], *A Letter to the Right Honourable George Grenville in Defence of J. Wilkes* (London, 1763).

allegiances are apparent in the tone of the paper he conducted, and in his other publications. In the early 1780s, writing as 'An Independent Whig', Almon launched a pamphlet campaign against North's ministry and the 'interior cabinet' supposedly headed by Charles Jenkinson.[84] In *The Revolution in MDCCLXXXII Impartially Considered*, the promise of 'oeconomy and reformation' under the new Rockingham administration was celebrated and contrasted with the 'extravagance and corruption' of North's government, when 'the national character was degraded and debased in every instance of their conduct'.[85] Although Almon 'retired' from press involvement in 1783, he married the widow of John Parker the following year, and proceeded to run Parker's *General Advertiser*.[86] By 1785, the paper tended to support Pitt, as the minister most likely to enact a reform of Parliament. On 5 February, it commented that 'there can be nothing plainer than Mr. Pitt's intention to support the Reform Bill with all his interest, and there can be nothing more certain than the intention of the Ex-Ministry to oppose him'. Almon's commitment to reform, so marked in the *London Courant*, was still apparent.

Henry Bate was another newspaper editor who expressed particularly strident political views, although usually in opposition to those espoused by Almon. He took charge of the *Morning Post* in 1775, but left in 1780 to found the rival *Morning Herald*.[87] His departure appears to have been the result of his conviction for a libel in the paper on the Duke of Richmond. It seems likely that Bate was responsible for numerous attacks which had labelled Richmond the 'Gallic Duke' and 'patriotic agent vender of his Majesty's dominions!'[88] Displaying typical bravado, the paper had subsequently claimed:

The Anglo-Gallic Duke and his confederates have pledged themselves to opposition, to hunt down the gentleman who is the reputed Editor of this paper, before the opening of the next sessions of parliament. This however is to be looked upon as nothing more than one of those hasty declarations made in the moment of patriotic phrenzy, because it requires something more than threats and vain boasting, to defeat the man, whom they have never yet been able to intimidate.[89]

---

[84] [John Almon], *A Letter to the Right Honourable Charles Jenkinson* (London, 1781); *The Revolution in MDCCLXXXII Impartially Considered* (London, 1782); *An Address to the Interior Cabinet* (London, 1782).
[85] Almon, *The Revolution in MDCCLXXXII*, 22.
[86] Maxted, *The London Book Trades*, 3 and 170.
[87] Grant, *The Newspaper Press*, 314.
[88] *Morning Post*, 9 Dec. 1779.   [89] Ibid. 3 June 1780.

However, since the printer of the *Post* refused to take responsibility for what was published, Bate was subsequently convicted of libel and was imprisoned for a short period.[90]

James Stephen, who worked for the *Post* as a parliamentary reporter during 1780, asserted that Bate's 'domineering spirit had so much subdued the Proprietors of the paper, among whom were Alderman Skinner and some other individuals of pecuniary consequence, that he was allowed to conduct it without controul as to its political tone or otherwise'.[91] The confusion caused by the Richmond Affair, however, seems to have upset this tight command. Richardson and his patron, Thomas Skinner, were almost certainly allied against Bate, particularly concerning his behaviour towards the Duke of Richmond. However, Bate's ability to dictate the *Post*'s politics as editor was apparently unassailable until he himself came under political fire. After Bate left the *Morning Post*, the paper sided with Fox.

In Bate's new venture, the *Morning Herald*, such conflicts did not arise, since Bate was both editor and proprietor.[92] The *Herald*'s political stance was very similar to (albeit slightly more cautious than) that of the *Morning Post* under Bate's editorship. On 17 January 1781, it commented in typical style: 'proudly as Opposition may boast of their strength, yet it is well known, that their influence every where, even with the mob, is decreasing, one or two families excepted; they are, in general, men of small properties, decayed estates, and as desperate in fortunes, as they are wicked in mind'. Throughout 1781, the *Herald* continued to attack the Opposition and the fledgling reform movement. It was a political stance which continued even whilst Bate was in prison and Alexander Chalmers was placed temporarily in charge.[93] However, in the later part of 1782, when Bate resumed control, the paper's opposition to the Shelburne Ministry became noticeably more marked. 'Legion' wrote on 18 July 1782, criticizing the new ministry thus: 'under the mask of patriotism, there are men of the most unmeasurable ambition, whose views are for power only, and who will unite with any set, or in any measures, to preserve it, it is again incumbent upon every man, who loves his country, to do his utmost in branding such men with contempt and detestation'.

During the constitutional crisis of 1783 to 1784, the *Morning Herald*

[90] Bate was finally sentenced to a year in prison in June 1781: Werkmeister, *The London Daily Press*, 48.

[91] Stephen, *Memoirs*, 288.

[92] There seems little evidence to support Werkmeister's assertion that money for this venture was received by Bate from the Rockingham Whigs: *The London Daily Press*, 42.

[93] Grant, *The Newspaper Press*, 316.

underwent something of a political transformation, even though Bate was editor throughout. In 1783, and in line with its earlier political allegiance, the *Herald* was hostile to what it described as the 'abominable coalition',[94] which 'may render us the *jest* of Europe',[95] and to Fox in particular. On 10 May it commented: 'Nothing can equal the duplicity of the man of the people [Fox]: in his speech on the parliamentary reform, his sole object seemed to be to prevent that measure being carried . . . How long will this deluded country suffer such Orators to insult their feelings with impunity?' At the same time, the *Herald* gave Pitt favourable coverage, being a man who 'abhors the principles that gave birth to the coalition so much that he will not hear of any such proposition [as joining it]'.[96]

By early 1784 the situation had altered a great deal. It was now Pitt upon whom the paper hurled abuse, and Fox who was defended. On 6 March, the *Herald* asserted that 'nothing can be more miserable than the attempts made by the present unconstitutional Ministers to obtain popularity in Westminster, a strong proof of this appeared on Thursday, when Mr. Fox was received with the most triumphant acclamations at St. James's gate, and the Minister of the Crown with a general hiss'. The *Herald*'s new allegiance did not seem to be an attempt to court a popular line, since it remained unaltered throughout 1784 and 1785, when Pitt's popularity was firmly established. The paper also adopted this stance despite the fact that the Treasury was paying it.[97]

The *Herald* might have changed its party-political allegiances between 1783 and 1784, but in other ways, the paper's politics remained consistent. In 1783, the coalition had been attacked as the 'oil and vinegar administration', guilty of 'political hypocrisy'[98] and interested only in power. North, whose previous administration the paper had supported, was told by 'Brutus' that 'If you formerly had any claim to the approbation of your fellow-subjects, you have now abandoned it for ever'.[99] Indeed, the *Herald* suggested that 'whoever seizes the reins of government, will prefer his own sordid views to the interest of the commonweal'.[100] Pitt, on the other hand, was described as one who 'bids fairest to be the Minister of this country; and considering his abilities and his virtues, the station of a premier will admirably become him'.[101] By February 1784, Pitt had

---

[94] *Morning Herald*, 3 June 1783.   [95] Ibid. 23 June 1783.
[96] Ibid. 29 July 1783.
[97] Secret Service Account [1784], in Rose's hand, printed in *Later Correspondence of George III*, i. 116–18.
[98] *Morning Herald*, 1 July 1783.
[99] Ibid. 7 Aug. 1783.   [100] Ibid. 18 Mar. 1783.   [101] Ibid. 9 June 1783.

become the 'prerogative Minister',[102] who 'at present lords it over the state, in open defiance of the Commons'.[103] By apparently overriding the constitution, Pitt was deemed to have lost his virtue. This was a sin which the Coalition, for all its odiousness, had never committed:

Lord North has always declared, that, however unfortunate he has been in the pursuit of his political measures, the honour, dignity, and interest of the nation have been the objects in view, and it should be always remembered that his Lordship acted under the authority of a majority of the House of Commons, and that when he found that majority fail him, he did not seek a resource in the House of Lords, but resigned.[104]

Pitt's only hope to regain his credibility was in his plan for parliamentary reform, of which the *Herald* argued 'unless he speedily gratifies the public in their well-founded expectations on this important point, his professions will be found to have been merely delusive, and the wreck of his popularity be the inevitable consequence'.[105] When Pitt failed in this, the paper was unforgiving. On 19 January 1785, it commented, 'Mr Pitt is now said not to have pledged himself, as a man and a minister, to support the reform in parliament; but as a man only, the effects of this kind of support, the public have been already acquainted with, and therefore will not be surprised to see the young Premier divide on the question without a single companion from the Treasury Bench'.

Henry Bate was, without doubt, the most prominent, and the most notorious, newspaper editor in London during the 1780s. He featured in many contemporary satirical prints, and was credited with a great deal of political power. In 'Ministerial Purgations, or State Gripings' (1780; Plate 4), Bate is set alongside both leading figures in the government and the Devil, who refers to him as 'my best child of all'.[106] The implication that Bate could influence the nation's affairs through his newspaper was repeated in another hostile print from 1780. In 'Political Stag Hunt, or the M[inisteria]l Hounds in Full Cry' (Plate 5), both the government and Bate are once again under attack. In this instance, rather than defecating on the country, ministers are presented as hounds, chasing the deer of the constitution who flees to the Whigs for protection. Bate is depicted here as the huntsman egging on the pack. In his bag, he carries materials for his newspaper—satire, malice, scandal, and falsehood—and his pocket contains a work on 'the art of living made easy'.[107] Although Bate's fame was

---

[102] *Morning Herald*, 11 Feb. 1784.   [103] Ibid. 2 Feb. 1784.
[104] Ibid. 17 Feb. 1784.   [105] Ibid. 16 Mar. 1784.   [106] 1780, BM, DG 5632.
[107] BM, DG 5676. Bate is also featured in two other prints from 1780: 'The Balance of Power', BM, DG 5666; and 'A Baite for the Devil', BM, DG 5550. From 1784, see 'The Loves of the Fox . . .', BM, DG 6369; and 'The Political Sampson', BM, DG 6620.

unusual, many of the capital's newspaper editors were public figures, in the sense that their identity was widely known, and writers to their papers would address letters directly to them. Such public recognition would have ensured that individual editors were identified with particular politics. No doubt this situation would have encouraged editors to maintain particular political positions in order to retain credibility. In addition, if readership could be determined by the politics of a newspaper, then the identification of certain editors with particular views would have been a positive selling point, particularly if the editor was a celebrity like Bate.

Newspapers run by Bate and Almon were particularly emphatic in their political stance. This was not the case with all successful papers, even if run by well-known editors. The *Morning Chronicle*, edited by William Woodfall, has already been noted as a self-consciously uncommitted paper. Woodfall was a celebrated figure, noted especially for his ability to memorize long parliamentary debates, a gift which earned him the nickname 'Memory Woodfall'.[108] His brother, Henry Woodfall, was also a newspaper editor, and ran the *Public Advertiser* for most of his life. Although this paper did not appear as neutral as that of his brother, it was not nearly as partisan as other newspapers. Not only were the editorial sections less virulent, but the paper was also composed of a much larger proportion of letters than most others. It appears that Henry may have had a policy similar to his brother's concerning the impartial publication of letters, since these often represented a political mix which detracted from any real firmness of political line. To eighteenth-century newspaper editors, impartiality did not mean a lack of bias in all coverage, but a willingness to publish letters and paragraphs partisan to both sides of the political debate. Henry and William Woodfall's father had also been a newspaperman, and had handed the *Public Advertiser* to Henry in 1758.[109] Both brothers seem to have received their entire livelihoods from the newspapers they ran, which may explain their apparently cautious approach.[110] But then again, not all editors could be as politically motivated or as flamboyant as Almon and Bate. Nor did they need to be, since the Woodfall brothers clearly found a market for their papers.

Most newspapers were run by professional newspapermen rather than propagandists in the pay of politicians, like Jackson. However, such

---

[108] Grant, *The Newspaper Press*, 199.   [109] Bourne, *English Newspapers*, i. 191.

[110] William had run the *London Packet* before he founded the *Morning Chronicle*. Although Henry had published the letters of 'Junius' in the 1770s, and consistently refused to reveal the writer's identity, the discussion of anonymity above makes it clear that he was probably prudent to keep silent.

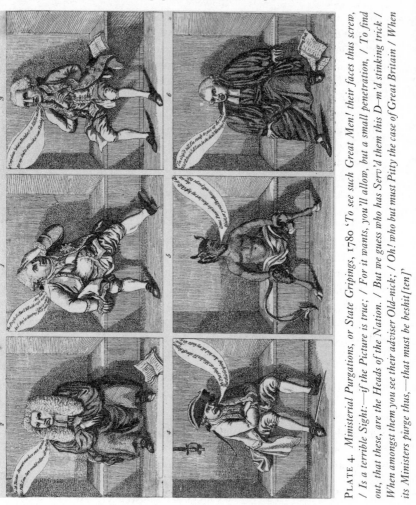

PLATE 4. *Minsterial Purgations, or State Gripings*, 1780 'To see such Great Men! their faces thus screw, / Is a terrible Sight:—if the Picture is true; / For it wants, you'll allow, but a small penetration, / To find out, that these, are the Heads of the Nation. / But me guess who has Serv'd them this D–m'd stinking trick / When amongst them you see their adviser Old-nick; / Oh! who but must Pitty the case of Great Britain / When its Ministers purge thus,—that must be beshit [ten]'

PLATE 5. *Political Stag. Hunt, or the M[inisteria]l Hounds in full Cry*, 1780 'Hungry Dogs the old Proverbs say / Eat dirty Pudding, when in their way / So will these Dogs as oft we are told / Catch at any thing which looks like Gold. / Or bears the least Aspect of doing / Good for themselves and their Country ruin. / 'Tis little Rogues submit to fate / Whilst ye Great enjoy ye World in State'

'hacks' should not be ignored. Despite the fact that they rarely commanded editorial control of newspapers, they did contribute to their
contents, and as such played an important part in determining newspaper
politics. In addition, their other activities, particularly as pamphleteers,
would have helped to shape the general nature of public political debate in
the capital. The authors of political pamphlets tend to be easier to identify
than those of paragraphs and letters in the papers, although it seems clear
that many writers performed both tasks. It has been suggested that James
Macpherson, the poet and 'translator' of Ossian, was paid £600 in 1776 to
supervise the ministerial papers, rising to £800 in 1781.[111] A similar claim
was repeated in the *Morning Herald* on 5 July 1784, whilst Walpole
charged him with getting £800 per year from the Court for inspecting the
newspapers and inserting 'lies' in a 'daily column'.[112] Another source
maintains that after settling in London in 1766, Macpherson was 'at once
employed by the government as a political writer', contributing to the
attack on 'Junius' by writing in newspapers as 'Musæus' and 'Scævola'.[113]
In the same year Macpherson was made Surveyor-General with a sinecure
worth £200 per year, which his biographer has claimed was 'on the
condition, so far as can be gathered, that he should devote himself henceforth to political writing'.[114] On 26 March 1782, when he was just about to
leave office, North wrote to the King suggesting that Macpherson be
given pensions which totalled over £500, a request which was apparently
granted:[115]

Mr James Macpherson has for many years been a most laborious and able writer
in favour of Government. The History of the Opposition, the best defence of the
American war, and almost all the good pamphlets on the side of Administration
were the production of his pen. When Lord North succeeded the Duke of
Grafton, he found Mr Macpherson on the private list of pensioners. He is now in
possession of a pension of £500 a year, and has lately lost the place of Secretary to

---

[111] John Nichols, *Literary Anecdotes of the Eighteenth Century*, 9 vols. (London, 1812–15),
ii. 17 and 483.
[112] Walpole, cited in Lutnick, *The American Revolution and the British Press*, 18; letter
from Walpole to the Countess of Ossory, 7 Jan. 1782, *Walpole's Correspondence*, xxxi. 320.
[113] Baily Saunders (ed.), *The Life and Letters of James Macpherson* (London, 1894), 215.
See also Edward Porritt, 'The Government and the Newspaper Press in England', *Political
Science Quarterly*, 12 (1897), 666–83.
[114] *The Life and Letters of James Macpherson*, 213.
[115] J. A. Cannon, in *History of Parliament*, iii. 96, records that Robinson sent a note
affirming this request, published in *The Parliamentary Papers of John Robinson, 1774–1784*,
ed. W. T. Laprade, Camden 3rd ser. vol. xxxiii (London, 1922), 50.

the province of West Florida, worth near £300 a year. He will certainly meet with no mercy from the new Administration, who are much irritated against him.[116]

In 1776, Macpherson wrote *The Rights of Great Britain Against the Claims of America*, a pamphlet defending the policy of the North administration which went into several editions. In 1779 he produced another pamphlet, entitled *A Short History of the Opposition During the Last Session*. This was another defence of the Ministry's American policy, and contained a strong attack on the parliamentary Opposition, claiming that England's worst foes were 'nursed in her own bosom' under the mask of patriotism, by an Opposition whose 'eagerness to thwart the measures of Government has expelled all regard for the opinions of the people'.[117] Macpherson was a close friend of Henry Woodfall, and wrote for the paper as an 'Independent Englishman',[118] as well as being a partner in the paper.[119] A letter from Woodfall's brother, William, to Caleb Whitefoord in 1775 reveals his plan to engage Macpherson in a campaign against Dr Johnson's *Journey to the Western Islands of Scotland*, which had offended Woodfall with its anti-Scottish tone:

I mean, as often as opportunity will admit, to say a word or two respecting the literary Dictator's Tour; and I think the attack would gain strength if Mr Macpherson and you were occasionally to join me. I presume the Morning Chronicle is the [best?] field to take post in, for if we began to fire away from the Packet, it might be discovered that Mr M. was one of the crew, and it might produce disadvantages.[120]

Macpherson's association with the *London Packet* was obviously common knowledge, whilst the *Morning Chronicle* provided a more anonymous setting for his writing. In 1780, Macpherson became MP for Camelford in Cornwall, apparently acting on behalf of the Nabob of Arcot, whose official London agent he became in 1781 upon the resignation of his relative, Sir John Macpherson. A 1779 pamphlet defending the nabob, *The History and Management of the East India Company . . . In Which the*

---

[116] *Correspondence of King George the Third*, v. 414.

[117] [James Macpherson], *A Short History of the Opposition During the Last Session* (London, 1779), pp. iii and 4.

[118] H. S. Woodfall's correspondence contains two undated letters from Macpherson: one is an invitation to dinner, the other advised that Woodfall 'may leave out the Postscript to the *Independent Englishman*. I'll send it in another shape', and included 'several scraps of intelligence': BL, Add. MS 27780, fos. 53–4.

[119] Macpherson is listed as one of 14 partners in the minutes of the *London Packet* for 1770: BL, Add. MS 38729, fos. 165–6.

[120] BL, Add. MS 36593, fo. 118.

Rights of the Nabob Are Explained, and the Injustice of the Company Proved, has been attributed to Macpherson, a man whose pen seemed permanently poised to defend his patrons.

Another prolific pamphleteer was Thomas Lewis O'Beirne, who wrote in defence of the Whigs. In 1780, he appeared as 'A Country Gentleman' in Almon's *London Courant*, and Almon also published O'Beirne's pamphlets. In the same year O'Beirne wrote *A Short History of the Last Session of Parliament*, parts of which were taken from his letters to the *Courant*. This was an attack on the Ministry, particularly in terms of its refusal to enact reform, and an appeal, in the expectation of a general election, for voters to elect an alternative government: 'if by their suffrages, they return to the next Parliament a majority of those men, who for the last six years, have held themselves independent of their Constituents, and acted as the representatives of the Minister, and not of the People, they will set the last seal to their own slavery'.[121] This was followed by a discussion of the Gordon Riots in *Considerations on the Late Disturbances*,[122] which attributed them to the unrest caused by the petitions of the Protestant Association (at a time when many ministerialists were blaming the Opposition). A year later, O'Beirne defended Admiral Keppel and Sir Hugh Palliser against court-martial.[123] In 1785, O'Beirne answered a pamphlet on Pitt's plan to establish a commercial system in Ireland,[124] attributed to George Rose, with *A Reply to the Treasury Pamphlet*, whilst in the same year, he produced *A Gleam of Comfort in This Distracted Empire, in Despite of Faction, Violence, and Cunning, Demonstrating the Fairness and Reasonableness of National Confidence in the Present Ministry*. Despite its title, this was an attack on Pitt's ministry and on the dissolution of Parliament, supposedly caused by the secret influence of the 'King's friends'.

O'Beirne's political writings appear, like those of Macpherson and O'Bryen, to have secured him patronage and preferment. Croly claimed that his association with the Whig hierarchy was accidental, the result of a chance meeting in a country inn, but that 'in a short period O'Beirne enjoyed all the advantages of the first society of the empire. What his graceful appearance and manners gained in the first instance, was kept by his literary acquirements and the usefulness of his services', and that

---

[121] T. L. O'Beirne, *A Short History of the Last Session of Parliament* (London, 1780), 6.
[122] T. L. O'Beirne, *Considerations on the Late Disturbances* (London, 1780).
[123] T. L. O'Beirne, *Considerations on the Principles of Naval Discipline and Courts-Martial, in Which the Doctrines of the House of Commons and the Conduct of the Naval Courts-Martial on Admiral Keppel and Sir Hugh Palliser are Compared* (London, 1781).
[124] T. L. O'Beirne, *The Proposed System of Trade With Ireland Explained* (London, 1785).

O'Beirne's career 'might have made an instructive and curious biography, and no imperfect manual of "the art of rising in the world" '.[125] This pattern emerged when O'Beirne acted as chaplain to Lord Howe during the American War. On his return to England, he defended his employer in *A Candid and Impartial Narrative of the Transactions of the Fleet Under the Command of Lord Howe*.[126] In 1782, O'Beirne became private secretary and chaplain to the Duke of Portland, who was to give him two valuable livings when he left office, in Northumberland and Cumberland, both of which he gave up in 1791 when, again via the Duke's influence, he received the rich benefices of Temple-Michael and Mohill from the Archbishop of Tuan. In December 1794, O'Beirne accompanied Lord Fitzwilliam to Ireland, first as his chaplain, then as his private secretary, and was rewarded with the bishopric of Ossory in 1795, which three years later he was to exchange for that of Meath.[127]

In contrast to O'Beirne's varied career, John Scott acted as propagandist for a single patron. In 1781, he returned to England from India to act as Warren Hastings's political agent. On 14 January 1784, a letter from Scott was published in the *Morning Chronicle*, defending himself against a claim made by 'The Reasoner' that the newspaper had received £1,000 in the preceding year to defend Hastings:

Mr Woodfall, I pay you no compliment, when I say I have at all times found you ready to insert whatever letters, &c. I may have sent to you, and you will do me the justice to say, that I never desired my name might be concealed, and that I never offered you the smallest compensation for inserting any article respecting Mr. Hastings, beyond the trifle which you would have had an undoubted right to demand, for advertisements from any citizen of London or Westminster.

Whilst denying that he bribed Woodfall, Scott freely admitted his role in defending Hastings in print. Scott was also a prolific pamphleteer, carrying out a campaign in favour of his patron, and attacking his main antagonist, Edmund Burke.[128] In his attempts to defend Hastings, Scott

---

[125] George Croly, *The Personal History of His Late Majesty George the Fourth*, 2nd edn. (London, 1841), 159 and 161.

[126] T. L. O'Beirne, *A Candid and Impartial Narrative of the Transactions of the Fleet Under the Command of Lord Howe* (London, 1779); [John Almon], *Biographical, Literary, and Political Anecdotes, of Several of the Most Eminent Persons of the Present Age* (London, 1797), 95.

[127] Henry Cotton, *Fasti Ecclesiæ Hibernicæ*, 4 vols. (Dublin, 1845–50), ii. 289.

[128] Amongst those pamphlets written by Scott were: *A Short Review of Transactions in Bengal During the Last Ten Years* (London, 1782); *A Letter to . . . Edmund Burke* (London, 1783); *A Letter to the Right Honourable Charles James Fox* (London, 1783); *The Conduct of His Majesty's Late Ministers Considered* (London, 1784); *A Reply to Mr Burke's Speech of the*

concentrated his efforts at influencing opinion not just in Parliament, as MP for West Looe in Cornwall, but also in his political writing.

One other writer who seems to have obtained preferment through his literary efforts in the newspapers was Hugh Boyd, the man whom both John Almon and Boyd's biographer, Lawrence Dundas Campbell, tried to identify as 'Junius'.[129] In 1779 and 1780, Boyd wrote in the *London Courant* as 'The Whig', and in the *Public Advertiser* as 'Democrates', attacking North and Sandwich.[130] In 1779, he also wrote to Henry Woodfall and asked him to oblige his 'old correspondent' by inserting several reports.[131] Two years later, Boyd became secretary to Lord Macartney,[132] and in October of that year, went to India to act on the East India Company's behalf in negotiations with a local ruler.[133]

The efforts of politically patronized propagandists, or 'hacks', and the direct intervention of politicians would have had an important influence on the content of London newspapers. However, those in high politics were rarely able to control the politics of the capital's press. Newspapers' reliance on extensive distribution rather than political subsidy meant that they were far less subservient to politicians than has been assumed, and instead were more dependent upon satisfying their readership. Consequently, the manner in which newspapers presented politics was an important editorial strategy. As the next chapter will discuss, political appeals to readers could be made not just in terms of party-political allegiances, but also in the representation of the wider political nation and the influence which was attributed to it.

First of December, 1783, On Mr Fox's East-India Bill (London, 1784); *Major Scott's Charge Against . . . Edmund Burke* (London, 1789); *A Letter to . . . Edmund Burke, in Reply to His 'Reflections on the Revolution in France', &c* (London, 1790).

[129] Andrews, *The History of British Journalism*, i. 223; Hugh Boyd, *The Miscellaneous Works of Hugh Boyd, the Author of the Letters of Junius*, ed. Lawrence Dundas Campbell, 2 vols. (London, 1800).

[130] Boyd, *The Works of Hugh Boyd*, i. 63.

[131] BL, Add. MS 27780, fo. 30.

[132] *DNB*, ii. 1000.

[133] BL, Add. MS 38408, fos. 320–1.

3
LONDON NEWSPAPERS
AND REFORM

In London, newspapers were associated with the wider political nation not only by those who sought to determine their influence, but also by the newspapers themselves. Their commercial nature, and the importance of sales to newspaper finances, created a newspaper press which was keen to appeal to as wide a readership as possible. To do this, newspapers needed to represent, or at least be seen to represent, the political nation. By articulating public opinion, the capital's newspapers could claim popular backing and were apparently ensured economic success. The degree of accuracy with which they were able to fulfil this task is impossible to measure with any certainty, but was presumably tested in the long run by the financial health of individual titles. This link between newspapers and the public suggests that readers had a significant, albeit an indirect, role to play in shaping the contents of the press. For this reason, newspapers provide an insight into public opinion, or perceived public opinion, as they provided one of the main forums of popular debate in the late eighteenth century.

There are, however, difficulties with an examination of the London press and popular opinion which are not apparent to the same degree in the study of the provincial press which follows. These stem from the unique nature of both the political community and the newspaper press in London. The large, socially diverse, and mobile urban population generated political debate which was extremely varied and frequently polarized. This was reflected in the newspapers the capital supported, which were themselves numerous and politically divided. Because of the character of the press in London, no clear picture emerges from it about the nature of public opinion concerning reform, but this is precisely because newspapers collectively represented the breadth of the political community in the capital. This situation was further complicated by the fact that London politics were not localized in the same way as in the provinces, but were conceived very much in national terms. Neither this aspect of popular politics in the capital nor its lack of consensus were new, since the type of political activity which took place here traditionally differentiated London from the rest of England.[1]

The disparity between the audience for newspapers in the capital and that in the provinces reflected the ways in which readership was constructed and mediated. In part, this was connected to the unique form of the London newspaper press: not only was it very large, both in terms of the number of titles produced and copies available, but at its core was a daily press which had no provincial equivalent. The continuity of debate which this provided and the immediacy between newspapers and their readership which would have been engendered are extremely important. However, perhaps more significant to the differences between a provincial and metropolitan readership was the social composition of both newspaper readers and the political nation in London. The extent of both literacy and the franchise in the capital made its population distinct from that of the rest of the country, and helped to broaden the character of the public in London. The literacy rate was much higher here than elsewhere in eighteenth-century England.[2] Cressy has shown that 92 per cent of the capital's traders and craftsmen were literate in the early part of the century, compared with only 65 per cent in the diocese of Norwich,[3] a figure which can also be set against Houston's figure of 66 per cent for the same group in the north of England, although this figure rose significantly by the 1760s.[4] The tendency which a higher rate of literacy afforded for a larger section of society to read newspapers in London than in the provinces may also have been greater still, since wages were generally higher in the capital (although the cost of living in general was also greater here than elsewhere).[5]

The peculiarly broad franchise which existed in London would also have encouraged political involvement amongst a more socially diverse

---

[1] For the study of popular politics in London, and in particular, the political activities of 'the crowd', see: Rudé, *Hanoverian London* and *Wilkes and Liberty: A Social Study of 1763 to 1774* (Oxford, 1962); G. Holmes, 'The Sacheverell Riots: The Crowd and the Church in Early Eighteenth-Century London', in P. Slack (ed.), *Rebellion, Popular Protest and the Social Order in Early Modern England* (Cambridge, 1984), 232–62; Tim Harris, *London Crowds in the Reign of Charles II: Propaganda and Politics from the Restoration until the Exclusion Crisis* (Cambridge, 1987); Rogers, *Whigs and Cities*.

[2] R. S. Schofield, 'Dimensions of Illiteracy, 1750–1850', *Explorations in Economic History*, 10 (1973), 437–54, p. 444; Cressy, *Literacy and the Social Order*, 145–54.

[3] Cressy, *Literacy and the Social Order*, 147 and 154.

[4] R. Houston, *Scottish Literacy and Scottish Identity: Illiteracy and Society in Scotland and Northern England 1600–1800* (Cambridge, 1985), 40. This figure had risen to 81% by the 1760s: ibid. 33.

[5] John Rule, *Albion's People: English Society, 1714–1815* (London, 1992), 168–76.

body than outside the capital, and have served as a form of political education. Although the right of voting in the City of London itself was in the Livery, it effectively behaved as a freeman borough, with an electorate of over 7,000.[6] Westminster was the largest urban constituency in the country with 12,000 'scot and lot' voters, whilst Southwark was another populous constituency of 2,000 voters with the same franchise qualification as Westminster.[7] The two county constituencies of Middlesex and Surrey which bordered the London boroughs were themselves significantly metropolitan in character.[8] In the counties, the franchise was ambiguous and was theoretically attached to freehold property worth over 40s. per annum in land tax assessment. In practice 'freehold' was broadly interpreted and although, like the 'scot and lot' qualification, which rested upon the payment of the poor rate, it excluded the lowest and the poorest inhabitants, the freehold franchise allowed a large proportion of the relatively wealthy male population in and around London a direct say in the political affairs of the nation.[9] O'Gorman has shown that in places with such large urban franchises, sheer size and the absence of controlling patrons allowed the political tendencies of these constituencies free play.[10]

The belief that only propertied wealth could provide a stable foundation for both law and government was widely held in eighteenth-century England.[11] Indeed, such was the tendency to view all social and political relations in terms of property that Langford has argued 'it became impossible to conceive of rights and liberties except in terms which implied individual proprietorship'.[12] However, the accepted link between property ownership and political authority, which, as we shall see, underlay much of the debate concerning the political nation and reform at this time in the provincial press, was less evident in London, where attitudes towards property and political rights were more ambivalent. This is not surprising given the nature of the political community in the capital. It is

---

[6] *History of Parliament*, i. 13; Susan E. Brown, 'Politics, Commerce and Social Policy in the City of London, 1782–1802' (University of Oxford D.Phil. thesis 1992).

[7] *History of Parliament*, i. 336 and 387.

[8] Ibid. 9–17. John Cannon has shown that a majority of the Middlesex electorate were urban (63% in 1802). Surrey was less urban in character, with 34% of its voters classed as urban dwellers in 1826: John Cannon, *Parliamentary Reform 1640–1832* (Cambridge, 1973), 293–4.

[9] O'Gorman, *Voters, Patrons, and Parties*, 59–65.

[10] Ibid. 55–6.

[11] See H. T. Dickinson, *Liberty and Property: Political Ideology in Eighteenth-Century Britain* (London, 1977); Paul Langford, *Public Life and the Propertied Englishman, 1689–1798* (Oxford, 1991).

[12] Langford, *Public Life and the Propertied Englishman*, 1.

clear from the particular reluctance of the London press to define the social boundaries of the wider political nation that newspapers here were aware of its great social diversity. Since the press linked newspaper readers with the public, its ambivalence concerning the social definition of the political nation reflected a desire not to exclude or alienate any of its readers by denying their right to a say in how the country's political affairs were managed. When compared to the provincial press, London newspapers reveal the existence of a socially more varied and less propertied public in the capital than elsewhere in the country.

During the early 1780s, newspapers in the capital, and the reformist press in particular, sought to challenge traditional limits upon the political influence of public opinion. A radical ideology of popular sovereignty and the role ascribed to extra-parliamentary activity defined the public and public opinion in ways which were increasingly broad and which were credited with greater influence in the nation's political life and constitutional structure. Though the short-term aims of the reformers failed, what emerged at the end of the contest was arguably a more politically informed public with a wider social base. Even those papers which opposed reform did not question either the existence or the positive potential of public opinion as a political force, although they did try to define the public in more explicitly respectable and socially elevated ways.

The London press as a whole gave the reform movement a great deal of coverage. This was not surprising considering the importance of the reform issue in terms of national politics, and the fact that the capital was so underrepresented in the Commons. However, although a reformist stance is visible in many of the London newspapers of the period, there was also a marked degree of opposition to the reform cause, showing that popular politics in the capital were not dominated by the reformers to the degree that has been supposed. Although newspaper interest in reform peaked between 1779 and 1780, it remained at a relatively constant level until 1785. Those papers which appeared sympathetic to the cause of reform were used by various county committees to publicize meetings, resolutions, and petitions, and to a lesser extent those newspapers which were hostile to such bodies carried similar advertisements placed by groups of anti-reform protesters. Newspapers were often paid to include such material. However, this was probably not true of much of the coverage given to the reform movement elsewhere in papers: in letters and amongst the editorial comment. Here the subject of reform was covered extensively and in detail, particularly during those periods when the movement was most active or appeared at all likely to make headway in Parliament.

Between 1779 and 1785, a significant proportion of the capital's press produced a powerful and coherent argument in favour of parliamentary reform by fusing elements of an older Country ideology with newer radical theories which challenged the acceptability of the Revolution Settlement. This combination of ideas is apparent in discussions of the relationship between taxation and representation, and in the hostility and suspicion shown towards executive power. The language of Country politicians is evident in appeals to 'virtue' and 'patriotism', and in the constant attack on corruption in high places. But a distinctively radical approach was used in the discussion of another Country ideological staple, the ancient constitution. Before the Norman Conquest, it was asserted, Englishmen had enjoyed considerable political liberty. In this distant past, Parliament had been elected annually, all men possessed the vote (and not just freeholders), and sovereignty had rested firmly with the people. This radical reinterpretation of the Anglo-Saxon constitution did not accept, as the Country thinkers had, that the Glorious Revolution had restored the constitution along pre-Norman lines, and that successive governments since then had acted to corrupt and distort it. Rather, it was argued that from 1066 onwards, the ancient constitution had been constantly degraded until it had reached its present, unrecognizable state, in which the influence of the Crown was huge, and that of the people had become inconsequential. According to this school of thought, what was needed was not a relatively minor readjustment to reinstate the constitutional arrangements of 1689, but a much greater reform of the political system. Tinkering with the existing structure of government was not enough; what was needed was a complete constitutional overhaul in order to restore the ancient constitution to its proper state. To this end, radicals demanded a 'return' to annual parliaments, secret ballots, universal suffrage, equal representation, and popular sovereignty.[13]

This new radical platform, part of Britain's growing radical popular political culture, did not owe its origins to the reform movement, but to

---

[13] On the country tradition, see Dickinson, *Liberty and Property*; J. G. A. Pocock, *Virtue, Commerce and Society* (Cambridge, 1976); Linda Colley, *In Defiance of Oligarchy: The Tory Party, 1714–1760* (Cambridge, 1982), chap. 4; P. S. Hicks, *Neo-classical History and English Culture: From Clarendon to Hume* (New York, 1996). For a typical description of the destruction of the Anglo-Saxon constitution, see 'An Admirer of Alfred', *London Courant*, 5 Apr. 1780.

the constitutional controversies surrounding George III's early reign and the ideological debates over relations with the American colonists.[14] Even before the first Yorkshire meetings gained national publicity, newspapers in the capital were expressing some of the same Lockean-inspired sentiments. In the *London Courant*, a letter addressed to 'the people of England' from 'Caradoc' discussed the sorry state of the constitution and asserted that 'the dignity of the crown is but a borrowed lustre, reflected upon the throne by the majesty of the people'.[15] 'A Country Gentleman' argued that Americans were fighting to defend their constitutional rights, and expressed the hope that the British public would also 'arise and assert its rights'.[16] These expectations were echoed by 'Miltiades' on 18 December 1779, who argued that 'when any government becomes destructive of the end it is meant to promote, it is the right of the people to resist it'. But although the reform movement did not prompt such appeals to popular sovereignty, debate on the reform issue in the early 1780s did help to define and shape the nature of the radical programme in this decade. The following discussion is limited to an examination of the press, but it should be noted that the type of radical ideas found here not only had currency in newspapers, but were the subject of discussion elsewhere, for example in public debating societies, such as the one held in Coachmaker's Hall, Cheapside. In December 1779, it advertised a debate on the question, 'Is not the restoration of annual parliaments, and of an equal representation, indispensibly necessary to preserve this country from its present dangers, secure the constitution, and perpetuate the glory and freedom of Englishmen?'[17]

Even though the debate on reform in the London press reached a fever pitch in December 1779 and in 1780 which was not to be repeated, it continued to assume importance. The *General Advertiser*, having taken on the mantle of the metropolis's leading radical paper from the defunct *London Courant* in 1782,[18] was particularly keen to keep the issue alive. On 8 January, it assured its readers that

The Herald and ministerial papers are rejoiced at the present seeming inactivity in the different counties relative to the Petition and Remonstrance; but his [*sic*] joy

---

[14] Brewer, *Party Ideology and Popular Politics*; O'Gorman, *Voters, Patrons, and Parties*, 300–16.

[15] *London Courant*, 7 Dec. 1779.   [16] Ibid. 2 Dec. 1779.

[17] *Gazetteer*, 7 Dec. 1779. For a discussion of London debating societies in 1780, see Donna T. Andrew, 'Popular Culture and Public Debate: London 1780', *Historical Journal* 39 (1996), 405–23.

[18] On 12 May 1783 the *General Advertiser* proclaimed that it hoped to take the *Courant*'s place in 'the glorious cause of liberty'.

will be but short-lived. The spirited citizens of London will again rekindle a spirit of patriotism, which will find a free admission into the very hearts of the people, and beget a general glow and warmth of integrity and resolution, which will, at last, triumph over Lords Bute and North.

The *Advertiser* carried a continuous stream of letters and editorial paragraphs in favour of the main points of the radical platform: annual parliaments, universal (male) franchise, and equal representation, and along with other newspapers, and the *London Courant* in particular, it helped shape the radical reformist stance after the frenzied activity of the national reform movement's first months.

Reformist newspapers like the *London Courant* were eager to promote the radical platform of parliamentary reform and made frequent references to the importance of restoring the ancient constitution. The call for annual parliaments was to become one of the *Courant*'s most consistent political themes. Letters from 'Alfred', 'Drusus', and 'Buckingham' repeatedly demanded that elections be held every year. This, 'Drusus' claimed on 10 May 1780, in a letter to 'the People of England', was an historically based right.[19] Another correspondent suggested that gaps of seven years between general elections were too great, and that 'woeful experience ought . . . now to convince us, how dangerous and imprudent it is for the nation to trust its deputies so long, so liable they may be to forget what they owe to their constituents'.[20] A writer in the *General Advertiser* stressed the need, 'at this alarming juncture', to 'stop the progress of corruption and venality, to restore the freedom of election, and the liberties of the people to their ancient purity'.[21] In further appeals to historical precedent, letter-writers in various newspapers used pseudonyms both to add authority to their argument and give important indicators of their political sentiments. Ancient Roman names such as 'Metellus', 'Gracchus', 'Mutius', 'Drusus', 'Aristides', 'Brutus', and 'Junius Brutus' reminded readers of the ideals of republicanism, democracy, and radical and populist reform.[22] Also popular, of course, were

---

[19] See also *London Courant*, 22 Mar. 1780.   [20] Ibid. 5 May 1780.

[21] *General Advertiser*, 4 Jan. 1780.

[22] The following are the most probable classical referents of these pseudonyms: 'Metellus' = Quintus Caecilius Metellus Pius (Scipio), who passed into republican legend for his attacks on Caesar; 'Gracchus' = the Gracchus brothers (or Gracchi), who were radical, populist reformers; 'Mutius' = Mutius Scaevola, a friend of the Gracchi; 'Drusus' = Marcus Livius Drusus, who proposed, alongside various democratic measures, to give the franchise to the Italian allies; 'Aristides' = an Athenian statesman famous for his honesty and moderation, and known as a populist; 'Junius Brutus' and 'Brutus' = Marcus Iunius Brutus, the tyrannicide who was famed for his patriotism: N. G. L. Hammond and

appeals to the mythical Saxon past, so prevalent in the thought of the London radicals,[23] and evident from the signatures 'Alfred', 'An Admirer of Alfred', and 'An Anglo-Saxon'.[24]

One of the most significant developments in the radical ideology put forward by London newspapers occurred when the impetus for reform was removed from Parliament and placed with the public. Although it was still largely accepted that any restructuring of the constitution would have to be a parliamentary procedure, parliamentary politicians were increasingly held to be too corrupt to enact such change unless powerful extra-parliamentary force was bought into play. This major shift followed the failure of the first round of petitions in 1780. Prior to this, 'Metellus' had claimed that 'If our constitution has any chance, it is by the people resolving to demand of Parliament, a strict examination into the expenditure of public money, and a reduction in all exorbitant salaries and useless places. Then, and only then, can we hope for the Crown to be kept within its proper limits'.[25] After North had made clear his intention to resist the petitioners' calls for reform, the *London Courant* despaired at the level of parliamentary corruption, but stated that 'what the people at large will do, is not so certain. The matter now lies upon them'.[26] In a letter addressed to North in April 1780, 'A Country Gentleman' asserted that against the corruption of Parliament, 'Our great hope is in the *determined virtue of the people*'.[27] The same author repeated these sentiments on 2 May, when he claimed that the parliamentary defeats of Dunning's motions and Burke's bill 'have shut those doors against us for ever. All our exertions must henceforth be made *without*'. These sentiments echoed those expressed in the *London Evening Post* in February, which stated that 'The *whole* business of *redress* now lies upon the body of the people, and upon them

---

H. H. Scullford (eds.), *The Oxford Classical Dictionary*, 2nd edn. (Oxford, 1970); and M. C. Howatson (ed.), *The Oxford Companion to Classical Literature*, 2nd edn. (Oxford, 1989). For examples of letters with these signatures see: *London Courant*, 1 and 4 Jan., 31 Mar., 22 and 25 Apr., 10 May, 8 June 1780; *General Advertiser*, 4 and 14 Jan., 29 Mar., 18 Apr., 28 May, 3 June, 20 July 1782, 27 Feb., 26 Mar. 1783; *Public Advertiser*, 5 and 12 Feb. 1780, 9, 16, and 24 Apr., 1, 15, and 22 May 1783, 16 Feb. 1784.

[23] See R. J. Smith, *The Gothic Bequest: Medieval Institutions in British Thought, 1688–1863* (Cambridge, 1987).

[24] For examples of the use of these pseudonyms see: *London Courant*, 29 Jan., 3 and 27 May, 7 Oct. 1780, 8 Feb., 9 Mar., 24 Sept. 1781; *St. James's Chronicle*, 20 Apr. 1780. Many of the letters which appeared in the papers from 'Alfred' were actually written by Jebb himself. Some of the addresses 'to the people of England' which appeared in the London press are found in Jebb's collected works: *Works of John Jebb*, iii. 285–342.

[25] *London Courant*, 1 Jan. 1780.

[26] Ibid. 16 Feb. 1780.　　[27] Ibid. 13 Apr. 1780.

only'.[28] In April, the *Courant* portrayed the struggle for reform as a contest between the government and the people, upon which 'the very existence of the constitution, as it now stands, must depend'.[29] A letter from 'A Consistent Whig', almost certainly written by Almon himself,[30] pressed home his radical ideas about popular sovereignty:

Nothing great or glorious ever was or will be achieved in this country without a popular Government, much less in scorn and defiance of the people; nor will any beneficial change to the nation be effected, till the people recover their consequence, with their original rights; and influence and party are both finally lost in annual parliaments, freely chosen by the equal suffrages of the whole community.[31]

More starkly, the *London Evening Post* commented that 'there is a period in all histories, when the people who are aggrieved should stop *complaining* and begin to *act'*.[32]

Increasingly, parliamentary politics and party divisions were portrayed as secondary considerations to the main issue of reform, which was dependent on extra-parliamentary support rather than high-political patronage. 'Let the People of England be from hence convinced', wrote a correspondent in the *London Courant*, 'that on themselves alone they must rely for salvation; that from the generosity of parliament they can expect nothing . . . that from a government founded on corruption, acquiescence is ruin; submission, slavery; and resistance only, is redemption'.[33] Indeed, Parliament was incapable of reforming the constitution, since 'in the present corrupt state of affairs, the member [of Parliament] is indeed the representative of himself, and the voice of an assembly so constituted is anything else but the voice of the people'.[34] Thus a 'Consistent Whig' argued that 'The recovery of the people's rights is their own immediate business and concern. It originates properly with them, not with a party, or the leaders of a party. If those gentlemen wish to restore the purse to the nation, and with it liberty and legal independence, let them join the county meetings'.[35] Similarly, the *General Advertiser*, advocating annual parliaments and equal representation in 1782, argued that without these

---

[28] *London Evening Post*, 17 Feb. 1780.   [29] *London Courant*, 24 Apr. 1780.
[30] Almon had used this pseudonym in various pamphlets: see *Letter to the Right Hon. Charles Jenkinson*; *Address to the Interior Cabinet*; *The Revolution in MDCCLXXXII*.
[31] *London Courant*, 24 Oct. 1780.
[32] *London Evening Post*, 22 Jan. 1780.
[33] *London Courant*, 30 May 1780. See also *Public Advertiser*, 13 May 1780.
[34] *London Courant*, 3 July 1780. See also *St. James's Chronicle*, 22 July 1780.
[35] *London Courant*, 5 Jan. 1781.

'the most virtuous Administration, to stem the tide of corruption, and preserve the Freedom of the People, will avail nothing.'[36] The paper also asserted that

The object which the people have always in pursuit, and which we as the servants of that public shall ever most assiduously pursue, is the recovery of that [ancient] constitution, of which, by the artifices of bad men they have been so totally deprived. An equal representation, and short parliaments, are the measures by which they mean to accomplish that object; and if they procure these, they will be satisfied, without enquiring whether they came from a man of this party or that party.[37]

With the focus removed from 'high' politics, the relationship between Parliament and the people was represented in simple and radical terms. Again departing from traditional Country ideology, the radical press ignored arguments concerning parliamentary sovereignty which permeated elite political circles, and asserted instead that sovereignty was held by the people. The *London Courant* maintained that 'The very right of electing representatives, declares the origin of power to be in the people. The people chuse a parliament to govern them, and to tax them; but not to abuse the authority delegated for the purpose of government and taxation'.[38] In the current state of affairs, according to the *St. James's Chronicle*'s correspondent, 'Amen', 'the servant is now become the master and usurps the Right of the People, and exercises an arbitrary authority over his ancient and natural Lord'.[39] Not only was the non-payment of taxes advocated, following the American example,[40] but by the middle of 1780, demands for universal male suffrage had become a regular feature in the *Courant*, as writers such as 'An Anglo-Saxon' urged a reform to 'reinstate the whole people to their rights of election'.[41] According to one writer in the *Courant*, 'property . . . does not always confer consequence; for property by no means necessarily connects with itself integrity or ability'.[42] Another letter, this time in the *Gazetteer*, and addressed 'to such of my countrymen as are not represented', asserted that 'if it must be confessed that the poor are the most patriotic, why exclude them from the pale of society?'[43] According to 'Drusus', writing in the *General Advertiser*,

---

[36] *General Advertiser*, 11 June 1782.
[37] Ibid. 16 July 1782. See also *General Advertiser*, 11 Apr. 1783.
[38] *London Courant*, 4 Feb. 1780.
[39] *St. James's Chronicle*, 23 Dec. 1780. See also *London Courant*, 19 May 1780.
[40] *London Courant*, 30 Mar. 1780 and 24 Mar. 1781.
[41] Ibid. 7 Oct. 1780. See also ibid. 15 July 1780.
[42] Ibid. 15 Jan. 1780.   [43] *Gazetteer*, 9 June 1780.

'the title of an honest Commoner' was 'more glorious than any which royalty can bestow'.[44]

Such was the emphasis placed upon popular sovereignty that the formation of popular representative bodies which might supersede Parliament was defended. Since Parliament had no authority but that delegated to it by the people, once it failed to properly represent the wishes of the people, it became constitutionally redundant:

a Committee of Delegates from Associated counties, even that which has excited so many invectives and complaints, and armed with all the powers imputed to it of influencing Parliament, is neither unconstitutional nor inexpedient, for that so long as the Representatives of the People speak the language of their constituents, and deliver their sentiments and wishes, the Delegation which has given umbrage must remain a lifeless and inactive body, existing in name only; but in the moment that the Deputies of the People in Parliament deviate into *mis*representation, and, instead of fulfilling, contravene the Ends and purposes of *their* Delegation, their Principals inherit a Right to controul and over-awe them, in whatever shape, and by whatever instruments they shall judge fit.[45]

Yet despite such strong assertions of popular sovereignty, newspapers which supported radical parliamentary reform usually stopped well short of advocating revolution. The *London Courant* argued that 'the business of the committees is particularly specified; it is to pursue the object of the petition, the reformation of abuses respecting public money. The mode of pursuing this object will be constitutional and legal, not by acts of violence, by *insurrections*, *confusion* and *anarchy*; but by a modest and moderate, yet determined, application to Parliament for redress'.[46] Indeed, the *Courant* of 25 February 1780 asserted that it was those who opposed reform, the Protestors, rather than those who promoted it, who threatened civil unrest with their meetings: 'What are we to think of such proceedings? Are they not *factious*? Are they not *inflammatory*? *Do they not tend to sow the seeds of sedition*? Are they not *calculated to lead the nation into rebellion*?'

The weight given to extra-parliamentary activity by the radical press made it unlikely that politicians or political parties would be trusted to enact reform. The *London Courant* argued that the country needed to be rescued from 'the cross of parliamentary corruption, where she has too long been crucified between two thieves, the Ins and the Outs'.[47] But in

---

[44] *General Advertiser*, 8 Mar. 1782. See also ibid. 29 Mar. 1782.
[45] *London Courant*, 16 Nov. 1781.
[46] Ibid. 4 Feb. 1780.   [47] Ibid. 7 Apr. 1781.

their distrust of politicians' ideological sincerity, if not in their belief in the need for constitutional reform, the radical and the conservative press were in some agreement. As the *Morning Post* concluded in 1784, those in high politics merely used the issue of reform as a rhetorical tool to attack their opponents, without ever being seriously committed to the principle: 'No Minister has ever been a friend to reform, and yet many Ministers, when in Opposition, have strenuously contended for the necessity of it, and talked the hour away in logical arguments on this subject—with no view but to embarrass the men in power'.[48] The *Morning Herald* claimed in 1783 that 'the people are perfectly indifferent as to the issue of the present political struggle, convinced from the general apostacy of our modern statesmen, that whoever seizes the reins of government, will prefer his own sordid views to the interest of the commonweal'.[49] Although the *Herald* was hostile towards the prospect of reform, Pitt's failure to institute it once in office was heavily criticized. On 23 March 1785, the paper commented that

The first and fastest impression Mr. Pitt made upon his country, has been by the Reform of Parliament. He figured in it with a most bewitching gallantry, and appeared as earnest in promoting it, as Cæsar in suppressing Cataline's plot. Twice in two years he has been in power, and all we heard from him touching the Reform, during his Ministry, was taunting those who brought it forward with envy and malice, or pouring showers of invective upon Lord North, for fear his Lordship should freeze in his long declared opposition to that scheme. But the moment his Ministry ceased, he relapsed back into Reform fever, and boiled and bubbled for its success . . .[50]

This level of cynicism about high politics was not always apparent in London newspapers, but it was a constant feature which appeared to be on the increase in the first half of the 1780s. Of course, one has only to look at the controversy surrounding George III's accession and the role of Bute to see that distrust of politicians was nothing new. However, there are grounds to suggest that this trend became more marked in the later period, and reflected not only a lack of faith in politicians in general, but a questioning of their position at the centre of the political world.

The tendency both to distrust politicians and doubt their constitutional legitimacy and importance was evident in the radical press's response to Wyvill's moderate campaign which sought to appeal both to the respect-

[48] *Morning Post*, 18 Mar. 1784. See also *Public Advertiser*, 19 Jan. and 24 May 1780.
[49] *Morning Herald*, 18 Mar. 1783. See also *General Advertiser*, 27 Mar. 1783.
[50] See also *Morning Herald*, 16 Mar. 1784.

able section of the population and to reform-minded politicians. This was largely overlooked in favour of more sweeping proposals, free from the taint of high-political 'corruption'. In the split which occurred between London radicals and the other elements of the reform movement, papers like the *London Courant* allied themselves with the former. In November 1780, the *Courant* sided openly with the radical writer John Cartwright, who accused Sir George Savile, the York Committee's parliamentary advocate, of despondency, and proclaimed 'away then, with triennial parliaments, additional knights, and all such trumpery', proposing instead annual parliaments, universal franchise, and equal representation.[51] 'Drusus' described triennial parliaments as 'an imperfect and ineffectual approach to the safe and wholesome usage of the constitution'.[52] 'Nil Desperandum' responded to the York Committee's moderate statement of policy in January, which attempted to appeal to the Rockinghamites,[53] and to the failure of the radicals to influence proceedings at the second series of meetings of deputies in London, by attacking the York Committee:

instead of firmness, I see a timidity, which betrayed itself very early in the Yorkshire address, and which in the moment of trial has shrunk back from demands, which yet they had avowed to be just . . . Let any reader compare the reports and resolutions of the Westminster Committee, with the address from the Yorkshire Association, and he will immediately see the difference to which I allude. How came this difference to be so easily adjusted? By what mode of reasoning have those, who call themselves friends of the people, been induced to relinquish their own idea, and acquiesce in a plan which goes no farther than the wishes of the friends to one particular party?[54]

The *Courant* of 28 June 1781 criticized the York Committee for addressing electors only, rather than advocating universal franchise, whilst a letter 'to the Deputies' which appeared the following day attacked the Yorkshire reformers' moderate programme:

we may waste our time in self-deception, by seeking salvation where salvation cannot reside—in triennial parliaments, with additional knights, or in any other capricious project; but so long as God shall be pleased to continue in force the present laws of nature, our grievances cannot be redressed, nor the evils we complain of be removed, until the whole mass of the people shall have recovered those sacred, unalienable rights of election, the loss of which is the SOLE cause of all our woe.

[51] *London Courant*, 9 Nov. 1780.   [52] Ibid. 23 May 1780.
[53] See Christie, *Wilkes, Wyvill and Reform*, 126.
[54] *London Courant*, 14 May 1781.

The radical reforming ideas of certain prominent writers in the capital were highly influential in public debate. John Cartwright, John Jebb, Capel Lofft, Granville Sharp, and Thomas Day formed the Society for Constitutional Information (SCI) in April 1780, as a means of spreading propaganda in favour of a radical reform of Parliament. Many of their ideals rested on belief in the natural right of representation, which it was argued was held by all Englishmen, regardless of status or wealth. Their aims were explicitly set out in one of the SCI tracts:

the design of this Society is to diffuse throughout the kingdom, as universally as possible, a knowledge of the great principles of Constitutional Freedom, particularly such as respect the election and duration of the representative body. With this view, Constitutional tracts, intended for the extension of this knowledge, and to communicate it to persons of all ranks, are printed and distributed GRATIS, at the expense of the Society. Essays, and extracts from various authors, calculated to promote the same design, are also published under the direction of the society, in several of the news-papers . . .[55]

For the SCI, newspapers were essential organs for the expression and dissemination of radical ideology. Jebb's letters in favour of annual parliaments and other reforms appeared in the *London Courant* and the *St James's Chronicle* under the pseudonym 'Alfred',[56] whilst he wrote on other political issues as 'Mentor' and 'Lælius'.[57] Cartwright also wrote letters for publication in the papers.[58] It appears that on at least one occasion in 1782, he too used the pseudonym 'Alfred', to address Pitt on the subject of reform.[59] Letters from Jebb, writing as 'Aristides', appeared in the *General Advertiser* on 28 May 1782, calling for annual parliaments and a vote for all taxpayers; on 27 February 1783, again supporting annual parliaments, as well as equal representation; and in the *Public Advertiser* on 23 May 1783, calling for equal representation, annual parliaments, and voting by ballot.

The SCI also used the *General Advertiser* as a vehicle for more explicit propaganda. This included extracts from Cartwright's pamphlet *Give Us Our Rights*,[60] and Burgh's *Political Disquisitions*.[61] But in Jebb's private

---

[55] *Tracts Published and Distributed Gratis By the Society for Constitutional Information, With a Design to Convey to the Minds of the People a Knowledge of Their Rights; Principally Those of Representation* (London, 1783), p. i. Also cited in *Works of John Jebb*, i. 156.

[56] See examples of letters signed 'Alfred' in *Works of John Jebb*, iii. 285–333, and in the following: *London Courant*, 29 Jan. 1780, 8 Feb., 9 Mar., 24 Sept. 1781; *General Advertiser*, 26 Mar. 1783.

[57] *Works of John Jebb*, iii. 350–61.

[58] Cartwright, *Works*, i. 149.   [59] Ibid. 155.

[60] *General Advertiser*, 2 Sept. 1782.   [61] Ibid. 23 Sept. 1782.

correspondence with Cartwright, he complained that the editor of the *Advertiser* had rejected the first half of a letter from 'Aristides' for being 'too strong', and added that 'I have taken it from him, but what to do I know not: the *people* have no paper'.[62] The capital's radical newspapers were clearly more in tune with the SCI than the Wyvillites or the parliamentary politicians, but their contents were still decided more independently of political organizations than might first appear. If the government could not control newspaper politics, then it is unlikely that bodies such as the SCI could either.

A few newspapers did side (at least at times) with the more moderate proposals of the Yorkshire reformers. In such cases, the emphasis was usually placed on reforming the existing constitution by the efforts of a people whose political legitimacy came from their property ownership. On 2 February 1780, the *Gazetteer* maintained that the petitioning counties represented 'four-fifths of the landed and commercial property of the whole kingdom, and full seven-eighths of the land-tax'. Its letter-writers tended to advocate triennial as opposed to annual parliaments,[63] as did those in the *London Evening Post*. Its issue for 20 April 1780 noted

The nation looks up to the County Associations and Committees for relief, against the infernal machinations of an abandoned, wicked Ministry . . . Every true Briton will, there can be no doubt, solemnly engage (by the most sacred ties) to oppose, and reject, with scorn, any candidate for a seat in Parliament, who will not pledge himself to give his vote against any supply or tax whatever, till one hundred, or more, county members shall be added to the House of Commons, and till the act for Septennial Parliaments is repealed, and Triennial Parliaments renewed; and till the enormous, all destroying influence of the Crown is reduced by œconomy, justice, and prudence.

However, the Wyvillite stance was rare in London papers, and was certainly overshadowed not just by radical claims, but also by the weight of material published which was hostile to reform per se.

Those papers which were opposed to parliamentary reform espoused a coherent set of arguments to defend the constitutional status quo. As Burke was to do far more eloquently a decade later, newspapers like the *Morning Post* and the *Morning Herald* maintained that prescription and practicality were much better guarantors of political stability than theoretical propositions. For all its faults or imperfections, the British constitution, as it stood, provided the best form of government possible: as the

---

[62] Cartwright, *Works*, i. 155.
[63] See, for example, *Gazetteer*, 2 Mar. and 1 Apr. 1780.

Post termed it, 'the best modelled constitution in the world'.[64] 'An Englishman' wrote in May 1780:

What can be more absurd than to suppose that the resolutions of inexperience, and often of intemperance, can bear any competition with those which are debated with so much solemnity, and resolved upon with so much consideration as in the parliament of a nation? The harmony between the King and the parliament in a good administration, and between the parliament and the people, is an undeniable proof of this; of which, thank God, no nation has more experience than ourselves . . . I hope therefore the people of England, at so alarming a conjuncture, will hold by the pillars of the constitution: I hope they will keep its ancient land-marks in view, and not suffer themselves to be carried about by every vain wind of doctrine, by the flight of men, and craftiness, whereby they lie in wait to deceive.[65]

Another writer in the *Post* questioned the notion of natural rights, which he supposed 'was never thought of or imagined till Mr. Locke found it out',[66] whilst 'Julius', in the *Herald*, disputed the historical basis of Englishmen's 'ancient rights'.[67]

Moreover, the spurious doctrines of the reformers, it was argued, were not only theoretically unfounded, but more importantly, they threatened to upset those most precious of conservative principles, the rule of law and the protection of property. 'Modern patriotism', claimed the *Morning Post*, had been so perverted from its former character that it was now the preserve of 'a set of *hungry ravenous* vultures, who make a merit of *knawing* the vitals of their country'.[68] Usually 'patriotism' and 'republicanism' seemed interchangeable. 'The fact is', asserted the *Post* in April 1780, 'that far greater danger is to be apprehended to the happy constitution of this country from the malignant growing influence of the spirit of *Republicanism*, rais'd, cherish'd, and matur'd by the artful machinations of ambitious, disappointed, evil minded demagogues, than from the influence of the Crown'.[69] The *Public Advertiser* claimed that 'the rage of patriotism' had deluded 'many well-meaning people' to support the petitions, committees, and associations which had brought the country 'to the very verge of a civil war'.[70] Reporting on the first York meeting, the

---

[64] *Morning Post*, 4 Apr. 1780.   [65] Ibid. 22 May 1780.   [66] Ibid. 2 June 1780.

[67] *Morning Herald*, 18 Sept. 1782.

[68] *Morning Post*, 6 Dec. 1779. See also 2, 14, and 28 Dec. 1779, 29 Apr. 1780, 3 Aug. 1784. Similar arguments are to be found in the *Gazetteer*, 14 and 28 Dec. 1779; and *Public Advertiser*, 10 May 1780 and 18 Aug. 1783.

[69] *Morning Post*, 8 Apr. 1780. See also ibid. 10 Apr. and 20 July 1780; *Public Advertiser*, 3 Mar. 1781; *Morning Herald*, 3 Jan., 22 Mar., 27 Apr., and 4 May 1781, 1 and 14 July 1783.

[70] *Public Advertiser*, 22 Apr. 1780. See also ibid. 29 June 1780; *St. James's Chronicle*, 22 Aug. 1780; *Morning Post*, 8 Dec. 1780; *Morning Herald*, 3 and 23 Jan. 1781.

Morning Post suggested that 'it may be a very pleasant amusement for orators, gamesters, and adventurers of all sorts; but they who have titles, fortunes, families, and characters, should think twice before they open the floodgates of rebellion, and let loose the floating humours of the land. They who love peace will not assist at these infernal ceremonies, which forbode nothing but disorder, horror, fear, and mutiny'.[71]

According to the *Public Advertiser*, 'every illegal meeting of the populace is a step towards insurrection and rebellion, and it may be left to the commonsense of any man of property, whether he is no more likely to lose all than to gain anything in such events'.[72] The Gordon Riots in June 1780 were, the conservative press argued, further proof of the link between constitutional reform and civil unrest. In July 1780, the *Post* commented that

The petitioners are at length at mum, and the associators (in the language of the times) are fairly done up. Time had discovered the nakedness of the Patriots, and Opposition are retired in despair . . . Out of evil good sometimes is produced; and [t]he late unhappy disturbances are a proof of it. The people are now quieted in their minds as to those infamous reports propagated by the patriots, that government sought to be arbitrary; and they perceive how nearly they were to falling into an error that might have destroyed the best constitution in the world. Thus convinced that opposition were the great enemies of our peace, prosperity, and happiness, the false language of patriotism will no longer seduce the senses of the people.[73]

The *Morning Herald* was equally sarcastic about the patriotism of those who threatened the nation's stability. On 17 January 1781, it commented on 'Committees, Deputations, Associations, and County meetings, the *glorious* result of whose *constitutional* doctrines and deliberations are too recent in every man's mind to be repeated'. On 12 March, the paper remarked:

It is most earnestly hoped, by every well-wisher to the peace of this metropolis, that some immediate stop may be put to those rebellious associations now on foot, and that the Delegates may not be permitted to kindle another flame in the metropolis. How obvious does the intention of the Delegates meeting in the capital appear! London, they well know, contains more vagabonds than any other part of England . . . They perceive the consequences of flying in the face of the law and the constitution, and yet they persist in doing so. What is to be the result? Not reformation, because their mode of seeking it is illegal—No, the result to be

[71] *Morning Post*, 31 Dec. 1779. See also *Morning Herald*, 10 and 12 Apr. 1781.
[72] *Public Advertiser*, 29 Jan. 1780. See also ibid. 27 Jan. 1780; *Morning Post*, 5 May 1780; and *General Evening Post*, 27 Jan. 1780.
[73] *Morning Post*, 12 July 1780.

dreaded, is such another rebellion, as seated Oliver Cromwell in the dictatorial chair; or such another convulsion as that which reddened the metropolis with fire and blood last summer.

Two years after the Gordon Riots, the *Herald*'s arguments remained unchanged. In 1782, the unrest of 1780 was still the subject of discussion:

> The opposition prints speak much of the wonderful effects that must ensue when the people feel the general glow and warmth arising from hearing patriotic petitions, and being assembled to mark them with their respective crosses; but it should be remembered that this is January, and not July; and that the recollection of the petitioning bonfires rather freezes than warms the blood of the people![74]

Not surprisingly, the charge that the reform movement was associated with the riots of June 1780 was strenuously denied by the reformist press, but it was clearly an accusation which carried with it a good deal of political capital.

Another recurrent theme in the conservative press was that the reform movement was the work of disappointed Opposition MPs, and lacked real or valid popular support. The traditional 'high' political focus of newspapers opposed to reform placed them in stark contrast to the reformist press, which concentrated so strongly on extra-parliamentary activity. On 14 December 1779, the *Morning Post* asserted that 'A *flaming* petition is now on the anvil, at which a certain Marquis [Rockingham] is and, the never-to-be forgotten *Charley Turner* [*sic*] are working day and night; it is to contain a variety of national grievances the unsuspecting freeholders of Yorkshire never even dreamt of'. Later that same month, the paper mocked the claim of the 'disinterested Marquis' that Opposition had nothing to do with the York petition, and referred disparagingly to Rockingham's 'indefatigable corps of Yorkshire petitioners'.[75] It was argued that the people would not have imagined 'any public evil' if the libels circulated by the Opposition had not 'set their imaginations at work, and made them dream and talk of evils which they never felt'.[76] 'An Old Freeholder', writing in the *General Evening Post*, claimed that committees and associations were the work of ambitious and disappointed men, who wanted to mislead 'the honest, uninformed multitude'.[77] The *Post* of 8 April 1780 argued that 'when a disinterested man is asked whether he feels the encreasing influence of the crown, and if he thinks the burthen is too heavy for him, he answers that for his part he don't attend to politicks; but

---

[74] *Morning Herald*, 9 Jan. 1782.
[75] *Morning Post*, 31 Dec. 1779. See also *Morning Herald*, 29 Mar. 1781.
[76] *Morning Post*, 28 Dec. 1779.　　　[77] *General Evening Post*, 28 Mar. 1780.

the members of opposition tell him so. His opinion, if from himself, would be that he was happy. Such is the real state of the petitions lately presented'.

Rockingham and his followers were depicted acting solely for party advantage. On 5 April 1780, the *Post* published an attack on Rockingham, which asserted that 'one of the morning papers informs us, that the Marquis——, the patriotic Marquis, is gone to York to quell an insurrection there: now we rather imagine, and the public opinion will justify us, that the noble Peer is gone down for the very opposite purpose. Hitherto he has aimed at rebellion—and we have no reason to think that he has yet changed his politics'. A letter from 'Fido' in the *General Evening Post* blamed the York meeting on 'a few mal-contents of the North-riding, from pique to their Lord Lieutenant', which 'the R——party . . . carefully fostered; and have at length by artifice and cabal formented a private pique to a county faction'.[78] 'Misostasis' wrote that the Opposition were using the country's dilemma to their own advantage,[79] whilst the *Morning Chronicle* accused the Minority Lords of wanting to use the York meeting as 'an instrument of mischief against Administration'.[80] Charles James Fox, an Opposition politician with a particularly high profile in the London reform movement, was accused of using the Westminster Committee merely to promote his own personal political ambitions:

The nonsensical petition of the Westminster Potwalloppers may now go to the devil for Master Charles Fox; their rag-tag, and bobtail Convention he thinks sufficient for his own private views, and therefore he leaves their flaming motion for the redress of public grievances to the patriotic gouts, who delight in such chimerical drudgeries, while he contents himself with canvassing the inhabitants for their vote against the next election.[81]

On 12 March, the *Herald* remarked that 'the public cannot be too often reminded that Mr. Fox's assemblies in Westminster-hall, were succeeded by the greatest insurrection that ever happened in this kingdom since the civil war; this should be a caution both to the ministers and magistrates to prevent these tumultuous meetings, where the minds of the populace are worked up to a degree of phrensy, by the republican doctrine of disappointed faction'. Significantly, the conservative press did not dismiss the importance of the wider political nation as such, but simply doubted that the reform movement commanded true popular support. As the *Post*'s

---

[78] Ibid. 28 Dec. 1779. See also *Gazetteer*, 6 Jan. 1780.
[79] *General Evening Post*, 8 Feb. 1780.
[80] *Morning Chronicle*, 31 Dec. 1779.   [81] *Morning Post*, 9 Feb. 1780.

discussion of Rockingham reveals, such papers clearly believed that public opinion existed as a legitimate political and social force, and indeed, used it as a form of sanction. But their discussion of the reform movement's supporters implicitly equated popular sovereignty with mob rule. Anti-reform newspapers differentiated between the general population and 'the people' in a way which their radical counterparts, with their more demo-cratic definitions of the public, did not. Thus 'Socius' warned the *Post*'s readers against mistaking 'faction for patriotism and the turbulence of the mob for the *majesty of the people*'.[82]

Conservative newspapers suggested a more propertied, respectable definition of the people, but seemed wary of defining it too clearly. Most often, 'the public' was identified in terms of what it was not. Thus, the *Morning Post* described a Middlesex Committee meeting in April 1780 as consisting of 'two or three republican Members of Parliament, and some of the lowest of the *canaille*'.[83] The *Morning Herald* was also fond of referring to the crowds at reform meetings, particularly in London, as 'mobs'.[84] However, at other times the people were explicitly equated with property owners, in the form of freeholders, such as in the report of a Westminster Committee meeting which commented that 'It was observed yesterday at the meeting of the mobille at Westminster-hall, that when the hands were held up, such a number of dirty fists never before appeared in that place. The assemblage consisted of the lowest dregs of the mob; and stating the fact justly, they disgraced the very idea of freeholders'.[85] 'Anti-Petitioner' in the *General Evening Post* protested that petitioners were neither respectable nor freeholders,[86] and the *Public Advertiser* claimed that

Nothing . . . can more clearly demonstrate that the outed party have not the sense of the freeholders of any county with them, in their present attempts to involve this country in all the horrors of anarchy, than that in their late advertisements they invite all persons whatsoever, paying taxes, to their tumultuous meetings. Even these will not assemble in any considerable numbers round the banners of sedition; therefore, the next address of the party will probably extend to beggars, vagrants, footpads and highwaymen.[87]

But such clear equations of political rights and property ownership were rare in the London press. As will be shown, the provincial press was more

---

[82] *Morning Post*, 9 Nov. 1782. See also ibid. 24 Apr. 1780. [83] Ibid. 13 Apr. 1780.
[84] See, for example, *Morning Herald*, 4 and 11 Apr. 1780.
[85] *Morning Post*, 7 Apr. 1780.
[86] *General Evening Post*, 19 Feb. 1780. [87] *Public Advertiser*, 2 Feb. 1780.

ready to describe the people or the public according to a much narrower and more rigorous, propertied definition. However, in the capital, where the newspaper-reading public appears socially broader than in the provinces, such an emphatic line, bound to have alienated readers, was avoided.

Those newspapers, such as the *Public Advertiser* and the *General Evening Post*, which included material from both sides of this very polarized debate over reform suggest deep political divisions within the capital's newspaper-reading public, and the existence of a vigorous debate, which was divided along the lines of political allegiance rather than those of social status. The *Public Advertiser* claimed to print whatever material was sent to it,[88] and the mixture of opinions it expressed suggests that a concerted propaganda campaign was being undertaken both by those opposed to reform and those in favour of it. However, the contents of the press as a whole, and that of the partisan papers in particular, suggest that none of the interested and organized political groups could direct the political contents of the capital's newspapers fully.

The complex factors which determined the politics of individual London newspapers meant that no paper could ever claim to be truly independent. However, the role that the readership had in shaping the politics of the press, albeit indirectly, means that the contents of newspapers can give us some indication of the nature of popular public debate. In the case of the reform movement, this has been shown to have been both vigorous and diverse. Despite what might have been expected, a significant proportion of London opinion was hostile to reform. The majority of newspaper readers would have been excluded from direct participation in the political process, yet many of these readers appeared unconvinced even by the persuasive promises of the reformers to give them a greater say in how the country was run. Rather like those who gathered behind the banner of 'Church and King' in the following decade, many in the 1780s held the protection of property and the rule of law to be more important than extending individual rights.

However, significant numbers were still attracted by a radical ideology of constitutional reform, where a growing focus on extra-parliamentary activity reflected the overriding importance of popular sovereignty.

---

[88] The *Public Advertiser* carried calls for annual parliaments and universal suffrage (see 9 Apr., 2 May, and 30 Oct. 1783) and defences of the county committees (25 Dec. 1779, 4 and 21 Feb. 1780), as well as claims that the reform movement was orchestrated by the Opposition (30 Dec. 1779, 28 Jan., 1 and 12 Feb. 1780) and that reformers threatened the constitution (22 Apr., 10 May, 29 June 1780).

Moreover, even those who were hostile to reform did appear to accept the central role of 'the people' in political life, and both sides in the reform debate tried to lay claim to public opinion as a prime legitimating force. Differences did not arise over the function or the utility of public opinion, but in the way in which the public was constituted and the degree to which the reform movement could claim to have popular support. Although conservative newspapers maintained a traditional allegiance to individual politicians at Westminster, they were increasingly likely to voice doubts as to their sincerity. Like radical papers, the conservative press shifted its gaze somewhat, and presented politics in a manner which incorporated both 'high' and 'low', and indeed would often blur the distinctions between the two. Increasingly, the individual politician, and even the King himself, earned their stature according to the extent to which they represented the sense of the people. Although the reform movement did little to alter the parliamentary constitution, the debates which it engendered acted to change the ways in which political life was perceived and actually functioned, as 'the people' and public opinion played an increasingly influential part in the nation's politics. As the rest of this book will show, such developments were not limited to the capital. The rapidly expanding provincial newspaper press also had a part to play in constructing and redefining the political process in late eighteenth-century England.

4
PROVINCIAL NEWSPAPERS
AND NEWSPAPER READERS

Eighteenth-century England witnessed a dramatic increase in the production of provincial newspapers. The scale of this development was such that whilst at least forty titles were available in 1770, this figure had nearly doubled by the end of the century. Yet despite their rapid proliferation, provincial newspapers were restricted by the small size of individual operations and a lack of manpower. Without journalists of their own, papers produced in the provinces were forced to use the London press as a source of much of their published material. The result was that eighteenth-century provincial newspapers appeared (at least superficially) neither original nor politically independent—in stark contrast to many of the capital's papers at the time, as well as to provincial newspapers of the nineteenth century.

The provincial press's apparently 'parasitic' relationship with its London counterpart in the eighteenth century, coupled with the less developed structure of provincial papers, both in terms of size and frequency of publication, has won them harsh treatment from historians. This is certainly true of Aspinall, who, in *Politics and the Press*, dismissed provincial newspapers for having low circulations and for filling their pages with advertising or with material copied from the London papers. He remarked that even at the end of the eighteenth century, very few provincial newspaper editors were capable of writing a leading article, since most were printers 'whose skill lay in a technical direction', and therefore depended upon London newspapers to supply the contents of their own publications.[1]

[1] Aspinall, *Politics and the Press*, 350. See also D. Read, 'North of England Newspapers (c.1700–c.1900) and their Value to Historians', *Proceedings of the Leeds Philosophical and Literary Society*, 8 (Nov. 1957), 200–15, and *Press and the People, 1790–1850: Opinion in Three English Cities* (London, 1961); D. Clare, 'The Growth and Importance of the Newspaper Press in Manchester, Liverpool, Sheffield and Leeds', *Transactions of the Lancashire and Cheshire Antiquarian Society*, 123 (1963), 101–23; D. Fraser, 'The Press in Leicester c.1790–1850', *Transactions of the Leicestershire Archaeological and Historical Society*, 42 (1966–7), 53–75; Feather, *The Provincial Book Trade*, 37. There are also a number of useful localized studies of individual newspapers or the press of single towns, but their narrowness of focus is problematic in terms of a broader understanding of the provincial press in the late 18th cent. and its relationship with its London counterpart. A large number of such works

Historians have largely accepted that provincial newspapers were small-scale, amateurish, 'scissors-and-paste' operations. As such they have generally struggled to explain their appeal. Their accounts stress the provision of local news of a non-political, uncontroversial nature, local advertising, and the relative cheapness of a weekly provincial paper, as compared with those from the capital, which appeared more frequently and may also have been less accessible. Yet the emphasis that most provincial papers put upon obtaining news from London 'by express', and the large sums expended in this endeavour,[2] suggest that readers placed great

take the form of articles which appear in local historical publications, many of which are referred to in the following pages. More substantial works include: J. D. Andrew, 'The Derbyshire Newspaper Press, 1720–1855' (University of Reading MA thesis, 1954); K. G. Burton, *The Early Newspaper Press in Berkshire* (Reading, 1954); D. Clare, 'The Growth and Importance of the Newspaper Press in Manchester, Liverpool, Sheffield and Leeds between 1780 and 1800', (University of Manchester MA thesis, 1960); D. F. Gallop, 'Chapters in the History of the Provincial Newspaper Press, 1700–1855' [on Bristol] (University of Reading MA thesis, 1952); J. J. Looney, 'Advertising and Society in England, 1720–1820: A Statistical Analysis of Yorkshire Newspaper Advertisements' (Princeton University Ph.D. thesis, 1983). The research undertaken on the earlier part of the century, however, particularly that by Cranfield and Wiles, does provide a solid basis upon which to examine the operations of the provincial press as a whole in later years: G. A. Cranfield, *The Development of the Provincial Newspaper 1700–1760* (Oxford, 1962); R. M. Wiles, *Freshest Advices: Early Provincial Newspapers in England* (Columbus, Ohio, 1965); whilst Christine Ferdinand's work on the *Salisbury Journal* gives important insights into the workings of a provincial newspaper over several decades: C. Y. Ferdinand, *Benjamin Collins and the Provincial Newspaper Trade in the Eighteenth Century* (Oxford, 1997). See also Black, *The English Press*. Some more recent historical work has begun to challenge the extent to which the provincial press was conditioned by London: J. Money, *Experience and Identity: Birmingham and the West Midlands, 1760–1800* (Manchester, 1977); J. Barry, 'The Press and the Politics of Culture in Bristol, 1660–1775', in J. Black and J. Gregory (eds.), *Culture, Politics and Society in Britain, 1660–1800* (Manchester, 1991), 49–81—though for a recent restatement of the dominance of the capital's newspapers, see Harris, *Politics and the Rise of the Press*, 82.

[2] See the records of the *Chelmsford Chronicle*: ERO, Acc. 5197, D/F, 66/1; Clare, 'The Growth and Importance of the Newspaper Press', 42; Andrew, 'The Derbyshire Newspaper Press', 67. In order that the *Northampton Mercury* should receive the news published in London in time to copy it and send its own editions off by the evening, the editor, Dicey, apparently 'had a London man who collected the papers every Saturday and came to Northampton on horseback, armed with a brace of pistols for fear of highwaymen, reaching Dicey's office four hours before the London coaches brought the news. It was a feat which meant changing horse every six or seven miles': 'Northampton Mercury', *Newspaper World*, 2160 (3 June 1939), 5. In 1786, the mail coach took approximately 26 hours to reach Leeds from London: [F Beckwith], 'Extracts from the Leeds Intelligencer and the Leeds Mercury 1777–1782', *Publications of the Thoresby Society*, 40 (1955), 1–110, p. ix. However, the *Leeds Intelligencer*, published on a Tuesday, could boast the inclusion of Monday's news 'by express': *Leeds Intelligencer*, 7 Dec. 1779. The *York Chronicle* of Friday, 23 Mar. 1781 claimed to have announced an important army victory on Thursday morning, sixteen hours faster than was possible by post, because of the paper's express. In Jan. of the same year,

importance upon the inclusion of very recent news. This might seem to give a competitive advantage to the more up-to-date newspapers of the capital, which appear to have been readily available in the provinces; however, the success of provincial papers in the face of opposition from the London press shows that this was not the case.

An examination of both the contents of provincial newspapers and the way in which they were run forces a major reassessment of the provincial newspaper press and of the basis of its appeal. A study of its economics shows that far from being small-scale or amateurish, the provincial press constituted much bigger business than has been thought. Provincial news-papers emerge as potentially highly profitable commercial ventures, which could be successful, money-making concerns. It seems likely that producing a paper capable of securing a readership large enough to make a profit was no easy task, but one which demanded entrepreneurial flair combined with a sensitivity towards local opinion. These requirements, coupled with the size of the operation (in economic if not in structural terms), ensured that the successful provincial paper was operated in a much more professional manner than has been assumed.

An examination of the newspapers themselves makes more apparent the skills which seem to have been necessary to run them. Certainly, the way in which provincial newspapers were distributed and the timing of their publication decided appear to have been carefully calculated. It is also likely that what actually appeared in print was of great importance, not only in the more predictable coverage of local news, but also in the way national news was treated. Historians have not paid sufficient attention to the political character and content of the news carried in provincial news-papers. By studying these elements of the provincial press, it becomes clear that it did not follow blindly the political leads set by the capital's newspapers. It is true that provincial papers made extensive use of mate-rial from London. However, this appears to have been on a selective basis, so that the contents of the provincial publications often reveal identifiable and consistent political stances, distinct from those found in any of the capital's newspapers. Indeed, the material found within provincial news-papers suggests that by displaying a uniquely local set of political preoc-cupations and opinions, they could successfully ward off competition from papers produced elsewhere. Thus, the provincial press may have

however, the *Chronicle* had to apologize to its readers since snow had delayed the arrival of the express, and the paper had been printed without receiving the latest news: *York Chron-icle*, 26 Jan. 1781.

been localized not just in its production, but also in the views and opinions which it expressed. As such, it confirms recent historiographical arguments about the vitality and independence of provincial culture and politics.[3]

The Economics of Provincial Newspapers

Although those studying eighteenth-century English newspapers are blessed with an abundance of surviving copies, they are equally cursed by the paucity of other extant material concerning the newspaper press. One of the major problems facing historians of the provincial press has been the scarcity of evidence about newspaper production; in particular, a lack of financial accounts has left large gaps in our knowledge of newspaper circulation, profitability, and general business practice. Hitherto, the only provincial newspaper account books located belonged to those who ran financially unstable, and ultimately unsuccessful, papers. It seems unlikely that these records are representative of the provincial press as a whole in the eighteenth century.

Although such failure appears not to have been uncommon, it was not typical. Of the 220 provincial newspapers which can be traced, almost a third do seem to have failed, and lasted for less than a year. However, for those which ran for longer periods, over 80 per cent appeared for at least five years, with many of these running for a considerably longer duration and almost half continuing into the nineteenth century.[4] This suggests that a typical provincial newspaper, representative of those which would have been read most frequently by a majority of provincial newspaper readers, was one which displayed a degree of longevity. Business interests appear to have provided the main motivation for those who produced

---

[3] See, for example, Dickinson, *Politics of the People*; O'Gorman, *Voters, Patrons, and Parties*; Rogers, *Whigs and Cities*; Wilson, *The Sense of the People*; Peter Clark (ed.), *The Transformation of English Provincial Towns 1660–1800* (London, 1984); John M. Triffitt, 'Politics and the Urban Community: Parliamentary Boroughs in the South West of England 1710–1730' (University of Oxford D.Phil. thesis, 1985).

[4] See J. G. Muddiman, *A Tercentenary Handlist of English and Welsh Newspapers, Magazines and Reviews* (London, 1920); R. S. Crane and F. B. Kaye, 'A Census of British Newspapers and Periodicals, 1620–1800', *Studies in Philology*, 24 (1927), 1–205; G. A. Cranfield, 'A Handlist of English Provincial Newspapers and Periodicals 1700–1760', Cambridge Bibliographical Society Monographs, 2 (Cambridge, 1952), and 'Handlist of English Periodicals, 1700–1760: Additions and Corrections', *Transactions of the Cambridge Bibliographical Society*, 2 (1956), 269–74; R. M. Wiles, *Freshest Advices*, and 'Further Additions and Corrections to G. A. Cranfield's Handlist of English Provincial Newspapers and Periodicals 1700–1760', *Transactions of the Cambridge Bibliographical Society*, 2 (1958), 385–9; G. Watson (ed.), *The New Cambridge Bibliography of English Literature* (Cambridge, 1971).

newspapers in the provinces, at least before the 1790s. Therefore it seems likely that the long life of those papers described as successful and typical was due to their profitability, and conversely, that those papers termed failures because they did not last were unprofitable.

The records concerning the circulation of Christopher Etherington's *York Chronicle* for 1772–7, as cited in Davies' *A Memoir of the York Press*, are not those of a successful paper, but previously gave the greatest insight into the economics of eighteenth-century newspapers. Since Etherington's poor business practice eventually led him to bankruptcy, the tale told by his accounts is a cautionary one. They represent the financial record of a newspaper which was in decline after just over one year in existence. Etherington finally went bankrupt in February 1777 and the paper was turned over to William Blanchard.[5] The accounts of the *Chronicle* do not therefore give an example of the economics of a more representative provincial newspaper, for which it is unlikely that such dramatic fluctuations of fortune would occur.

The discovery a few years ago of the account books recording the finances of the *Hampshire Chronicle* between 1778 and 1783 is therefore useful, although these documents, produced by a business in severe financial trouble, present similar problems to the records left of the *York Chronicle*. When James Linden, the *Hampshire Chronicle*'s proprietor, went bankrupt the business was bought by a partnership of five, which included Benjamin Collins, owner of the *Salisbury Journal*. Another of the new owners, the Winchester bookseller John Wilkes, was entrusted with running the paper. The *Chronicle* changed hands for only two hundred guineas.[6] This very low figure suggests the degree of the paper's financial trouble;[7] moreover, the *Chronicle*'s prosperity did not improve under its new management. Put candidly, under Wilkes' control the newspaper was a financial disaster. Thus, while these records give us more information than those of the *York Chronicle* about the way in which provincial newspapers were run, one must be extremely careful in accepting the

[5] R. Davies, *A Memoir of the York Press* (London, 1868), 331–4.

[6] PRO, E140/90–1. See Ferdinand, *Benjamin Collins*, and 'Local Distribution Networks in Eighteenth-Century England', in R. Myers and M. Harris (eds.), *Spreading the Word: The Distribution Networks of Print 1550–1850* (Winchester, 1990), 131–49. I am grateful to Christine Ferdinand for lending me her microfilm copy of the *Hampshire Chronicle* account books.

[7] Most papers went for much higher sums: see below. This figure is so low that probably it covered only the paper's press and print, allowing very little for the purchase of the paper's copyright. It certainly did not include 'goodwill', since Linden soon attempted to set up a rival: Ferdinand, *Benjamin Collins*, 4.

Chronicle's accounts as being in any way representative of provincial papers as a whole. Indeed, the survival of the paper's records is due to their being exhibits in a lawsuit brought by Wilkes against his former partners in an attempt to regain some of the money which he claimed to have lost in the enterprise.[8]

The business records for two far more successful papers, which appear to have escaped the scrutiny of historians until now, give valuable new insights into the organization of eighteenth-century provincial newspapers. These consist of the minute-book of the proprietors of the *Chelmsford Chronicle*, which covers the period between 1777 and 1784 and gives detailed quarterly accounts;[9] and that of the proprietors of the *Salopian Journal*, which records proceedings at shareholders' meetings between 1793 and 1799 and gives a thorough financial record of the paper from December 1793 to March 1795.[10] Both papers' records provide a far more complete picture of the internal workings of a provincial newspaper than has hitherto been presented. Those of the *Chelmsford Chronicle* are particularly important because they represent what is likely to have been a far more typical eighteenth-century newspaper. During the periods of accounting for each paper covered by the various sources, the *York Chronicle*, *Hampshire Chronicle*, and *Salopian Journal* were all unprofitable. Only the records of the *Chelmsford Chronicle* depict a financially healthy, and therefore far more representative, provincial newspaper of the late eighteenth century.

The *Chelmsford Chronicle* was probably started in 1764 and continued as the *Essex Chronicle* into the twentieth century. It was first printed by William Strupar, who was joined in partnership a year later by L. Hassall, a bookmaker and stationer. By June 1768, the paper had been taken over by T. Toft and R. Lobb, but before April 1771 it was again under new ownership, and by February 1777, when the minute-book begins, it was split between William Clachar, Samuel Gray, and Charles Frost and Elizabeth Griffiths who co-owned a third share.[11] These four were

---

[8] Ferdinand, 'Local Distribution Networks', 131.

[9] ERO, Acc. 5197, D/F, 66/1.

[10] SRRU, MS 1923. The minutes are contained within one book (Book I), and the accounts within another (Book II), although the two are bound in one volume.

[11] See the article in the 200th anniversary edn. of the *Essex Chronicle* on 14 Aug. 1964, by its editor, R. A. F. Handley. However, it is not clear that the paper owned by Clachar *et al.* was a direct descendant of Toft and Lobb's paper: see the first edn. of the paper under Clachar's management, *Chelmsford Chronicle*, 5 Apr. 1771. In this issue only Clacher's and Frost's names are mentioned, which suggests that Gray and Griffiths may have become shareholders later on.

proprietors until May 1784, when Griffiths' name disappeared from the list of shareholders and the other three remained partners. Throughout the period covered by the minute-book all the proprietors were involved in some way with running the paper. Clachar appears to have been the *Chronicle*'s printer, and was paid a regular sum which amounted to between £67 4s. and £67 12s. per year. In common with Frost and Gray, Clachar also claimed various expenses connected with the paper's operation.[12]

In terms of sales, circulation area, and profits, the *Chelmsford Chronicle* would not have been one of the largest provincial newspapers in England in the late eighteenth century. It was not as established as many of its counterparts and its immediate audience in Chelmsford was not particularly numerous. Positioned as it was, the *Chronicle* would also have been challenged by the older *Ipswich Journal*, which listed agents in both Chelmsford and Colchester,[13] and by the London papers. It seems unlikely, then, that the *Chronicle* was an unusually successful provincial newspaper, and, in common with other newspapers, it was not a risk-free investment.[14] Yet it did provide a relatively rewarding return for its shareholders, averaging dividends of £104 13s. for each of the three shares per year: enough to place the owners firmly within the middling rank of society.[15]

The *Chelmsford Chronicle*'s affairs stand in stark contrast to the financial situation of the *Hampshire Chronicle*. The ledger shows that the Hampshire paper consistently lost money. When the partnership involving Collins was brought to an end in 1783, it was noted that over £935 had been 'sunk in this undertaking'.[16] On average, the *Hampshire Chronicle* made a loss of £191 10s. per year, compared with the *Chelmsford Chronicle*'s average profit of £313 13s. Despite the dangers inherent in treating the economics of the *Hampshire Chronicle* as in any way typical of provincial newspapers as a whole, its failure paradoxically tells us something about the way in which successful papers functioned. This is especially true if its workings are examined in comparison with those of a paper like the *Chelmsford Chronicle*. The disparity between the profits of the two is huge (over £500 per year) and is related to significant differences in net income from sales and advertising. However, the disparity between the

---

[12] ERO, Acc. 5197, D/F, 66/1.   [13] *Ipswich Journal*, 4 Dec. 1779.
[14] Losses were recorded at the meetings held on 10 Feb. 1777 and 24 May 1784: ERO, Acc. 5197, D/F, 66/1.
[15] P. Langford, *A Polite and Commercial People* (Oxford, 1989), 62–5.
[16] PRO, E140/90.

papers of income from these sources was only £30, and does not explain a difference in average monthly profits of over £40.[17] Indeed, the profit levels of the *Chelmsford Chronicle* suggest that a smaller paper like the *Hampshire Chronicle*, which would presumably have had slightly lower running and distribution costs because of the comparative size of its operation, should have at least been able to break even, given its sales and the amount of advertising which it attracted.

In the light of this, the only reason for the large and consistent losses made by the Hampshire paper seems to be mismanagement. This explanation is certainly borne out by the state of the paper's financial records. Unlike the *Chelmsford Chronicle*, whose finances were recorded in quarterly accounts by double-entry bookkeeping, the *Hampshire Chronicle*'s accounts were much more haphazard, and appeared in the form of a cash book which recorded day-to-day expenses and a separate ledger for the paper's advertising. Upon the dissolution of the partnership in 1783, a whole page of the final account had to be devoted to accounting errors which had been discovered. One of these mistakes meant that the £100 profit recorded in the paper's first six months under the partnership was in fact a loss. This formed part of the paper's large deficit of over £900, which in turn provided the basis for the lawsuit which followed.[18]

The records of the *Salopian Journal* (1793–9) also show it to have been a loss-making concern. However, this appears to have been a temporary position, maintained only whilst the paper established itself. The first edition of the *Salopian Journal* appeared in Shrewsbury on 29 January 1794. Another paper, the *Shrewsbury Chronicle*, had been published in the town by Thomas Wood since 1772, and would have been a serious rival for the newcomer. Indeed, the *Journal* lost a large amount of money during the first years of its existence. However, it remained in business for many years, which suggests that at some point it did begin to make a profit. Both the minute-book of proprietors' meetings and the record of the paper's financial transactions cover the period of the *Journal*'s early life, giving a uniquely detailed account of the launch of a provincial newspaper in the eighteenth century.[19] When the *Journal* began, it was owned by a consortium of eleven prominent Shrewsbury gentlemen and businessmen, nine of whom owned a full share, and two who jointly held

[17] The *Chelmsford Chronicle*'s average monthly profit was £26 2s., whilst the corresponding loss made by the *Hampshire Chronicle* was £16: ERO, Acc. 5197, D/F, 66/1 and PRO, E140/90.

[18] PRO, E140/90.   [19] SRRU, MS 1923, Books I and II.

the tenth share of the paper.[20] Each share was purchased for £100.[21] At the initial proprietors' meeting on 21 December 1793, it was agreed that the shareholder Joshua Eddowes and his son William would act as 'printers, treasurers, and secretaries',[22] almost certainly in view of their established involvement in the print trade.[23] Three days later, Isaac Wood, another investor, was given the job of 'the compiler of the paper', for which he was to receive one guinea a week.[24]

The proprietors of the *Salopian Journal* expended a considerable amount of time and money in publicizing their new venture during December 1793 and the first two months of 1794. The minutes for December 1793 record that advertisements were placed in the London daily papers; the *Sun*, the *Star*, and the *Morning Chronicle*; and in the *Gentleman's Magazine*. In addition, handbills and large bills were produced to be distributed and posted up 'throughout this and the neighbouring counties'.[25] More bills were produced in January 1794, for the windows and shop walls of the paper's agents, and the first edition of the *Journal*, numbering two and a half thousand copies, was given away free, with some of the copies sent to London coffee-houses.[26] On 21 January, it was decided to provide uniforms for the men employed to distribute the paper

---

[20] Captain Jonathan Scott, Joseph Loxdale, John Flint, Thomas Lloyd, William and Joshua Eddowes, John Probert, William Coupland and Robert Pemberton who jointly owned a share, Isaac Wood, and Revd Edward Blakeway, Mayor of Shrewsbury. Blakeway was also the Rector of St Mary's: Joseph Morris, 'The Mayors of Shrewsbury', *Shropshire Archaeological Society Transactions*, 4th ser., 9 (1923), 5. By 2 Nov. 1796, he had died and his widow, Mercy, inherited his share of the paper. The new articles of agreement which this necessitated have survived. They show that all the shareholders used the title 'esquire', except the Eddowes, who were both described as 'bookseller and printer', and William Coupland, who was dubbed a 'gentleman'. Isaac Wood was described as a watchmaker as well as the paper's editor: SRRU, D2713. The Eddowes were both burgesses: Llewelyn C. Lloyd, 'The Book Trade in Shropshire', *Shropshire Archaeological Society Transactions*, 98 (1935–6), 65–142 and 145–200, pp. 106–8.

[21] Minutes of meeting of 21 Dec. 1793: SRRU, MS 1923, Book I.

[22] The accounts in SRRU, MS 1923, Book II are in Joshua's hand.

[23] Joshua Eddowes had been a printer and bookseller in Shrewsbury from 1749, when he was admitted a Freeman of the Booksellers' Company. His son William served as his apprentice, and followed him into the Company in 1785, when he also went into partnership with his father: Lloyd, 'The Book Trade in Shropshire', 106–8.

[24] Meeting of 24 Dec. 1793. Wood gave up his share in Feb. 1794, and the paper was then divided between 9 others, but he retained his position as 'compiler'/'editor' of the paper: SRRU, MS 1923, Book I.

[25] Minutes of 21 Dec. 1793, SRRU, MS 1923, Book I.

[26] Minutes of 10 and 21 Jan. 1794, ibid. The minutes recorded that only 2,000 copies be printed, but the account books show that 2,500 were produced. The coffee-houses listed were the London, Chapter, Peele's, Oxford, Salopian, and Wright's coffee-houses.

in the countryside. The minutes noted that 'each newsman be furnished with a blue coloured upper coat with a red collar; a Hat edged with a lace band and a horn'. The costs of these attempts to publicize the *Journal* were listed in the paper's accounts, and totalled over £72.[27] It was suggested that 'the members for the county and town be solicited for leave to make use of their names to circulate papers thro' the Post Office',[28] though it does not seem that this attempt to exploit parliamentary privilege was successful. The proprietors themselves were also urged to make applications to their friends 'for their encouragement and support', and a circular letter was printed for this purpose.[29]

However, these efforts went unrewarded at first, for the paper was not profitable in its first years. Apart from the initial investment of £100 made by the shareholders, they were asked to provide further sums between 1793 and 1795 to offset the paper's cash flow problems, which amounted to £80 for each of the ten shares.[30] An entry in the account book for 1 January 1795 notes that an additional £132 9s. was needed in order to balance the account.[31] Therefore by March 1795 almost £2,000 had been invested in a paper which was producing no return for its owners. The reasons why the *Journal* was not making a profit in its early years are not as obscure as in the case of the *Hampshire Chronicle*. The Shrewsbury paper was simply not achieving high enough sales, nor attracting sufficient advertisers. Between February 1794 and March 1795, the *Salopian Journal* seems to have averaged sales of under 680 copies a week,[32] which was only one-third of the *Chelmsford Chronicle*'s average circulation figure.[33] The revenues the Shrewsbury paper received from advertising and sales combined were not enough to cover even its production costs.

In spite of this initial poor showing, the *Journal* did not follow the *Hampshire Chronicle* into bankruptcy, but continued well into the nineteenth century. The fact that it survived for so many years suggests that at some stage it did begin to make money, and since the Eddowes continued to run the paper, it does not seem that poor management was to blame for such an apparently inauspicious infancy. As a new paper, the *Journal* had not yet built up a sufficient readership and advertising base.

---

[27] SRRU, MS 1923, Book II.   [28] Minutes of 7 Jan. 1794, SRRU, MS 1923, Book I.
[29] Minutes of 7 and 10 Jan. 1794, ibid.
[30] Each shareholder paid £10 on 21 Dec. 1793, 28 Jan., 8 Apr., and 10 June 1794, and £20 on 2 Sept. and 16 Dec. 1794: SRRU, MS 1923. The Sept. payment was requested because the paper had received a bill for £83 for duty on advertisements and for 'other expenses': proprietors' meeting, 2 Sept. 1794: SRRU, MS 1923, Book I.
[31] SRRU, MS 1923, Book II.
[32] Ibid.   [33] ERO, Acc. 5197, D/F, 66/1.

More established newspapers, which could rely for their financial health on a strong foundation in these areas, appear to have been, as we shall see, extremely valuable commercial assets. Those who chose to invest in them paid large sums to do so, presumably because they could expect to see healthy returns. In the case of a new venture, it is unlikely that those involved would have held such hopes. On the contrary, they would expect to be out of pocket until the paper grew to a sufficient size. The costs and risks involved in setting up and establishing a new paper meant that the value of older successful newspapers was considerable.

The provincial newspaper often appears as the poor relation to London papers, but this was not necessarily the case. With profit levels which averaged over £300 a year, the *Chelmsford Chronicle*, probably a relatively small provincial paper, was almost as financially rewarding as one of the capital's newspapers.[34] The valuation of £1,400 made by the owners of the *Chronicle* may not have been particularly exact (although it was probably based upon the purchase price), but it does at least indicate the broad worth attributed to the paper.[35] To put it in relative terms, it is much lower than the value of £5,200 attributed to the *Salisbury Journal*,[36] or the £4,000 figure put on the *Bath Chronicle* by its owner.[37] Although there does not appear to be any concrete evidence of the price at which shares in the *Chelmsford Chronicle* changed hands, if we use the paper's valuation as a guide, and compare this with the dividends which are recorded, it appears that it gave its proprietors a large annual return of 22 per cent on their investment. This is remarkably close to the figure calculated for the London newspaper, the *Gazetteer*,[38] and suggests a level of profit which would generally have been expected by those investing in newspapers. However, the *Salisbury Journal*'s dividends appear to have been lower. In the 1770s its estimated profits and the price of its shares gave its proprietors a return of 15 per cent. This figure may have been smaller than that of both the *Gazetteer* and the *Chelmsford Chronicle* because it represented a more secure investment in a well-established newspaper, whose profits were more predictable and less likely to fluctuate.

---

[34] ERO, Acc. 5197, D/F, 66/1. The London paper, the *Gazetteer*, had annual profits which averaged £366 during the 1780s: PRO, C104/67, Book H.

[35] This figure was supposed to represent 'the Chelmsford Chronicle and printing materials, wherewith it is printed': ERO, Acc. 5197, D/F, 66/1. The sum of £1,400 was cited as the value of the paper throughout the period covered by the minutes.

[36] Cranfield, *The Development of the Provincial Newspaper*, 256.

[37] Feather, *The Provincial Book Trade*, 104.

[38] Here a return of 23% on the original investment during the 1780s was calculated: PRO, C104/67.

An examination of those who owned provincial newspapers is further suggestive of the profitability of this type of venture. John Feather has argued that provincial newspaper ownership provided the basis of the wealth enjoyed by several eighteenth-century businessmen. Before his death in 1778, Robert Goadby, who owned the *Western Flying-Post*, amassed a 'considerable fortune' due to his involvement in the paper. William Jackson, of *Jackson's Oxford Journal*, also died a wealthy man: he left £13,000 in cash legacies. Much of this had come from his involvement in banking in later life, but it was, Feather maintains, his newspaper which started Jackson off.[39] A similar picture emerges from Christine Ferdinand's study of Benjamin Collins and his association with the *Salisbury Journal*. Collins was one of the *Journal*'s founders in 1736, and went on to assume sole ownership of the paper. He soon diversified into various ventures associated with the print trade, most notably bookselling, and later turned his hand to banking and moneylending. When he died in 1785, he left an estimated £85,000–£100,000 and had assumed the status of a 'landed gentleman'.[40]

In 1784, Thomas Slack, who had started the *Newcastle Chronicle* in 1765, left four houses to his daughters and an estate worth £500.[41] The owner of the *Northampton Mercury*, Thomas Dicey, made enough money to enable him to afford the lifestyle of a country squire.[42] George Burbage, who owned the *Nottinghamshire Journal*, was made a sheriff in 1773 and elected to the Senior Council of the Corporation in 1790. He also worked as an auctioneer and had his own paper mill.[43] James Simmons, who founded the *Kentish Gazette* in 1768, was at various times Sheriff of Canterbury, the Government's Distributor of Stamps for Kent, and MP for the area, whilst apparently making his fortune.[44] Robert Raikes, who ran the *Glocester [sic] Journal* between 1757 and 1802, sold it for £1,500, as well as receiving an annuity of between £300 and £500.[45] William Pine,

---

[39] Feather, *The Provincial Book Trade*, 22–3.

[40] Ferdinand, *Benjamin Collins*, chap. 1.

[41] J. Hodgson the Younger, 'Thomas Slack of Newcastle, Printer, 1723–1784, Founder of the "Newcastle Chronicle" ', *Archaeologia Aeliana*, 3rd ser., 17 (1920), 145–52; R. Welford, 'Early Newcastle Typography. 1639–1800', *Archaeologia Aeliana*, 3rd ser., 3 (1907), 1–134.

[42] Rather than live above his printing shop, Dicey bought Claybrook Hall, near Lutterworth, which was 20 miles from Northampton: W. W. Hadley, *The Bi-centenary Record of the Northampton Mercury* (Northampton, 1920), 37.

[43] W. J. Clarke, *Early Nottingham Printers and Printing*, 2nd edn. (Nottingham, 1953), 17–22.

[44] C. H. Timperley, *A Dictionary of Printers and Printing* (London, 1839), 826–7.

[45] The smaller figure is given in an MS note written by W. H. Black which was printed in the *Antiquary* (Dec. 1876), and was reprinted in *Gloucestershire Notes and Queries*, 3 (1885),

the owner of the *Bristol Gazette and Public Advertiser*, was a waywarden for two Bristol parishes in the 1770s and regularly gave to charity. On his death he left £2,000 to his widow and an invested sum of £4,000, all being the profits of his printing and newspaper business.[46] The success of such individuals does not provide clear evidence that provincial newspapers generated high profits. However, what is apparent is that many wealthy and socially prominent provincial businessmen were also newspaper proprietors and that part of the reason why they were so successful may have been due to their involvement in such ventures. Even though the degree to which this was true cannot be tested, it is significant that those who had proved, or would go on to prove, their financial acumen and business skills in other areas also chose to invest in newspapers. This suggests that newspaper ownership offered an attractive opportunity to those with the commercial ability and entrepreneurial flair needed to achieve business success.

An examination of two types of ownership commonly associated with provincial newspapers—family and partnership—indicates further what valuable commodities newspapers were. Those papers run as family businesses appear to have been treated as important inheritances. For example, Robert Goadby was so convinced of the value of the *Western Flying Post*, which he left to his brother and nephew, that he forbade them to sell it in order to pay his bequests out of the income.[47] Newspapers were almost always left to members of the owner's most immediate family. These would have been the proprietor's dependants, the widow, sons, and daughters, who would have been expected to receive most from the estate. More often than not, newspapers appear to have formed the central part of the legacy and continued to be run by the recipients. Robert Raikes inherited the *Glocester Journal* from his father in 1757 and controlled it until his retirement in 1802.[48] The *Leeds Intelligencer* was founded in 1754 by Griffin Wright, who ran it until 1785 when he handed it over to his son, who in turn passed it to his son twenty years later.[49] John Drewry took over the *Derby Mercury* after his uncle's death in 1769 and ran it until 1794.[50]

210. It was also cited in A. Gregory, *Robert Raikes: Journalist and Philanthropist* (London, 1877), 18. The larger sum is given in R. Austin, 'Robert Raikes, the Elder, & the "Gloucestershire Journal"', *The Library*, 3rd ser., 6 (1915), 1–24, p. 24.

[46] Gallop, 'History of the Provincial Newspaper Press', 100.

[47] Feather, *The Provincial Book Trade*, 23 and 104.

[48] Austin, 'Robert Raikes', 24.

[49] [Beckwith], 'Extracts from the Leeds Intelligencer and the Leeds Mercury'; Mildred A. Gibb and Frank Beckwith, *The Yorkshire Post, Two Centuries* (Leeds, 1954), 1–5.

[50] *The Newspaper World and Advertising Review*, 8 July 1939.

William Lee ran the *Sussex Weekly Advertiser* from 1745 until 1787 when he died and the paper was taken over by his sons.[51] Robert Trewman, the owner of *Trewman's Exeter Flying Post*, left the paper to his son, Robert, and his widow in 1802,[52] and Solomon Hodgson, owner of the *Newcastle Chronicle* until 1784, left the paper to his widow, Sarah, having inherited it from her father, and she in turn bequeathed it to her sons.[53]

Although newspapers were valuable businesses that could produce handsome profits for their owners, they were also capital-intensive, as the records of the *Salopian Journal* show: a large amount of money had to be expended initially before any return could be expected. This is no doubt why groups of individuals often joined together in order to purchase or begin a paper. This form of cost-sharing would not only reduce the financial burden on owners, but also divided the amount of risk taken. The ill-feeling which could be caused by the failure of such arrangements reveals the amount that those involved had at stake. For example, the *Ipswich Journal* was taken over in about 1777 by a partnership composed of a Mrs Craighton, who had inherited the paper from her brother, Stephen Jackson, her nephew, who acted as editor, and John Shave, a printer. Ownership of the paper became the subject of a fierce legal battle in the early 1780s when Craighton fought with her former co-proprietors over her rights to an annuity and a share in the paper.[54] The same type of animosity was aroused over the inheritance of *Felix Farley's Bristol Journal* in 1774, when its owner, Sarah Farley, died, and her niece Hester took over. Two of Sarah's former employees, Samuel Bonner, the foreman printer, and Richard Middleton, her clerk, claimed to be the paper's true inheritors. A bitter dispute followed that was never resolved, and both parties brought out rival papers.[55] A similar squabble took place in Exeter in the 1760s between R. Trewman and W. Andrews, who were employed by Andrew Brice, the proprietor of *Brice's Weekly Journal*. Trewman, an apprentice, and Andrews, a journeyman printer, claimed

[51] Arthur Beckett, 'The First Sussex Newspaper', *The Sussex County Magazine*, 15 (Aug. 1941), 247–54, pp. 247–9.

[52] Robert Dymond, 'Trewman's Exeter Flying Post', *The Western Antiquary*, 5 (1886), 163–6.

[53] E. Mackenzie, *A Descriptive and Historical Account of the Town and County of Newcastle Upon Tyne* (Newcastle upon Tyne, 1827), 728.

[54] *History of the Ipswich Journal*; S. F. Watson, 'Some Materials for a History of Printing and Publishing in Ipswich', *Proceedings of the Suffolk Institute of Archaeology and Natural History*, 24 (1949), 182–227.

[55] Gallop, 'History of the Provincial Newspaper Press', 82.

that Brice had promised to retire and leave them the paper. When he did not, they set up the rival *Exeter Flying Post*.[56]

The potential value and profitability of provincial newspapers challenges the notion that they were merely sidelines to the more important business activities of local printers. Cranfield has stated that, at least for the earlier part of the century, newspapers did not provide enough profit to be a printer's main source of income and were only subsidiary interests.[57] This suggests that running a paper was, and could only be, a part-time affair. Such a view has widespread implications for the importance of provincial newspapers, not only in terms of their circulation, but also in the way in which they were produced. But provincial newspapers were not generally insignificant business enterprises, as has been shown. Moreover, they were often produced in a much more professional manner than the image of a printer's part-time interest suggests. As in London, their management by editors, rather than by the printer and/or owner, was not uncommon. Clachar, although he may well have been involved in other ventures, was given a salary to run the *Chelmsford Chronicle*. His position was not unique. Even John Wilkes received payment, perhaps unjustly, for his management of the *Hampshire Chronicle*.[58] Charles Pugh, who founded and owned the *Hereford Journal*, was able to live in London whilst he paid a man called Rathbone to act as editor, 'who wrote the paragraphs and in general superintended the publication'.[59] Ann Ward, who owned the *York Courant*, appears to have employed David Russell to run the paper on a day-to-day basis.[60]

What evidence there is, then, suggests that provincial newspapers were generally run in an efficient and professional manner, in stark contrast to their amateurish image. Far from being merely sidelines to more significant enterprises, provincial newspapers constituted big business in late eighteenth-century England. They could be valuable commodities which produced large profits and appear to have contributed significantly to the

[56] Dymond, 'Trewman's Exeter Flying Post'; and T. N. Brushfield, *The Life and Bibliography of Andrew Brice, Author and Journalist: With some Remarks on the Early History of the Exeter Newspaper Press* ([Exeter?], 1888), 39–42.

[57] Cranfield, *The Development of the Provincial Newspaper*, 246.

[58] The paper's account books record regular payments for his role, which was variously described as being that of 'printer', 'publisher', and 'editor': PRO, E140/90.

[59] MS notes by John Allen, a Hereford printer and bookseller, which appear in the first bound volume of the *Hereford Journal* held at the Hereford Reference Library. His remarks are expanded by F. C. Morgan in 'Hereford Printers and Booksellers', *Transactions of the Woolhope Naturalists' Field Club, Herefordshire* (1941), 106–27.

[60] YCA, Acc. 1663 M25 and M32.

wealth of their owners. However, although this reassessment of the provincial press has challenged some of the ways it has been portrayed in previous historical accounts, the basis of its economic strength remains obscure. Without an understanding of why provincial newspapers were successful, their significance to late eighteenth-century society remains unclear.

Provincial Newspapers and their Readers

The dramatic increase in the number of provincial newspapers produced in England during the eighteenth century (see Fig. 4) can be linked to the more general trend in the production of reading matter of all sorts which took place in this period, which in turn has been associated with the 'commercialization of culture'.[61] James Raven has shown that there was a steep rise in the number of publications as the century progressed and has noted a watershed in the 1780s.[62] Cranfield has suggested that the proliferation of papers, at least before 1760, could be linked to periods of particularly vigorous activity in the country's domestic or foreign affairs.[63] However, the pattern of growth for the whole century does not support such an argument. Although there appear to be periods in which a rapid increase in titles coincided with important political events, there are also times when this did not happen. For example, it would appear that more provincial newspapers were produced in response to tensions in the early 1740s and to those caused by the French Revolution, but there was no reaction to the political instability of the early 1760s or to the American Revolution; moreover, it is difficult to understand why the production of papers rose so steeply in the early 1770s and late 1780s, but not in other periods when more important political events occurred. The most striking trend in Fig. 4 is of an underlying and steady increase, which does not suggest that the proliferation of papers was determined by the changing nature of politics, although this may have influenced it at certain times. A decade-by-decade comparison of the geographical spread of provincial newspapers offers little by way of new interpretation. The timing of their appearance does not indicate that the production of new papers was determined by proximity to the capital or by the development of the turnpike road system. There is some evidence to suggest that the general

[61] N. McKendrick, J. Brewer, and J. H. Plumb, *The Birth of a Consumer Society: The Commercialization of Eighteenth-Century England* (London, 1992).
[62] James Raven, *Judging New Wealth: Popular Publishing and Responses to Commerce, 1750–1800* (Oxford, 1992), 32–5.
[63] Cranfield, *The Development of the Provincial Press*, 20–1.

Fig. 4. The proliferation of provincial newspapers in eighteenth-century England

Sources: J. G. Muddiman, *A Tercentenary Handlist of English and Welsh Newspapers, Magazines and Reviews* (London, 1920); R. S. Crane and F. B. Kaye, 'A Census of British Newspapers and Periodicals, 1620–1800', *Studies in Philology*, 24 (1927), 1–205; G. A. Cranfield, *A Handlist of English Provincial Newspapers and Periodicals* 1700–1760, Cambridge Bibliographical Society Monographs, 2 (Cambridge, 1952), and 'A Handlist of English Provincial Newspapers and Periodicals, 1700–1760: Additions and Corrections', *Transactions of the Cambridge Bibliographical Society*, 2 (1956), 269–74; R. M. Wiles, 'Further Additions and Corrections to G. A. Cranfield's *Handlist of English Provincial Newspapers and Periodicals 1700–1760*', *Transactions of the Cambridge Bibliographical Society*, 2 (1958), 385–9, and *Freshest Advices*; George Watson (ed.), *The New Cambridge Bibliography of English Literature* (Cambridge, 1971).

economic situation in the country played some part in influencing the establishment of new papers; however, this is far from conclusive. The spread of provincial newspapers in England did not seem to conform to any neat pattern, and although the underlying trend throughout the century suggests a steady expansion in the market for provincial newspapers, this does not explain the sporadic pattern of growth. To do this, we are forced to examine the circumstances surrounding the founding of individual papers.

Over fifty newspaper titles appeared regularly in the provinces in the years between 1779 and 1785. The papers represented towns across the whole country, sixteen of which supported more than one newspaper

(Fig. 5). Although many of these towns were provincial centres, such places did not automatically produce their own papers: there were notable exceptions, such as Lincoln, Colchester, and Carlisle. The factors which dictated the existence of a provincial newspaper in a particular area were complex. What mattered most was not necessarily a town's position as an

FIG. 5. English provincial newspapers, 1779–1785

Sources: Same as for Fig. 4.

administrative, economic, judicial, or social centre, but whether the location afforded a sufficiently large readership, and whether a paper's establishment was viable given the nature of the existing competition. Even if these conditions were favourable, they could not be exploited successfully by everyone. The possession of particular skills and entrepreneurship appear to have been essential for those involved in newspapers. In many ways, then, the provincial press functioned exactly like its London counterpart.

Indeed, the frequent failures witnessed amongst provincial newspapers in the late eighteenth century mean it is far more probable that producing a successful paper and attracting high sales was a complicated matter, and not one which involved merely cobbling together bits of the London press and hoping for the best. There are plenty of examples of provincial newspapers which were not successful. As the discussion of the *Hampshire Chronicle* has shown, Etherington's failed attempt with the *York Chronicle* is by no means a solitary example. In Coventry, the *Coventry and Birmingham Chronicle* lasted only a few years until the early 1760s, and *Piercy's Coventry Gazette* only ran between 1777 and 1778.[64] *Harrison's Derby Journal*, set up to rival *Drewry's Derby Mercury*, lasted for four years from its start in 1776.[65] Henry Cox's *Nottingham Gazette* ran for only eight months in 1780. Its failure was blamed by its proprietor on insufficient sales.[66] Feather claims that Etherington's *York Chronicle* collapsed because 'even a city of the importance of York could not support two newspapers'.[67] However, when the paper was bought from Etherington by Blanchard, it became highly successful. This suggests that poor management was to blame in the first place, rather than the size of the market. The same is almost certainly true of James Linden's failure with the *Hampshire Chronicle*, and of the subsequent financial losses generated under John Wilkes's management of the same paper. Just as Etherington's failure was not unique, neither was Blanchard's rescue of a paper. In Chester, John Poole and a Mr Barker set up the *Chester Chronicle* in 1775 as a rival to the more established *Chester Courant*. The *Chronicle* apparently struggled to compete with the *Courant*, and, on 8 August 1783, printed a declaration that it was going out of business. However, the paper

---

[64] *Victoria County History of Warwick. Vol. VII: The City of Coventry and the Borough of Warwick*, ed. W. B. Stephens (Oxford, 1969), 223. After this date Piercy joined forces with Swinney of the *Birmingham Chronicle*, but this seems only to have lasted until 1781: Joseph Hill, *The Book Makers of Old Birmingham* (Birmingham, 1907), 78.

[65] Andrew, 'The Derbyshire Newspaper Press', 220–43.

[66] Clarke, *Early Nottingham Printers and Printing*, 24.

[67] Feather, *The Provincial Book Trade*, p. 95.

reappeared the following week, having been purchased by John Fletcher, who was able to make the *Chronicle* profitable.[68]

Like their London counterparts, provincial newspapers were financially dependent upon two main sources of income: advertising and sales. Although the former formed a crucial part of a newspaper's total revenue, circulation figures were still the key to newspaper profits, and the economic strength of a provincial paper depended upon its ability to secure a large readership. Even a well-run provincial paper would have barely managed to survive on weekly sales of just over 1,000 copies. The records of the *Chelmsford Chronicle* show that its figures were over twice this, whilst other papers claimed even higher circulations.[69] Christopher Etherington's *York Chronicle* appears to have reached circulation levels of up to 2,500 between 1772 and 1777.[70] This has led Cranfield to suggest that in the mid-eighteenth century, larger provincial papers would have sold around 2,000 copies per week, with lower figures of about 1,000 for most newspapers, and much less for some others.[71] But the examination of the *Hampshire Chronicle* suggests that even a well-run provincial paper would only just have managed to survive on sales of slightly over 1,000 copies. The *Salisbury Journal* was claiming to have a circulation of 4,000 by 1780,[72] and *Creswell and Burbage's Nottingham Journal* cited sales of over 2,000 in the following year.[73] The *Manchester Chronicle* reported its sales as 2,000 in the autumn of 1782, reaching 2,500 by 1786.[74] James Bowling, editor of the *Leeds Mercury* and 'a gentleman of considerable talent', was credited with increasing the circulation of the paper to 3,000 copies in the 1790s.[75]

Press historians have noted that eighteenth-century printing was an extremely slow process, and that the handpress could manage only 250 sheets per hour.[76] However, this did not necessarily mean that circulation

[68] Nuttall, 'A History of Printing in Chester', 62–6.

[69] ERO, Acc. 5197, D/F, 66/1. See also 'The Leeds Mercury', *Effective Advertiser* (Mar. 1886), 27; Clare, 'The Local Newspaper Press and Local Politics in Manchester and Liverpool', 23–4; Clarke, *Early Nottingham Printers and Printing*, 20.

[70] Davies, *A Memoir of the York Press*, 331–4.

[71] Cranfield, *The Development of the Provincial Newspaper*, 176.

[72] Ferdinand, *Benjamin Collins*, 128.

[73] *Nottingham Journal*, 6 Jan. 1781, cited in Clarke, *Early Nottingham Printers and Printing*, 20.

[74] Clare, 'The Local Newspaper Press and Local Politics in Manchester and Liverpool', 23–4.

[75] 'The Leeds Mercury', 27.

[76] See Andrew, 'The Derbyshire Newspaper Press', 144; Burton, *The Early Newspaper Press in Berkshire*, 5.

would have been so restricted by production methods.[77] As Clare argues, provincial newspapers, as weekly publications, would have had time to print large quantities, and may have had more than one press.[78] John Feather has shown that this was true for several provincial newspapers. As early as the 1720s, John White, the printer of the *York Courant*, had three presses. In 1779, Myles Swinney, who owned the *Birmingham Chronicle*, had four, and T. A. Pearson, who ran the rival *Aris's Birmingham Gazette*, had five. Goadby employed three journeymen, which Feather claims would have been usual. This means he could have kept two presses working on his paper, and another on other printing jobs.[79] The *Chelmsford Chronicle*'s wage bill for its journeymen printers in the 1780s indicates that it also employed three men on a more or less regular basis.[80] Even though great emphasis was placed upon the speedy inclusion of news from the latest London post, production figures did not necessarily have to be small, since the page including such news would have been printed last.[81] Besides, printing methods did not seem to have been a problem in London, where publishers of daily papers produced over 2,000 copies a day of each title.

Estimating the number of newspaper readers in the provinces is necessarily a rather rough-and-ready procedure. In 1780 there were at least fifty provincial newspapers produced in England. If we assume a weekly print run of 2,000 copies for each, this means that an estimated 100,000 provincial newspapers appeared every week. The number of people who read each individual paper in the provinces was probably lower than in the capital, so if we use a multiplier of five instead of ten, then the estimated size of the provincial newspaper readership becomes 500,000, or about 8 per cent of the population in England outside London.[82] This suggests a much lower level of readership than in the capital, where it has been

---

[77] Burton uses the fact that one press could only have printed 1,500 sheets over an 8-hour period to argue that the circulation of the *Reading Mercury* was probably less than 1,000 copies by the end of the century: Burton, *The Early Newspaper Press in Berkshire*, 5.

[78] Clare, 'The Growth and Importance of the Newspaper Press in Manchester, Liverpool, Sheffield and Leeds', 2.

[79] Feather, *The Provincial Book Trade*, 99–102. Feather points out that the cost of type far outweighed that of a press: the amounts of type kept by various printers would have been worth about £600 in 1800, whereas a press cost about £20 in the 1780s.

[80] ERO, Acc. 5197, D/F, 66/1.

[81] The description of the production of the *Northampton Mercury* confirms this: *1720. 1901. History of the Northampton Mercury*, 63.

[82] The total English population in 1780 has been estimated at around 7 million: Wrigley and Schofield, *Population History of England*, 333–5 and app. 3. The London population was approximately 800,000: Law, 'Some Notes on the Urban Population in the Eighteenth Century', 24.

estimated that the newspaper audience could have constituted upwards of one-third of the inhabitants. However, these calculations do not take into account the degree of penetration by London newspapers in the provinces, nor do they show the undoubted importance of regional variation, and in particular the difference between urban and rural readerships. Whilst Christine Ferdinand has calculated that the *Salisbury Journal* may have been read by only 5 per cent of the population in its catchment area in the later eighteenth century,[83] Frank O'Gorman has estimated that press circulation usually reached between 10 and 15 per cent of the population of provincial towns in the early nineteenth century.[84] If we use the 1801 census returns to measure urban populations, and assume that 50 per cent of newspapers were sold outside their town of publication, then papers produced in places like Leeds, Cambridge, Newcastle, Oxford, Shrewsbury, and York could have been read by anywhere between 15 and 50 per cent of the urban population.[85] If this is the case, then given the national figure of 8 per cent, these findings suggest that a far greater proportion of provincial newspaper readers came from towns and their immediate environs, and that readership was spread more thinly in rural areas. In common with the capital, the joint purchase of newspapers and their availability in coffee-houses was common. Clare has noted that Manchester, Liverpool, Sheffield, and Leeds all boasted coffee-houses in which papers were available; and such places often had a special newspaper-reading room.[86] In Liverpool, large newspaper-reading rooms were established in the St George's and Pontack's coffee-houses by 1775, which are described as being situated in places 'of respectability'.[87] In Derby, the Derby coffee room was providing a similar service by 1768, and was joined in 1788 by Nelly's Coffee House, whilst Buxton had the Grove coffee-house from 1784.[88]

Given the pattern of newspaper proliferation throughout the century, it seems likely that the provincial press drew much of its readership from

---

[83] Ferdinand, *Benjamin Collins*, 131.

[84] O'Gorman, *Voters, Patrons, and Parties*, 288.

[85] B. R. Mitchell, *British Historical Statistics* (Cambridge, 1988), 26–7. Not only has the number of newspapers in each town been taken into account, but in places where more than one paper was printed, figures have been calculated according to whether they appear to have shared their readership or not.

[86] Clare, 'The Growth and Importance of the Newspaper Press in Manchester, Liverpool, Sheffield and Leeds', 17.

[87] Richard Brooke, *Liverpool as it Was during the Last Quarter of the Eighteenth Century: 1775 to 1800* (Liverpool, 1853), 163 and 269.

[88] Andrew, 'The Derbyshire Newspaper Press', 186–7. For a discussion of the place of coffee-houses in provincial urban culture see Peter Borsay, *The English Urban Renaissance: Culture and Society in the Provincial Town 1660–1770* (Oxford, 1989).

amongst the expanding middle classes. However, in the provinces as in London, there is anecdotal evidence which suggests that those fairly low on the social scale might have read newspapers as well. In 1791, the London publisher James Lackington described reading amongst 'the poorer sort of farmers, and even the poor country people . . . in short, all ranks and degrees now read'.[89] Even the author and publisher John Trusler reflected general anxieties about the spread of reading in the eighteenth century, and worried that printed matter in general was becoming so cheap that everyone would be able to afford it. In the country, where he claimed all men were learning to read, Trusler believed that they had started to 'sacrifice the wholesome food of the body for the pernicious poison of the mind'.[90] *Bonner and Middleton's Bristol Journal* carried a letter on 5 August 1780 which argued that newspapers gave 'our country villagers, the curate, the exciseman, and the blacksmith . . . the self-satisfaction of being as wise as our first minister of state'.[91]

The lists of subscribers to the *Salopian Journal* between 1794 and 1795 are of some interest here, although these records are incomplete and represent a newspaper which was struggling. In addition, it was almost certainly the case that those listed as subscribers were readers of higher social standing, since they were trusted with payment on (often very protracted) credit. From what information is given in the *Journal*'s records, it appears that two-thirds of recorded sales in Shrewsbury were made to subscribers. Amongst the 123 names listed, four appear to be innkeepers: Mr Yates of the Horse Shoe, Mr Lewis of the Still, Mr Griffiths of the Coach and Horses, and Mr Hughes of the Wine Vaults. Another subscriber is described as an Officer of the Excise, one as a painter, and two as cutlers.[92] A majority are given a title, and a great many have 'Esq.' placed after their names (not that this is necessarily indicative of very much): there are ninety-one 'Mr.'s, fifteen 'Rev.'s, and four 'Capt.'s. In addition, eight women are listed as buying the paper on their own account. Outside Shrewsbury, where the majority of recorded sales were made, just over one-half were to subscribers. Here a similar pattern of titles emerges, as far as the use of 'Mr.' and 'Esq.' are concerned. But, of a total of 161 names, only three women are listed, and, contrary to what one might expect, the names of only five clergymen appear. Perhaps

---

[89] Cited in S. H. Steinberg, *Five Hundred Years of Printing* (London, 1959), 166. .

[90] Trusler's memoirs, cited by James Raven in 'From Promotion to Proscription: Arrangements for Reading and Eighteenth-Century Libraries', in Raven *et al.*, *The Practice and Representation of Reading in England*, 193.

[91] Cited in Gallop, 'A History of the Provincial Newspaper Press', 173.

[92] Mr Price, Mr Prichard, and Mr Morris and Mr Richards respectively: SRRU, MS 1923, Book II.

predictably, the subscribers listed in the *Journal*'s accounts suggest a readership from amongst the middling sorts.[93] The identity of those who bought the paper for cash may have yielded more interesting evidence, but unfortunately, their social positions remain a mystery.

In order for newspaper proprietors to secure the level of sales necessary, they had to find customers from outside the town of publication.[94] The use of newsmen to deliver papers around the countryside has been well documented by Cranfield and Wiles for the earlier part of the century,[95] and more recently by Christine Ferdinand in the case of the *Salisbury Journal*.[96] These historians have stressed how important a well-planned distribution system was to the success of a provincial newspaper. Ferdinand has demonstrated how this operated on several levels: from the management of the paper, to a series of agents in local towns, and finally to the carriers and newsmen who delivered to villages and rural areas.[97] This final practice still seems to have been common in the 1780s. Newsmen, who usually travelled on foot rather than on horseback, would only have served relatively nearby areas of the surrounding countryside, but would probably have delivered the bulk of papers not sold in town. Andrew has noted that the *Derby Mercury*'s local distribution network ensured that the paper, which was printed on a Thursday morning, would reach most of its readers in nearby villages by the same evening, and the rest by the Friday morning.[98] Sometimes quite complicated local arrangements were involved. The Norfolk clergyman James Woodforde recorded that he received newspapers at his village of Weston Longville, from 'Sarah Grant from the Poor House on Hungate Common', after they had been left there for him by his butcher the night before.[99] It is also clear that provincial newspapers were distributed further afield.[100]

The records of the *Salopian Journal* give particularly detailed information about the paper's distribution during its first thirteen months in

---

[93] Mr Price, Mr Prichard, and Mr Morris and Mr Richards respectively: SRRU, MS 1923, Book II.

[94] Looney has suggested that over half of the copies of provincial newspapers produced were sold outside their town of publication: Looney, 'Advertising and Society', 41. However, there is no way to be sure of the proportions.

[95] Cranfield, *The Development of the Provincial Press*, 190 ff.; Wiles, *Freshest Advices*, 95 ff.

[96] Ferdinand, *Benjamin Collins*, and 'Local Distribution Networks'.

[97] Ferdinand, *Benjamin Collins*, chap. 2.

[98] Andrew, 'The Derbyshire Newspaper Press', 170.

[99] Diary entry dated 17 Feb. 1799. Woodforde also noted that severe weather had prevented the distribution of the Ipswich paper to some areas two weeks earlier: James Woodforde, *The Diary of a Country Parson, 1758–1802* (Oxford, 1978), 576 and 579.

[100] The *Chelmsford Chronicle* made regular payments for what appears to have been the carriage by coach of copies of the paper: ERO, Acc. 5197, D/F, 66/1.

existence. Because the *Journal* had yet to become established, the arrangements outlined were probably more modest than for other late eighteenth-
century provincial newspapers. However, they show that the paper's
proprietors were well aware of the importance of a good distribution
system, and provide some idea of the model upon which the paper's future
success was based. At the first shareholders' meeting on 21 December
1793, the geographical ambitions of the *Journal* were set out when it was
decided that advertising for the new paper, in the form of handbills and
posters, should be distributed throughout Shropshire and the neighbouring counties.[101] At a subsequent meeting, it was noted that five newsmen
were to be employed to carry the paper to 'Ludlow, Whitechurch, [Mar-
ket] Drayton, Broseley, and to Bishops Castle via Yockleton and Welsh
Pool'.[102] It was later agreed that John Jones, the newsman who took the
paper to Welshpool, should also take it to Llanfyllin, and that John Hall,
who went to Whitchurch, should extend his walk to Nantwich.[103] Both
Jones and D. Cowley, the Ludlow newsman, were given loans to buy
horses to use on their rounds.[104] The *Journal*'s account book lists weekly
payments of 2s. 3d. and 2s. 8d. for the newsmen's services. It also notes
the payment of 10d. per week for carriage of the paper to Oswestry and
Ellesmere.[105]

The *Salopian Journal*'s records also give figures for the amount of
copies produced each week, the number sold in Shrewsbury for cash
rather than on account (presumably either at the Eddowes's print shop or
via agents), those sold by the newsmen for cash, and payments by subscribers. These figures are problematic, since the number of copies
printed was far greater than the total of those recorded as being sold. On
average, between February 1794 and March 1795, 680 copies of the paper
were produced each week. However, an average of only 57 copies were
recorded as having been sold in Shrewsbury (for cash), and a further 153
by the newsmen out of town, in addition to the 285 subscribers listed
during the thirteen-month period.[106] The discrepancy between the
number of copies produced and those apparently sold is unexplained. It
does not seem that the proprietors were simply printing more copies than
they could sell, since the amount of stamps and paper purchased confirms
the figures given, and on one occasion, it was specifically recorded that the

---

[101] Minutes of the proprietors of the *Salopian Journal*, SRRU, MS 1923, Book I.
[102] Minutes of 21 Jan. 1794, ibid.
[103] Minutes of 13 May 1794, ibid.
[104] Minutes of 4 Feb. and 3 June 1794, ibid.
[105] SRRU, MS 1923, Book II.   [106] Ibid.

entire week's imprint had been sold.[107] It would not have made financial sense to waste money producing papers which would not sell, particularly since duty would still have to be paid on them. One can only assume that other sales were being made during the period covered which were not listed in the accounts. Given the limitations of the information available in the *Salopian Journal*'s surviving records, what remains is still useful and informative. It suggests a reliance upon sales outside Shrewsbury, with weekly cash sales in town under half of those made by the newsmen outside it. For the subscribers listed the bias is not nearly so emphatic: 123 appear to have lived in town, and 161 outside it. Fig. 6 shows the pattern of the *Journal*'s distribution, and reveals that the bulk of sales was made within a 25-mile radius of Shrewsbury. This is less than half the distance covered by the more established and successful newspapers in the Midlands, which are discussed below.

In line with the text-based approach used in the examination of the London press, the contents of provincial newspapers suggest a good deal about the ways in which they attracted readers and who these readers were. In addition, there are also clues as to why successful provincial newspapers sold so well in the face of potentially fierce competition from both the London papers and the rest of the provincial press.[108] An examination of provincial newspaper content suggests that those who

[107] The minutes for the proprietors' meeting for 3 June 1794 noted the sale of every one of the 775 copies printed the week before, which meant that some of the current week's papers had to be exchanged for the previous week's papers in order to 'complete sets': SRRU, MS 1923, Book I.

[108] These newspapers were easily available, as was demonstrated by an advertisement in the *Bath Chronicle* on 17 Feb. 1780, which was placed by the booksellers and stationers Pratt and Clinch. They promised that 'the Nobility, Gentry, and others, may be supplied with any of the *London Newspapers*, morning or evening, either weekly, monthly, quarterly, yearly, or with single papers, a day sooner than by post, and at a cheaper rate'. In addition, those who subscribed 10s. 6d. per year could use their library to look at the London daily and evening papers, and provincial papers from Bath, Bristol, Oxford, Cambridge, Gloucester, Salisbury, Birmingham, Sherborne, Reading, Worcester, Hereford, Exeter, Canterbury, Leeds, Liverpool, Whitehaven, Chester, and Southampton, as well as newspapers from Ireland and Scotland. On 19 Dec. 1782, the *Bath Chronicle* published an advertisement for a rival enterprise in the town. Hazard's Circulating Library charged 10s. 6d. per year, or 4s. per quarter, and purchased the *Morning Chronicle*, *Morning Post*, and *Morning Herald* daily for its readers, as well as supplying papers from Bath, Bristol, Salisbury, Winchester, Exeter, Sherborne, Reading, Worcester, Hereford, Leeds, Chester, and Birmingham. An advertisement placed in *Aris's Birmingham Gazette* on 18 Nov. 1782, by Mrs Ann London, promised 'the Nobility, Gentry, Clergy, &c. any of the London news-papers, sent to persons residing in the country, clean from the press, and free of postage, in the neatest and most punctual manner'. The advertisement listed all the daily, tri-weekly, and weekly London papers which were available on quarterly subscriptions and noted that 'the masters of taverns, coffee-houses, inns, &c. will do well to attend to my easy price'.

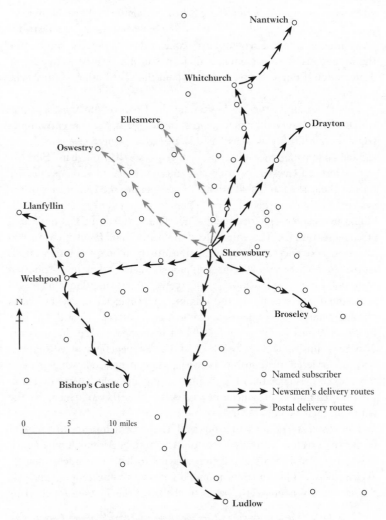

FIG. 6. Circulation of the *Salopian Journal*, 1794–1795

Source: SRRU, MS 1923.

produced them employed several strategies which contributed to their success. The distribution of papers and timing of publication appear to have been crucial factors in the promotion of sales. It was quite common for provincial newspapers to include lists of the main towns and villages to which they were distributed, as well as the names and locations of their

advertising agents. Although there is little reason to doubt such information, it gives only a general picture of the extent of newspaper distribution, either in terms of geographical scope or density of sales. But despite
the limitations of such evidence, there is still much to be gained by its
examination if one is trying to understand the distribution of provincial
papers.

This is certainly true for Wales and the English Midlands, a region
which was well served by newspapers. In the 1780s, the concentration of
papers was probably as dense in this area as anywhere else outside the
capital. Newspapers based in Hereford, Worcester, Birmingham, Shrewsbury, Derby, Leicester, Nottingham, and Coventry all gave specific details of their areas of distribution.[109] Fig. 7 shows the complexity of the
system of newspaper distribution. There is no neat pattern showing individual newspaper 'spheres of influence', but an extremely complicated
arrangement. In the Midlands at least, no paper could lay claim to an area
which was not encroached upon significantly by others and did not itself
trespass upon the territory of its neighbours. Such overlaps in distribution
were not a new phenomenon in the 1780s, but had no doubt increased
throughout the century as the number of provincial newspaper titles
expanded and circulation areas became more compact.[110] Yet the picture
in the Midlands is not as confused as it first appears, and the apparent
disorder is misleading. A closer look at the newspapers involved suggests
both an ordered relationship between some papers, allowing a more
peaceful co-existence than Fig. 7 implies, and an evolutionary pattern in
the proliferation of provincial newspapers which was influenced by the
nature of their potential markets.

The *Hereford Journal* stands out as the paper which seems to have had
by far the greatest unrivalled area of distribution. Although an English
newspaper, much of its circulation appears to have depended upon its
Welsh sales.[111] This apparent monopoly is slightly misleading, since although there was no Welsh paper to challenge the *Journal*, much of its

---

[109] The *British Chronicle, or Pugh's Hereford Journal, Berrow's Worcester Journal, Aris's
Birmingham Gazette*, the *Shrewsbury Chronicle, Drewry's Derby Mercury*, the *Leicester and
Nottingham Journal, Creswell and Burbage's Nottingham Journal*, and *Jopson's Coventry Mercury*. *Harrison's Derby Journal* and *Swinney's Birmingham Chronicle* were not used, as copies
for the period under discussion do not appear to have survived.

[110] See Feather, *The Provincial Book Trade*, 20–1, for the situation in 1730.

[111] The paper's list of advertising agents records individuals in 'Bath, Bristol, Gloucester,
Worcester, Tewkesbury, Ledbury, Bromyard, Shrewsbury, Ludlow, Bishop's Castle,
Leominster, Kingston, Norberth, Tenby, Swansea, Neath, Cowbridge, Pontypool,
Monmouth, Abergaveny, The Hay, Brecon, Londovey, Llandilo, and Camarthen': *Hereford
Journal*, 2 Dec. 1779.

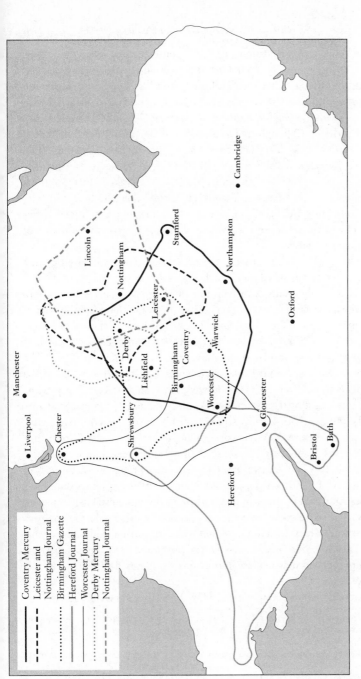

Fig. 7. Provincial newspaper distribution in England and Wales, 1780

Sources: Aris's Birmingham Gazette, 3 Jan. 1780; Berrow's Worcester Journal, 2 Mar. 1780; British Chronicle or, Pugh's Hereford Journal, 6 Jan. 1780; Creswell and Burbage's Nottingham Journal, 1 Jan. 1780; Drewry's Derby Mercury, 14 Jan. 1780; Jopson's Coventry Mercury, 19 June 1780; Leicester and Nottingham Journal, 1 Jan. 1780.

circulation in Wales was almost certainly contested by the *Glocester Jour-nal*, which unfortunately did not list its agents, and by Bristol newspapers. In addition, the fact that the Hereford paper had agents in Gloucester, Worcester, and Shrewsbury meant that some overlap also occurred with *Berrow's Worcester Journal* and the *Shrewsbury Chronicle*, as well as with papers in Bath. Although its circulation was not uncontested in Wales, then, there was far less competition here than in the Midlands. The *Hereford Journal*'s Welsh bias is evident in the advertisements which the paper carried during the 1780 and 1784 general elections. In 1780, these were placed by candidates in Pembroke, Carmarthen, Radnor, Glamor-gan, Monmouth, and Cardigan, as well as Ludlow, Worcester, and Here-ford. The same areas were represented in 1784, with the addition of Brecon and Gloucester.[112]

It is likely that the *Shrewsbury Chronicle*'s existence was based upon a similar dependence on sales in North Wales. However, the paper did not list its advertising agents or distributors in any great detail. It did claim to reach towns as distant as London, Glasgow, and Whitehaven, but gave little useful detail of its local distribution, except to state that it was 'circulated thro' Shropshire and the different Counties adjacent, particu-larly North-Wales; and to greater Distance by the General Post'.[113] Its circulation by post would explain references to distant towns, but these were likely to have represented relatively few readers. Like other provin-cial papers, most of its distribution would have been far more localized, and like the *Hereford Journal* would probably have covered the less con-tested area to its west. What connected the Hereford and Shrewsbury papers, apart from their relationship to a Welsh readership, was their relative youth. The *Shrewsbury Chronicle* was probably established in 1771, whilst the *Hereford Journal* was founded in 1773. This would have put them at a disadvantage in comparison to the more established papers nearby.[114] It seems likely that the area served by these older newspapers had become saturated and could not support further additions at this time. Thus in order to be successful, the proprietor of any new paper was forced to seek out new readers in previously underexploited areas: in this case, Wales.

What of these older newspapers? How could they survive, faced with so

[112] See issues of the *Hereford Journal* for Aug. and Sept. 1780 and Apr. 1784, and the 'mission statement' in the paper's first edn. of 9 Aug. 1770.

[113] *Shrewsbury Chronicle*, 19 Aug. 1780.

[114] The starting dates of the other papers shown on the map are as follows: *Berrow's Worcester Journal*, 1709; *Derby Mercury*, 1732; *Aris's Birmingham Gazette*, 1741; *Coventry Mercury*, 1741; *Leicester and Nottingham Journal*, 1753; *Nottingham Journal*, 1756.

many competitors and seemingly with no areas in which they could escape the rivalry of other papers? Although those newspapers in the Midlands and Wales are being examined in isolation, it must also be remembered that there were papers in the surrounding regions which would have further complicated the situation. Gloucester had its own newspaper, as did Bath, Bristol, Oxford, Northampton, Cambridge, and Stamford. To the north, Chester, Liverpool, and Manchester also supported newspapers which were distributed to some of the areas under immediate discussion. Faced with such apparently intense competition, it seems that individual provincial newspapers could still survive, and indeed thrive.

One explanation for this relates to the day on which the newspapers were published, which varied from paper to paper. For example, although the Birmingham and Coventry papers both appeared on a Monday, the *Derby Mercury* came out on Fridays. This gave readers geographically positioned between these places the chance to read a new local newspaper at half-weekly intervals, rather than once a week. The same situation would have been possible further west in areas covered by both the Coventry and Birmingham papers, and by *Berrow's Worcester Journal*, since the latter appeared on Thursdays. This type of publication pattern meant that provincial papers could co-exist without hostile rivalry. Indeed, it could even be argued that the newspapers involved were complementary to one another. Similar situations appear to have existed elsewhere, and even between papers produced in the same town. It is likely that York could support two similar newspapers, not because the city and its environs contained two audiences numerous enough to make both papers profitable, but because they appeared bi-weekly and thus shared their readership. The same was probably true in Bath, where the *Bath Journal* and the *Bath Chronicle* were published on Monday and Thursday respectively. However, such apparently cosy and symbiotic relationships between newspapers were not the rule, and other examples can be found where the timing and place of publication, in addition to the contents of papers, suggests direct and fierce competition.

Indeed, an examination of newspaper contents reveals much, not just about the relationship between papers, but also concerning other strategies which proprietors seem to have used to promote sales and ensure a paper's success. An overriding concern appears to have been to aim newspapers at a local market. This preoccupation is most apparent in the 'mission statements' which many provincial papers carried in their first issues. These outlined the proprietor's or editor's vision of their new paper, and whilst usually full of both self-congratulation of their owners

and obsequious praise for potential readers, they are nevertheless of interest. Within these 'mission statements' the importance of representing a
particular locality as distinct from other provincial regions was clear. The
first copy of the *Hampshire Chronicle*, begun on 24 August 1772, asserted
that

Amidst the extent and multiplicity of those various channels of communication,
which modern improvement hath opened to the commerce and correspondence of
these kingdoms; it hath been long a matter of equal surprize and complaint, that
the county of Hants, inferior to none with respect to natural situation and
incidents of national importance, should want the convenience of a WEEKLY
NEWS-PAPER. It is indeed with an impropriety, disgraceful to its ancient spirit
of emulation and industry, that Hampshire is at present under the necessity of
informing its inhabitants even of the business of their own county, by means of the
News-papers of the distant metropolis or the neighbouring counties.

The first edition of the *Hereford Journal*, which appeared on 9 August
1770, carried a similar address:

A recommendatory introduction to the present proposed undertaking of the establishment of a newspaper, in these parts, is, perhaps, less proper than an apology
would be for its not having been undertaken before.

   It has long been a just matter of surprise, and even of complaint, that, while
there is scarce a county in England that does not support a news-paper, a county
so opulent, so respectable in itself, as that of Hereford, and, especially, so happily
situated for immediate communication with a considerable part of Wales, into
which the circulation of a news-paper would, in course, be so ready and so
practicable, should remain in the want of so great and essential a convenience, of
its own proper growth or produce.

The first copy of the *Shrewsbury Chronicle* stated that 'it has long been [a]
just matter of admiration, that there has never been a paper of this kind
printed in the polite and opulent town of Shrewsbury; nor even in any
part of the large, rich, and populous county of which this town is the chief;
but the inhabitants have hitherto been beholden to the printers of other
counties for their political information'.[115] The papers' pleas stressed the
importance of a newspaper to a town or county of any prominence. The
appeal of the new papers was supposedly based upon their local production. But in this respect, although some references were made to the
greater accessibility of newspapers, there is no mention of their relative
cheapness. The case put to potential readers was based on the supposition
that any place of importance ought to have its own newspaper: that, in

---

[115] *Shrewsbury Chronicle*, 23 Nov. 1772. See also *Chelmsford Chronicle*, 5 Apr. 1771; *Bury
Post*, 11 July 1782; *Kentish Weekly Post*, 5 Sept. [1768]; *Maidstone Journal*, 25 Jan. 1786.

effect, it should be properly represented. This, then, was an appeal to civic pride which attempted to exploit local inhabitants' sense of regional identity.

This suggests that those who ran provincial newspapers believed that they could exploit a unique local appeal. But in this context, the emphasis historians have tended to place upon the inclusion of local advertising and local news in provincial newspapers to explain their popularity may not tell the whole story. There were other, less obvious editorial strategies to promote sales which are identifiable. One of these concerns the large coverage given to national and foreign news. Whereas the local news carried could appear uncontroversial and non-political in nature (although its importance should not be discounted), the former, at least in so far as national affairs were concerned, was nearly always openly political and frequently partisan in tone. The lack of overt political bias evident in the local news published by many provincial papers may have stemmed from a wariness on the part of their publishers about offending people in local positions of influence coupled with more practical constraints upon news-gathering and writing imposed by a lack of staff. These problems would not have been experienced in the case of national (or perhaps, more accurately, London) news, since the material printed in provincial papers was lifted for the most part straight from the pages of the capital's press.

However, despite the way in which national news was obtained by provincial newspapers, it is probably a mistake to view their appeal to readers as being simply in terms of providing a compendium of the London press. When examining provincial press contents, it soon becomes apparent that even if editorial control did not stretch as far as actually producing the coverage of national news independently, it did seem to govern the choice of material. The contents of provincial newspapers generally do not suggest an unthinking plundering of the capital's papers, but more usually a careful selection from these sources, frequently producing a political coherence that a more random sample would not have ensured. It was a concern for the paper's political contents which led the proprietors of the *Salopian Journal* to agree that the inclusion of 'all letters, essays, &c of a political nature' would be decided by a ballot.[116]

---

[116] Minutes of the proprietors' meeting, 24 Dec. 1793: SRRU, MS 1923, Book I. Between Dec. 1793 and Dec. 1799, only 3 instances were recorded at which the proprietors were asked to decide whether material should appear in the paper or not. At a meeting on 20 Feb. 1794, it was decided that extracts of Playfair's pamphlet entitled *Peace With the Jacobites* should be published; at another meeting 5 days later it was decided not to print letters signed 'A Briton' and one in answer to 'Candidus'; and on 20 May 1794, it was recorded that a Mr Fielding be told that 'the paragraph he wishes to be inserted in the Salopian Journal is too personal to be admitted': ibid.

John Money has already taken issue with both the idea that the provincial press was merely a register of local information and yesterday's events and the notion that, in consequence, provincial opinion was no more than a delayed and passive replica of attitudes in the capital.[117] He has argued that printers could play to a public already hostile to the Ministry by extracting material from the most sensational productions of the London Opposition press, and traces this tradition of opposition to government amongst the Midlands papers back as early as the 1730s.[118] In addition, he has outlined the particular political differences which existed between the various Coventry and Birmingham newspapers in the 1760s and 1770s,[119] whilst his study of Birmingham and the West Midlands as a whole has shown that provincial opinion here had its own dynamic and did not follow blindly that of London. In Jonathan Barry's study of the Bristol press and the politics of culture between 1660 and 1775, it is argued that the press can be viewed both as a source of evidence and as a central and integral aspect of cultural life in provincial towns. Barry claims that a political stance could be the result of the printer's politics or because a paper was sponsored to represent a particular position. 'There is little in the history of the Bristol newspapers', he argues, 'to support the common contention that the provincial press of this period was simply a scissors-and-paste affair'.[120]

Moreover, the movement of newspapers between London and the provinces was not one-way: by 1784, 3,090,948 newspapers were being dispatched from London, and 70,526 were received.[121] The flow into London is a small but by no means insignificant proportion of the total number of newspapers sent by post. The cash book detailing the financial transactions of the London paper the *Gazetteer*[122] demonstrates that one reason why provincial newspapers were sent to London was the demand of the capital's press. During the late 1770s and the first half of the 1780s, the *Gazetteer* paid to have newspapers sent to it from throughout Britain and from Ireland by applying directly to the printers. It is clear that the selection of papers bought was frequently altered as the subscription to one newspaper was cancelled (usually temporarily) and another taken up. However, during the period covered, the receipt of newspapers from the following places was recorded: Newcastle, York, Liverpool, Chester,

---

[117] Money, *Experience and Identity*, 52.   [118] Ibid. 53.   [119] Ibid. 53–72.
[120] Barry, 'The Press and the Politics of Culture in Bristol', 62.
[121] Brian Austen, 'British Mail-Coach Services 1784–1850' (University of London Ph.D. thesis, 1979), 20.
[122] PRO, C104/67, Book M.

Derby, Birmingham, Gloucester, Oxford, Ipswich, Bristol, Bath, Exeter, Salisbury, Canterbury, and Lewes. These towns represent almost half of those supporting newspapers at the time. The interest shown by the *Gazetteer* in provincial newspapers suggests that they were of greater importance and interest to both a national public and London readers than has been assumed.

The degree of editorial care which the news-gathering arrangements of provincial newspapers imply suggests that a paper's political stance may also have been used in order to appeal to readers. This certainly seems to have been the case in places where the publication of more than one paper appears to have resulted in fierce commercial rivalry rather than the types of complementary arrangements already mentioned. One such area of less than cordial newspaper relations was Leeds. The town supported two newspapers in the early 1780s which both appeared on a Tuesday: the *Leeds Intelligencer* and the *Leeds Mercury*. The main difference between the papers was political, as demonstrated by their choice of material concerning national politics. The *Intelligencer* was a pro-ministerial paper until the Rockingham Whigs came to power. Up to that point, the paper had been hostile to both the Opposition and those involved in the reform movement, whose ideas it claimed were 'entirely subversive of the principles of the constitution; and would, if well founded, be productive of the greatest confusion and mischief'.[123] With the formation of the Fox–North coalition, the *Intelligencer* became more ambivalent towards those politicians it had formerly admired. The paper also extended this ambivalence to Pitt once he was in office. In 1785 it described his failed reform bill as 'a mere parliamentary balloon' that Pitt had 'never intended . . . should rise, and therefore prepared his ingredients accordingly'.[124]

The *Intelligencer*'s rival, the *Mercury*, took an entirely different line. It was a staunch advocate of those involved in the reform movement, of whom it claimed 'a dignified moderation has marked their proceedings, and a steady perseverance in their original demands of redress promises a happy effect to their measures'. The paper also noted that 'it is yet some comfort that history affords no example in which the people, when under oppression, did not at length stand forth in their own cause, and in which the cause of the people did not therefore ultimately triumph'.[125] In contrast to the *Intelligencer*, the *Mercury* did not doubt Pitt's sincerity once in office.[126]

A very similar situation existed in Newcastle. The rival *Newcastle*

[123] *Leeds Intelligencer*, 1 Feb. 1780.   [124] Ibid. 26 Apr. 1785.
[125] *Leeds Mercury*, 13 Mar. 1781.   [126] See ibid. 12 and 26 Apr. 1785.

Chronicle and *Newcastle Courant* were both published on a Saturday and differentiated themselves by their political stance. The *Courant* attacked the Opposition and the reformers. On 24 March 1781, one of its correspondents commented: 'that there are at present in this country, associations of men combined for the horrid purpose of creating a civil war amongst us, is most notorious'. The *Chronicle*, on the other hand, was highly supportive of the 'public-spirited' reformers who set 'so virtuous and patriotic an example,'[127] whilst it remained critical of 'our squandering Ministry'.[128]

In Newcastle and Leeds there was apparently no complementary relationship between newspapers, but rather an intense rivalry which was demonstrated by the promulgation of opposing political views. This is in contrast to places such as York and Bath where papers were published bi-weekly and represented broadly similar political views. This suggests that in the former towns, the local newspaper readership was not shared by papers, but was split. Since political differences formed the clearest expression of division between such papers, it may have been this which newspaper proprietors hoped would determine readership choice. In other words, the particular political stance of a provincial newspaper was another device which proprietors used to attract readers. Given the emphasis which the press itself placed upon the local character of provincial papers, the way in which their political contents were moulded may well reflect something of the nature of local political divisions. As will be discussed in Chapter 6, both Leeds and Newcastle appear to have experienced bitter local political divisions in this period. A rare example of a provincial newspaper reader recording the reasons for his choice of paper is found in the diary of Matthew Flinders, a Lincolnshire surgeon. For Flinders, politics loomed large in his decision. In an entry made on 20 October 1775, he noted that he would buy the Stamford paper rather than the *Cambridge Chronicle*, since the latter was 'very barren of entertainment, and partial on the furious and patriotic side'.[129]

Other strategies which the producers of provincial newspapers appear to have used to enlarge their audiences were more explicitly localized in their appeal. The local news columns of papers often carried regular

---

[127] *Newcastle Courant*, 8 Jan. 1780.   [128] Ibid. 29 Jan. 1780.

[129] Diary of Matthew Flinders, Lincolnshire Archive Office. I am grateful to Paul Langford for this reference. Herbert Butterfield states that those opposed to the General Meeting in 1780 had to have their circulars printed in London since the Cambridge printer, presumably Hodson, who produced the *Chronicle* was 'a patriot': *George III, Lord North and the People*, 285.

reports of matters which would have been of particular interest to those in the area, such as crop prices, shipping, and racing news. The two New-castle papers regularly published material relating to agriculture, whilst the *Hereford Journal* listed grain prices at Hereford, and *Drewry's Derby Mercury* those at the Chesterfield and Derby markets. Both Bristol papers carried shipping information, as did the *Western Flying-Post*, whilst the Oxford and Cambridge papers contained university news. The *Cambridge Chronicle* also published detailed information concerning the racing at Newmarket, and the Bath papers printed regular lists of the arrivals of members of fashionable society in town during the season. Moreover, although the 'news' itself in such local sections often (although by no means always) appeared uncontroversial, this was frequently not the case amongst the letters published by provincial newspapers. These could concern both local and national politics and might be highly partisan in tone. The letters were supposedly from local readers, and often carried signatures and used modes of address which emphasized their local prov-enance and appeal. For example, 'A Man of Kent' who wrote frequently to the *Kentish Gazette* addressed his letters 'to the freeholders of Kent' and 'the gentlemen of the county of Kent'.[130] Readers of the *York Chron-icle* read appeals to 'the independent gentlemen, clergy, and freeholders of the county of York' from 'a fellow freeholder', and 'a Yorkshire freeholder',[131] whilst the *York Courant* published letters from 'a Yorkshire gentleman' and 'a freeholder of Yorkshire'.[132] As is the case with such letters in the London press, whether or not they can be termed 'genuine' is perhaps not as important as the sense of immediacy between a paper and its readership which they would have enhanced.

At no time would this have been more evident than during elections, when most provincial papers would be full of reports, letters, and adver-tisements concerning local politics. In places where the election was con-tested, readers were also supplied with regular reports of the state of local polls, and predictions of the results. Most of this material presumed to satisfy a very local interest, and much of it addressed all or part of the local readership directly. Advertisements by prospective parliamentary candi-dates seeking support were placed in newspapers which served the constituency in question, and were explicit in their appeal to the local

---

[130] *Kentish Gazette*, 22 Jan., 9 and 16 Feb. 1780, 30 Oct. 1782, 24 Mar. 1784.

[131] *York Chronicle*, 21 Jan. 1780 and 28 Mar. 1783; see also 3 Dec. 1779, 14 Jan. 1780, 3 Jan. and 26 Sept. 1783.

[132] *York Courant*, 7 Dec. 1779, 23 Sept. 1783, and 1 Mar. 1785; see also 25 Jan. 1780, 24 July 1781, and 21 Jan. 1783.

population. Henry Sampson Bridgeman, standing for Wigan in 1780, promised in *Aris's Birmingham Gazette* to 'promote the general welfare of the country, and the particular interest of this borough',[133] and in the same paper, a candidate for Warwick claimed that his 'constant object' was 'to pay the strictest attention to every concern of this great manufacturing and opulent county'.[134] In the *Kentish Gazette*, the 'worthy freemen and the Town and Port of Sandwich' were reminded of a candidate's efforts to preserve Sandwich's harbour, and were promised 'an unwearied attention to the interests of the community in general, and the Town of SANDWICH in particular'.[135]

Although provincial newspapers would carry election news from around the country, reports of local hustings and polls, and discussions of local electoral politics, were given greater space. Aside from letters, the coverage of local politics in the provincial press may have tended to be uncontroversial, but this was not always the case. The report of a nomination meeting in Reading discussed the merits of one of the candidates in a way which was anything but neutral:

> however gentlemen may differ from Mr. Hartley in his political opinions, every one must be compelled to acknowledge and admire the spirit, the firmness, and the ability wherewith he supports them. Surely the Freeholders who were witness of his manly conduct at the nomination meeting yesterday, must be encouraged to entrust their dearest interests with a man whose conscious integrity and uprightness of intention could support him against the torrent of abuse and illiberality, so undeservingly levelled against him on that occassion.[136]

But it was in the letters published by provincial newspapers that opinions concerning local elections were most strongly expressed, and the vibrancy of provincial political life was most evident. The political coverage supplied by letters could be both partisan and contradictory. During the 1780 election, the *Kentish Gazette* published a letter from 'A well-wisher of Sandwich' which defended the candidature of a Mr Brett, alongside another from 'A Sandwich Tradesman' which opposed him.[137] Letters in the *Bristol Journal* from 'A Freeholder' and 'Observator' in April 1784 attacked Henry Cruger, one of the candidates for the town, whilst another from 'A Freeman' supported him. Two weeks later, 'A Citizen' blamed rival candidates George Daubeny and Matthew Brickdale for local riots.[138] Such was the apparent deluge of letters which the *Kentish Gazette* re-

---

[133] *Aris's Birmingham Gazette*, 7 Aug. 1780.   [134] Ibid. 11 Sept. 1780.
[135] *Kentish Gazette*, 6 Sept. 1780.
[136] *Reading Mercury*, 5 Apr. 1784.
[137] *Kentish Gazette*, 6 Sept. 1780.   [138] *Bristol Journal*, 10 and 24 Apr. 1784.

ceived about the Sandwich election of 1780 that on 20 September 1780 it announced, 'the Sandwich election now being determined, we must beg leave to decline the insertion of any thing more on that subject, either for one party or the other'.

Such discussions and portrayals of local affairs gave provincial newspaper readers a picture of political life which was highly accessible. As in the capital, the provincial press's coverage of electoral politics presented public debate and local politics as something in which readers could participate. Newspapers provided their readers with a sense of intimate involvement in politics, both by the letters published, which were supposedly from readers, and by the nature of discussion, which usually implied that those following the debate had some legitimate part to play in it. A letter in the *Hereford Journal* from 'A. B.' which appeared in March 1780 noted that

The people have a legal right to seek redress of their grievances by applying to their Representatives in Parliament: and when they complain with justice, and steadily persevere in their complaints and remonstrances, they must be heard, and obtain redress; or confusion may be expected to ensue . . . Such representatives as have disregarded the petitions on the present occasion, and acted in direct opposition to them, it is to be hoped and expected, will be properly marked. In case of a dissolution of the Parliament, the people ought at this time to be particularly nice and careful in their choice, and not to return men who are under the immediate influence of the Crown.[139]

Newspapers like the *Cambridge Chronicle* made a point of publishing division lists on important parliamentary votes which noted how MPs who represented 'the counties, cities, and boroughs within the circuit of this paper' voted.[140] A letter to Somerset freeholders from 'A Freeholder' which appeared in the *Bath Chronicle* of 21 September 1780 advised electors to consider their choice of candidates carefully at a time of such public danger. Similarly, a paragraph in the *York Chronicle* before the 1784 election asserted, 'FREEHOLDERS OF YORKSHIRE COME FORWARD TO YOUR OWN RESCUE, YOUR LIBERTY, YOUR PROPERTY, YOUR ALL IS AT STAKE'.[141] The kind of uniquely localized political debate provided by a paper produced in the provinces was something which a newspaper brought from London could not offer, nor, for that matter, could a provincial paper produced elsewhere.

Whilst one must not ignore the significance of the wider distribution of

[139] *Hereford Journal*, 13 Apr. 1780. See also *Bath Chronicle*, 1 May 1783.
[140] *Cambridge Chronicle*, 4 Mar. 1780.   [141] *York Chronicle*, 19 Mar. 1784.

provincial newspapers, locally made sales were of overriding importance to a paper's profitability and survival. It was probably because provincial newspapers were so closely associated with their place of production that proprietors would often act as paid agents for papers published in other towns, even when their geographical areas of circulation appeared to clash. Amongst the Midlands papers in the 1780s for example, Samuel Drewry, owner of the *Derby Mercury*, acted in this capacity for *Aris's Birmingham Gazette*, the *Nottingham Journal*, and *Jopson's Coventry Mercury*. Robert Raikes, the proprietor of the *Glocester Journal*, was agent for the *Bath Journal*, the *Bristol Journal*, *Berrow's Worcester Journal*, and the *Hereford Journal*. Similar arrangements were evident amongst proprietors of the *Birmingham Chronicle*, the *Hereford Journal*, *Aris's Birmingham Gazette*, *Berrow's Worcester Journal*, and the *Bristol Gazette*.[142]

This study of both newspaper economics and politics reveals that the focus of provincial papers was directed at the town in which they were produced and its immediate environs. It is therefore likely that this bias would have been the basis upon which many a country reader would choose between one paper and another—according to the town with which he or she felt most affinity or whose affairs held most interest. If readership choice was decided by the strength of a paper's local appeal, then its contents may well have been shaped, at least in part, by the perception of those running newspapers of what constituted local sentiment or opinion. Their astuteness in this respect would have been tested in the longer term by the success of each individual paper. As in London, then, it appears that newspapers and public opinion may well have been linked. This was clearly the belief of many involved in provincial politics in the late 1770s and early 1780s, whose views and activities are discussed in the following two chapters.

[142] See *Jopson's Coventry Mercury*, 19 June 1780; *Creswell and Burbage's Nottingham Journal*, 1 Jan. 1780; *Berrow's Worcester Journal*, 2 Mar. 1780; *Aris's Birmingham Gazette*, 13 Jan. 1780; the *Leicester and Nottingham Journal*, 1 Jan. 1780; the *British Chronicle, or, Pugh's Hereford Journal*, 6 Jan. 1780; *Drewry's Derby Mercury*, 14 Jan. 1780; *Felix Farley's Bristol Journal*, 4 Dec. 1779; the *Bath Journal*, 6 Dec. 1779.

5
THE POLITICS OF
THE PROVINCIAL PRESS

In May 1780, Rockingham wrote to a York correspondent, John Carr, complaining of the 'radical' direction which the Yorkshire reformers were taking. Part of the blame for this he attributed to newspapers, which had helped to propagate the 'speculative propositions' of more frequent elections and the need for extra county MPs. Rockingham argued that as 'the calamities and distresses which this country now feels agitates men's minds exceedingly—reforms in the constitution are advertised in the papers either in letters or pamphlets—like quack medicines and the poor suffering patient rapidly catches at whatever is held out as a radical cure'.[1] Four years later, Rockingham's successor, Lord Fitzwilliam, received similar accounts of the undesirable influence of the press in the provinces. Richard Fenton informed him that 'the minds of the people are so poisoned by virulent letters & paragraphs in the news papers &c &c—that it seems to be apprehended the most serious consideration will be required—whether any effectual opposition can be made at present to this much to be lamented delusion'.[2] John Carr also bemoaned the continuing prominence of the Yorkshire newspapers: 'I wish we had a good paragraph put into the York & Leeds papers previous to the meeting, to state the dispute betwixt the K[ing] and parliament properly, for it is amazing to think how ignorant people are on the subject, they have no idea but that Mr Fox wants to get the better of the K. and be the Ld Protector and therefore he and all his abettors ought to be opposed'.[3] Others amongst Fitzwilliam's York correspondents attributed the earl's weakening political influence in the county not to misinformation, but to the high level of public knowledge about parliamentary affairs. Commenting on the increasing unpopularity of Fitzwilliam's proposed candidate for York, Lord John Cavendish, James Farrer noted that 'many of the citizens here, seem to be much informed about Ld John's conduct in ye House of Commons, respecting the Receipt Tax, as yr Lordship will see in this days York

---

[1] Copy of Rockingham to Carr, London, 22 May 1780, WWM, R1/1897.
[2] Fenton to Fitzwilliam, [Bank Top, Barnsley?], 14 Mar. 1784, WWM, F34/82.
[3] Carr to Fitzwilliam, York, 8 May 1784, WWM, F34/59.

Chronicle sent you'.[4] In the following month, Peregrine Wentworth observed that Fitzwilliam's own speech in the Lords in favour of the Receipt Tax would 'never be forgiven' in York, 'as it has done more hurt to the merchants'. In addition, Wentworth noted that many in York were 'so hot at present and angry with Charles Fox upon his India Bill that many of them are not to be talked to'.[5]

The influential role of newspapers in local politics was also acknowledged outside Yorkshire. In 1780, the Earl of Banbury advised Robert Thistlewaite that he must put an advertisement in 'our provincial paper' if he intended to stand for election in Hampshire.[6] In reference to a planned county meeting in Berkshire, Winchcombe Henry Hartley wrote to his brother on 15 January 1780, and argued that 'the meeting can hardly be this week yet, as it must be advertised in the Oxford and Reading Journals'.[7] A letter from Benjamin [?] Newson to George Selwyn in the same year described how electioneering in Gloucester caused opposing political groups to battle in the pages of the local newspaper.

I am happy to find, by your favour receiv'd this morning, that my poor attempt, to secure your name from the scurrilous attack made upon it in the last week's Gl. Journal, is honoured with your last approbation . . . Your opponent has certainly got an advantage, by having made the first canvass; but you must not estimate that advantage by the report of the Gl. Journal, which is no other than the report of your Opponent himself and of his adherents.[8]

The importance of an extensive and positive press coverage was evident to those involved in the local reform organizations from the start. In January 1780, Stephen Croft informed Rockingham that several local activists planned 'to publish a weekly paper called the Yorkshire Freeholder in order to keep up the ball'.[9] In April, Christopher Wyvill outlined his plan to use the York newspapers in a letter to William Gray, the clerk of the York Committee:

I think it will be of national use to our cause, to keep the York papers constantly well supplied with paragraphs & letters relative to the Association . . . I would

[4] Farrer to Fitzwilliam, York, 2 Jan. 1784, WWM, F34/28.

[5] Wentworth to Fitzwilliam, Wakefield, 11 Feb. 1784, WWM, F34/34.

[6] Banbury to Thistlewaite, Winchester, 15 Sept. 1780, Hampshire Record Office, Banbury/Knollys Papers, IM44/67/37.

[7] W. H. Hartley to David Hartley, 15 Jan. 1780, Berkshire Record Office, Hartley Russell MSS, D/EHy F88/1.

[8] Newson to Selwyn, Gloucester, 24 Apr. 1780, Castle Howard Archives, uncatalogued papers of George Selwyn.

[9] Croft to Rockingham, York, 10 Jan. 1780, WWM, R136/38.

advise a few of the best paragraphs relative to our cause to be selected from the London papers, & inserted in both the York papers every week; with the addition of such paragraphs as might be furnished by any members of the Committee, or by yourself, relative to what papers in Yorkshire [*sic*]. Short letters also would be of great use, adapted to the state of sentiments, objections, &c at the time.[10]

In common with its Yorkshire counterpart, the Gloucestershire reform committee resolved to use newspapers—in this case in Gloucester, Bristol, and London—to publicize their activities between 1780 and 1782. In February 1780, the committee also decided to enter into a debate in the *Glocester Journal* with an anonymous correspondent who was 'endeavouring to misrepresent their honest endeavours'. Despite the fact that the author's anonymity made him or her appear less than respectable, the committee's concern 'least a misrepresentation of facts might have an effect upon some persons' was such that they felt the need to publish a reply.[11] The importance of publicity was reiterated by the experienced politician Lord Mahon. As Chairman of the Kent Committee he wrote to Wyvill in 1781 concerning the recent Yorkshire petition: 'unquestioningly the most effectual way of giving a Piece of this particular Nature, the most general & universal circulation amongst those for whom it is principally calculated, is to get it inserted in all the Public Papers, both in Town and Country'.[12] Two years later, Christopher Wyvill asked a Cambridge correspondent to write a paragraph for his local newspaper concerning a forthcoming meeting at York, 'as an earlier and more extensive communication . . . would be useful to the cause'. Wyvill claimed that 'success can only be expected from mutual communication, and the general publication of whatever tends, in any degree, to animate our friends, and to interest the public'.[13]

As was the case in London, many individuals and groups in the provinces were eager to influence opinion in their own localities, and tried to use newspapers to do this. But, also as in the capital, the means which political activists sought to use, and the degree of success with which they met, are not immediately apparent. Some idea of the dealings between

[10] Wyvill to Gray, 25 Apr. 1780, YCA, Acc. 1663, M25.280.

[11] Proceedings of the Gloucestershire Committee, 1780–2, Gloucester Record Office, D1356. For details of the Yorkshire committee's activities, see Christopher Wyvill, *Political Papers, Chiefly Representing the Attempt . . . to Effect a Reformation of the Parliament of Great Britain*, 5 vols. (York, 1794–1802), i. 50, 98, 245, and 272, ii. 1 and 108. Protesters employed similar tactics: ii. 108.

[12] Mahon to Wyvill, 5 Nov. 1781, cited in Peter L. Humphries, 'Kentish Politics and Public Opinion 1768–1832' (Oxford University D.Phil. thesis, 1981), 111.

[13] Wyvill, *Political Papers*, iv. 284.

provincial newspapers and those seeking publicity can be gained from the records of the *Hampshire Chronicle*. Despite his failings in many other respects of newspaper management, its printer, John Wilkes, did keep detailed records of the money which the paper received for advertisements.[14] These show, for example, that the *Chronicle* received payment for letters from 'An Independent Freeholder' and 'A Hampshire Freeholder', concerning the Hampshire by-election, and published in December 1779.[15] However, despite partisan pieces like these being charged for as advertisements, subsequent material published concerning the reform movement does not appear to have been paid for in this way. The York petition, Richmond's letter calling the Sussex meeting, news about the Devon reform movement, Hartley's letter to the York meeting, the resolutions of the Dorchester Committee and the proceedings of Sussex and Winchester general meetings, as well as a piece from the 'York Freeholder' and a paragraph proclaiming that 'we hear that the Hampshire petition is already signed by 2600 very respectable Gentlemen, Clergy, and Freeholders, and others of considerable property in the county',[16] all appeared in the *Hampshire Chronicle* apparently free of charge. The records of the *Hampshire Chronicle* suggest that the political contents of a provincial newspaper could be shaped, in part, by anyone willing to pay to insert material, but that such commercial transactions clearly do not tell the whole story. For the *Chronicle* at least, other factors must have ensured that material appeared in print without having been 'sponsored' in the way that the electioneering letters had been.

Unfortunately, little more evidence concerning the operation of the *Hampshire Chronicle* has survived. However, there are more abundant sources for a study of the press in York. An examination of these reveals a complex picture of the way in which newspaper politics were fashioned. The *York Courant* and the *York Chronicle* were among the most eager supporters of the reform movement. While many provincial newspapers often appeared ambivalent, or remained silent, about reform, the two York papers maintained a more constant and favourable coverage of the issue throughout the period between 1779 and 1785. The uniqueness of the York press reflected the peculiar position of the town and the county within the national reform movement. In particular, the York papers represent a special case because of the activities of Christopher Wyvill. From 1779 onwards he worked hard to manipulate the York press and to

---

[14] PRO, E140/90.   [15] *Hampshire Chronicle*, 6 Dec. 1779.
[16] See *Hampshire Chronicle*, 10, 17, 24, and 31 Jan. and 7 Feb. 1780.

use it as part of his reformist propaganda campaign. That Wyvill succeeded in influencing the York papers is undeniable, but that he could not dictate the politics of either newspaper is equally clear. The reformers constituted one of a series of local factors which conditioned the response of the York press to political events. Arguably, it was above all the attempt to appeal to readers which produced the consistency of opinion displayed in the York newspapers. As a result, these papers demonstrated a peculiarly local view of events, based upon a particular perception of public opinion.

Like the rest of the provincial press, the York newspapers 'lifted' material from London papers. The reformist attitude of the York papers led them to use some of the capital's newspapers more than others. The *London Courant* appears to have been a particular favourite from amongst the daily press, whilst the *London Evening Post*, *St. James's Chronicle*, and the *General Evening Post* featured prominently in the list of tri-weekly newspapers used. None of the capital's evening papers were as overt in their politics as their daily counterparts, and indeed they were often ambivalent, whilst the *General Evening Post* tended towards a support of the Ministry in the early 1780s. But the manner in which the York press used them was highly selective. For example, on 17 December 1779, the *York Courant* published a paragraph which had appeared in the *St. James's Chronicle* on 9 December beginning, 'It is notorious that the monied interest of this country is equal to the landed, and yet the former does not contribute one shilling towards the support of Government', whilst on 24 March 1780, the *York Chronicle* borrowed a statement on Burke's Establishment Bill that 'the eyes of the nation are fixed upon the present Representatives in Parliament, and their success at the ensuing election will depend upon their conduct in the debates upon Mr Burke's Bills' from the *St. James's Chronicle* of the 16th. This paragraph had also appeared in the *London Courant* of the 17th, proving that even the most radical of newspapers was not always original. However, although it continued to use the *St. James's Chronicle*, the *York Courant* did not copy the paragraph that appeared in it a few weeks later accusing Burke's plan for economic reform of being merely the result of 'pique' against the Administration,[17] nor did it use the letter from 'Crito' which described the Opposition as merely masking private interest in their actions.[18]

Pieces concerning reform which reached the York press from London were generally very supportive of the campaign, but tended to be far more

[17] *St. James's Chronicle*, 13 Jan. 1780.   [18] Ibid. 18 Jan. 1780.

moderate than most of the material published by the reformist press in the capital. A diatribe on the fate of the petitions from the *London Courant* of 16 February 1780, which criticized the North administration and its supporters for upholding the influence of the Crown, later appeared in the *York Chronicle*,[19] as did a piece from the *Gazetteer* which argued that the county petitions were valid because of the amount of tax revenue and property they represented.[20] In January 1781, a letter from 'A Man of Ross' appeared in the *York Courant*,[21] one of a series in praise of the 'ancient' constitution and attacking corruption and secret influence, which had originally appeared in the *Gazetteer*. An extract from the *London Courant* commenting upon 'a remarkable instance of a borough's being bought and sold, at the late general election, submitted to the consideration of the associators, and all other advocates for a pure and uncorrupt parliament' was used by the *York Chronicle* on 2 March 1781. A letter from 'Pasquin' deploring the state of the economy and the continued war with America, which had also appeared in the *London Courant*, was repeated in both York papers a couple of months later.[22] In April and May 1784, the *York Chronicle* published several pieces entitled 'Abridgement of the State of Politics', which were taken from the *Whitehall Evening Post*.[23] The political commentary which these provided was blatantly hostile to the Coalition, whilst the first of these pieces carried by the *Chronicle* praised the men of the city and county of York who had 'given the severest blow to Faction it has yet felt, and that where its leaders expected their warmest friends.—Amongst these brave men the true AMOR PATRIÆ has triumphed over all the selfish views, private friendship, and predilectional'.[24] Since the mass of material taken from the London press by the York papers was consistently pro-reform, it is not surprising that there is little evidence that material was taken from either the *Morning Post* or the *Morning Herald* concerning any aspect of domestic news, although both papers were cited where reports of foreign events were concerned.[25]

This is not to say that the arguments put forward in these papers were

[19] *York Chronicle*, 25 Feb. 1780.

[20] *Gazetteer*, 2 Feb. 1780; *York Chronicle*, 3 Mar. 1780.

[21] *York Courant*, 2 Jan. 1781.

[22] The letter from 'Pasquin', which appeared in the *London Courant* of 21 Apr. 1781, was copied in the *York Courant* of 1 May 1781 and the *York Chronicle* of 4 May 1781.

[23] See *York Chronicle*, 23 Apr. and 14 May 1784; from the *Whitehall Evening Post* of 17 Apr. and 8 May 1784.

[24] *York Chronicle*, 23 Apr. 1784.

[25] See, for example, the *York Chronicle* of 7 Jan. 1780.

ignored by the York press. In December 1779, the *York Chronicle* published paragraphs in direct response to material printed in the *Morning Post*. On the 14th the *Post* had claimed that the Yorkshire petition was the work of members of the parliamentary Opposition, and of Rockingham in particular. The *York Chronicle* of the 24th carried a letter from 'E O' which described this report as 'false and wicked'. As we shall see, this letter was inserted by the York reformers. In another attack on the Yorkshire reformers, the *Post* asserted that the York meeting threatened civil war.[26] The *York Chronicle* of 14 January 1780 used a paragraph which had previously appeared in both the *London Courant* and the *London Evening Post* to counter the *Morning Post*'s claim.[27]

The traffic of material between the London and York papers was not one-way, and pieces which had originated in Yorkshire often found their way into the capital's newspapers. The use of news from the York press was more than a labour-saving exercise on the part of the London pressmen. Like their York counterparts, they were selective in the material that they chose to take. In the early days of the reform movement, when much of the important activity was centred upon York, the London press displayed a peculiar interest in events there, and in the content of the town's newspapers. But the role of the York papers in supplying the capital's press was not confined to the provision of the most basic information concerning York Committee proceedings and dry reports of county meetings. Material from York frequently provided the lead in a particular debate rather than following or responding to the capital's newspapers. The *London Courant* of 17 December 1779 included a report of the forthcoming York meeting and accompanied it with a paragraph from the *York Chronicle* of the 10th, which argued, 'Surely if a frugal expenditure of public money may ever be requested with propriety, it will be thought proper in the present general distress of this country, when trade, manufactures, and land-rents are in so rapid a decline'. Similarly, the *General Evening Post* of 18 December 1779, reporting on the circular letters which had been sent out by the York Committee, took a paragraph from the *York Courant* of the 14th, which stated, 'We are informed from good authority that so many answers have already been received, (fully approving the measure) that there is no shadow of doubt but the GENERAL MEETING will be a very respectable one'. The *London Evening Post* of 20 January 1780 published a letter from 'A Freeholder of Yorkshire' which

---

[26] *Morning Post*, 13 Dec. 1779.
[27] *London Evening Post*, 8 Jan. 1780; *London Courant*, 8 Jan. 1780.

had originally appeared in both York papers, seeking to counteract anti-association propaganda.[28] The writer asserted that 'the plan of Association recommended to the consideration of the Committee by the second resolution at the late County Meeting, is expressly limited by the words legal and constitutional. An Association on such grounds must be pacific; and having in view the correction of a gross abuse in the expenditure of public money, must be not only lawful, but laudable'. On 4 March the *Post* noted the appearance of a 'test' for MPs in the *York Courant*, and in May the paper quoted from the *York Chronicle* of 28 April that 'we hear the Form of Association has been circulated with great success in the West-Riding; having been signed by many persons who declined signing the petition'.[29] For its part, the *London Courant* of 7 July published a paragraph which had appeared in both the York papers denying that there was a link between the Gordon Riots and the county associations,[30] whilst on 2 December 1782, the *General Advertiser* reprinted a paragraph from the York papers which disputed the claim that Wyvill had been presumptuous and had instructed the Sheriff of Northumberland to call a county meeting.[31]

Despite borrowing material from each other, the York and London press clearly had differing priorities, reflecting differences in the political opinions of their readerships and again reinforcing the provinces' independence from metropolitan influence. These divergent concerns and interests are apparent in the coverage given to the initial York meeting in 1779. This event created various controversies, two of which, concerning individual participants Henry Goodricke and Leonard Smelt, became the subject of much newspaper scrutiny. However, the papers produced in York and in the capital chose to concentrate on completely different men, and, by implication, on very different issues. The anti-Smelt campaign which ran in the capital's reformist press following the York meeting was peculiar to London. Smelt, as one of the Prince of Wales's tutors, had royal connections which did nothing to endear him to those critical of the Crown when he spoke in defence of royal prerogative at the York meeting. Ironically, in the light of Smelt's subsequent treatment by the press, one of his complaints at York had been about newspaper hostility to the King. Smelt argued that the King's influence was demonstrably too small since 'he was unable now to curb that licentiousness with which he was every

---

[28] See *York Chronicle* and *York Courant*, 14 and 18 Jan. 1780, respectively.
[29] *London Evening Post*, 4 May 1780.
[30] See *York Courant* and *York Chronicle*, 4 and 7 July 1780, respectively.
[31] See *York Courant* and *York Chronicle*, 26 and 29 Nov. 1782, respectively.

day talked of in every company, and in every street. He was unable to put to silence the numerous libels with which he was daily insulted. He cannot even restrain the insertion of a paragraph in an ordinary newspaper'.[32] William Mason wrote to Horace Walpole from York that Smelt's speech 'will astonish you by its impropriety. He has torn the veil with a vengeance'.[33] A few days later, once Smelt's speech had been widely publicized in London, Walpole replied, 'Poor Mr. Smelt: how one may hurt a man by serving him'.[34]

Yet despite Mason's protestations, Smelt was given little coverage in the York press. In London, however, Smelt's arguments were repeated and debated at length, and used almost exclusively for propaganda purposes by the Opposition press. Far from being an eloquent defence of the Crown, Smelt's speech appeared as clumsy and sycophantic. A letter from 'A Yorkshireman', which appeared in the *London Courant* on 8 January 1780, formed part of the general cry against him: 'I really think it of some importance to the public to know if these are to be considered only as the empty and foolish fancies of a weak and shallow understanding; or whether they are despotic doctrines of a mind tainted with the mischievous and insatiable thirst of arbitrary power'.[35] Despite its signature, though, neither this, nor any of the other attacks on Smelt, ever reached the pages of the York press.

The York papers took far more interest in the behaviour of a local man and MP, Henry Goodricke, who arrived at the county meeting brandishing an alternative petition and expressing his wariness about anything more radical than inquiring into civil list expenditure.[36] Unlike Smelt, Goodricke was no stranger to political controversy in Yorkshire, having previously published an attack on Dr Price in York.[37] The debate surrounding Goodricke's behaviour, which can be found in both York papers

---

[32] Cited in Wyvill, *Political Papers*, i. 16.

[33] Mason to Walpole, 31 Dec. 1779, *Walpole's Correspondence*, xxviii. 492. Mason, a clergyman, was a well-known poet, political satirist, and polemicist, active in the Yorkshire reform movement. See Hartley Coleridge, *The Worthies of Yorkshire and Lancashire* (London, 1836); *DNB*, xii. 1322–6.

[34] Walpole to Mason, 4 Jan. 1780, *Walpole's Correspondence*, xxix. 1.

[35] See for example the *London Courant* of 8, 17, and 18 Jan., 8 and 22 Feb. 1780, and the *General Advertiser* of 10 and 21 Jan. 1780.

[36] *York Chronicle*, 7 Jan. 1780. Goodricke was MP for the Hampshire seat of Lymington between 1778 and 1780. Whilst in Parliament he voted mostly with the Opposition: *History of Parliament*, ii. 509. He came from a well-established Yorkshire family which held a baronetcy: Charles Alfred Goodricke (ed.), *History of the Goodricke Family* (London, 1885).

[37] Henry Goodricke, *Observations on Dr. Price's Theory and Principles of Civil Liberty and Government, Preceded By a Letter . . . On the Pretensions of the American Colonies in Respect of Right and Equity* (York, 1776).

at the beginning of 1780, took the form of a series of letters between Goodricke and his anonymous opponents: the former defending his refusal to sign the Yorkshire petition, the latter attacking his failure to join the rest of the county and unite in the struggle for reform.[38] James Preston informed Rockingham on 13 January that 'the Town have been much entertained here with the paper war that Mr. Goodricke has got engaged in'.[39] Stephen Croft had already contacted Rockingham about the affair, and noted that at least one of the perpetrators of the attack on Goodricke was a local reform activist. On 10 January he wrote: 'You not be [*sic*] displeased at seeing Mr Goodricke having got a good dressing for his silly publication the author is a secret but is Luke Farrar'.[40] Goodricke helped to prolong the debate by sending letters to the papers responding to his critics. He provided an important target for the Yorkshire reformers, symbolizing as he did what was at best inertia, at worst a dangerous opposition to reform. Unlike Smelt, who fitted neatly into the Opposition press's obsessive interest in royal prerogative and secret influence in London, Goodricke was of little interest to those in the capital,[41] but of great concern in Yorkshire, where he appeared to represent a more immediate threat to the reform movement. Even at this early stage in the reform movement's life, we see the metropolitan and provincial press displaying divergent interests, and reflecting the different forms which both reform agitation and the debate over reform took according to region.

This split between the London and York press was apparent throughout the period 1779 to 1785. It appeared equally striking when the second meeting of deputies from the various associated counties and boroughs took place in London in March and April 1781. Wyvill had written to Gray requesting coverage of the event in the York press.[42] However, it took over two weeks for a report sent by Wyvill to reach the pages of the York papers,[43] and subsequent material which he asked another member of the York Committee, a Mr Burgh, to arrange does not appear to have been published at all.[44] The lack of interest in these meetings displayed by the York press was not echoed in London newspapers, where the

---

[38] See *York Chronicle*, 7, 14, 21 Jan., 25 Feb. 1780, and *York Courant*, 4, 11, 18 Jan. 1780.

[39] Preston to Rockingham, York, 13 Jan. 1780, WWM, R136/41.

[40] Croft to Rockingham, York, 10 Jan. 1780, WWM, R136/38.

[41] However, a letter from Goodricke and one from 'A Single Individual' taken from the *York Courant* of 4 and 11 Jan. 1780 were reprinted in the *Gazetteer* of 14 Jan. 1780.

[42] Wyvill to Gray, 27 Feb. 1781, YCA, Acc. 1663, M25.359.

[43] See the *York Courant* of 13 Mar., and the *York Chronicle* of 23 Mar. 1781.

[44] Wyvill to Gray, 3 Mar. 1781, YCA, Acc. 1663, M25.360. No further material concerning the meeting of deputies appeared in either York paper.

meetings formed the subject of much debate.[45] A divergence of interest was also apparant in late 1783 and early 1784, when the pages of London newspapers were filled with reports and debates about the battle between Pitt and the Coalition. These events certainly did not go unnoticed in York (as is discussed below), but they occupied a less prominent place than in the capital's papers. Where the York press and the London papers really differed in these months was over the coverage of Wyvill's attempts to launch another national campaign and to produce a new petition. Very little of this was mentioned in a London press which was obsessed with the constitutional crisis.

Whilst this issue did feature prominently in the York papers, they remained more constant than their London counterparts in their commitment to the coverage of the reform movement during this period.[46] However, they too began to show signs of disenchantment with local reformers. A letter which appeared in the *York Chronicle* in August 1783 carried an attack on those 'imagined Friends of the Constitution in different parts of England, [who] are too much disheartened by the late rejection of their Petition for a MORE EQUAL REPRESENTATION, to renew their attempt next winter'.[47] Six months later, the same paper was highly critical of those who had removed their names from the York association, and whose 'specious excuses' would hereafter 'carry with them neither credit nor consolation'.[48] But the general move away from reform activity, which the York press was initially critical of, first in the country as a whole and then within Yorkshire, was reflected not long after by the papers themselves. By 1785, the York press appeared more ambivalent over the issue of reform. 'A Freeholder', writing in the *York Courant* in January, doubted whether those who made up Pitt's ministry would be likely to support any alteration in the constitution in favour of liberty, labelling them as 'men of high aristocratic principles, and proprietors of numerous boroughs'. He also attacked Wyvill for trying to drum up support for Pitt: 'beware of the insidious invitations of the great Leader of the Association to form a coalition with him [Pitt] and his associates, whose constant practice it has been to draw men in to sign their names to papers of some sort, and then tell them they are pledged to support all his

[45] See for example the *London Courant* of 12 Mar. and 7 Apr. 1781, the *Morning Herald* of 6, 7, 12, and 29 Mar. and 10 and 17 Apr. 1781, and the *St. James's Chronicle* of 6 and 17 Mar. and 12 and 21 Apr. 1781.
[46] See reform-related reports in the *York Chronicle*: 22 and 29 Aug., 19 Sept., 10 Oct., 7 Nov. 1783, 9, 16, 23, and 30 Jan., 5 and 19 Mar., and 16 Apr. 1784, and in the *York Courant*: 26 Aug., 2 and 16 Sept., 7 and 21 Oct., 11 Nov., 9 Dec. 1783, 16 Mar. and 20 Apr. 1784.
[47] *York Chronicle*, 22 Aug. 1783.   [48] Ibid. 16 Apr. 1784.

politics'.[49] Another letter, signed by 'A Freeholder', which appeared in the *York Courant* on 8 February, supported reform, but urged the county to proceed with caution following Wyvill's circular letter calling for another petition. In March, the same paper published a letter from 'A Freeholder of Yorkshire' which questioned again Pitt's sincerity concerning reform:

His friends are aware that no Reform will be carried thro' the House of Commons, and are afraid lest his hypocrisy should be seen through; the blame must be laid therefore upon Mr. Fox, and no doubt we shall have paragraph upon paragraph to prove it; but we trust that the freeholders of this great county have too much sense to be so misled; they must know that if Mr. Pitt is sincere he may carry his proposition for a reform, as well as his scrutiny for Westminster, even if he should be opposed by Mr. Fox . . .

This writer also criticized the York associators and the recent county meeting, commenting that 'they have no great reason to boast of either numbers or respectability'.[50] The following week 'A West-Riding Merchant' wrote critically of Pitt's administration, whilst on 3 May a correspondent attacked Pitt's motion for reform as 'the most palpable humbug'.[51]

Such sentiments clearly did not reflect those of the Yorkshire reformers. They had not lost their platform in the York press after 1783, but Association rhetoric appeared incongruous and far less convincing when coupled with these dissident voices. The reformers were pushed onto the defensive, and the grand campaigning language of the past was largely gone, to be replaced with a series of denials and attempts to explain the actions of the Associators. A paragraph in the *York Chronicle* of 4 February 1785 rejected the claim that the reformers were planning an innovation in the constitution rather than a restoration. In the same issue, the accusation that Wyvill had made public Pitt's promise to support reform 'as a man and as a minister' was also denied. The paper was still carrying Wyvill's defence of Pitt's failed bill as late as June 1785.[52] In the *York Courant*, 'A Member of the Yorkshire Association' wrote to correct the view put forward by 'the enemies of the proposed Reformation of Parliament' that 'the late county meeting at York was *not numerous*, and *not unanimous* for the petition'.[53] Within such an environment, the reformers' arguments, which had previously seemed forceful and optimistic, sounded unconvincing and strained.

---

[49] *York Chronicle*, 14 Jan. 1785.   [50] Ibid. 1 Mar. 1785.
[51] *York Courant*, 8 Mar. and 3 May 1785.
[52] See *York Chronicle*, 10 June 1785.   [53] Ibid. 15 Mar. 1785.

Yet despite later lapses, the York newspapers were generally extremely supportive of the reform movement. In part, this was because the York-shire reformers, and Wyvill in particular, maintained an important influ-ence over the York press. The nature of the relationship between Wyvill and the York press is not easy to determine, but from the evidence available, it appears to have been a complex one, certainly far more so than has been implied by Christie's work on the reform movement. Here, Wyvill is presented as able to control what material was published in a press that acted as a passive receptacle for the reformers' propaganda.[54] Clearly such an interpretation downplays not only the degree to which provincial newspapers acted as reflectors of local sentiment, but also the independence from the centre which local political culture assumed. The following examination of the Yorkshire reformers and York newspapers will reveal much more complicated arrangements between politicians and newspapers than Christie portrays. Christopher Wyvill was certainly an important figure in the formation of the York press's political coverage between 1779 and 1785, but he was just one of several factors in a complex equation of local influences and controls, not least of which was public opinion.

For much of the period that the association movement was active, Wyvill lived in the capital in order to co-ordinate pro-reforming efforts with the London committees, and to mediate with various Westminster politicians. Since the capital remained the centre of national political activity, Wyvill was also able to communicate with committees of associa-tion throughout England. During this period of exile, Wyvill did not lose touch with events in York (although at times it appears that his attention was diverted). Indeed, he sought both to foster, and maintain control of, the reform movement in his home county. One of the main methods by which he attempted to do this was by influencing local newspapers. The surviving correspondence between Wyvill and William Gray, the clerk of the York Committee, shows that Wyvill wrote frequently asking for pro-reformist material to be published in the York papers. The content of these letters was such that Gray, a particularly religious man, was troubled by them. Although he conceded that petitioning and forming an associa-tion were not contrary to 'the scriptures' he confided to Wyvill that

some of the measures intended to promote the success of these, appear to me to have a different tendency; such as the paragraphs &c. occasionally inserted in the News Papers, by way of animadversion on the conduct of the Ministry & their

[54] Christie, *Wilkes, Wyvill and Reform*. Christie cites only the *York Chronicle*.

adherents with respect to the concerns of the petitions & associations, and calculated, as I humbly conceive, to intimidate Ministry, and to hold them out in an
odious light to the people. . . . I know these are trifling *matters in politics*, and that
there is an *apparant* unliklihood to carry any great publick without what is called
Spirit, exerted in this way. . . . I would wish therefore, (if you will not be offended,) that the publication of occasional paragraphs might be committed to
Blanchard, who is very [trusty?].[55]

But it seems that Gray was appeased, and of ninety-two letters sent him
between April 1780 and June 1785, almost all mention (and most deal
exclusively with) paragraphs which Gray was to insert in the York newspapers.[56] During periods of particular reform activity, in the opening
months of 1781 for example, Wyvill sent pieces to Gray as often as twice
a week. In most cases, only the covering letter remains to indicate that
Wyvill had sent material to be published, with little suggestion of how it
was composed. It is almost certain that some of this was taken from the
London papers. Indeed, a reference to paragraphs from the *London
Courant* is made in a letter dated 23 February 1781.[57] There are also
pamphlets amongst the York Association papers which would have been
sent by Wyvill to use in the York press, such as an address by the MP
David Hartley, which Wyvill mentions in a letter to Gray on 17 January
1781.[58] However, it is clear from the few examples which did survive that
Wyvill himself wrote much of the material he sent.

   Pieces known to have been written by Wyvill were supplied ready to
publish, and were couched in appropriate editorial language. A letter
dated 13 December 1784, for example, contained a paragraph in Wyvill's
hand, which began, 'the following extract of a letter, which we publish
with pleasure, comes from a Gentleman on whose veracity we can rely'.[59]
On 19 January 1785, Wyvill sent a piece which opened thus: 'intelligence
is just received, that the opulent & unrepresented town of Birmingham
may be expected to co-operate on this occasion with the county of York'.[60]
In a paragraph contained in a letter dated 5 January 1783, Wyvill affixed

---

[55] Gray to Wyvill, York, 6 Nov. 1780, NYRO ZFW/7/2/8/3.

[56] YCA, Acc. 1663, M25.

[57] Wyvill to Gray, 23 Feb. 1781, YCA, Acc. 1663, M25.358. See also Wyvill to Gray, 25
Apr. 1780, YCA, Acc. 1663, M25.280.

[58] Wyvill to Gray, 17 Jan. 1781, YCA, Acc. 1663, M25.352. The address, in which
Hartley praises the actions of the York reformers, also appeared in pamphlet form: David
Hartley, *An Address to the Committee of the County of York, on the State of Public Affairs*, 2nd
edn. (London, 1781).

[59] Wyvill to Gray, 13 Dec. 1784, YCA, Acc. 1663, M25.516. See also Wyvill to Gray, 25
Apr. 1780, YCA, Acc. 1663, M25.280.

[60] Wyvill to Gray, 19 Jan. 1785, YCA, Acc. 1663, M25.523.

the following beneath a list of York freeholders who had signed the Association's petition:

In the preceding list, we observe with great pleasure the names of many Yorkshire families of great distinction, & Gentlemen of the first opulence in the commercial line. But to give the names of all the worthy, & independent Freeholders who have signed the Petition, with as honest a meaning to support the constitution as the first Esquire or Baronet in the list we have given would far exceed the limits of our Paper.[61]

Wyvill was not only careful to ensure that the coverage of reform was favourable, but also that the timing of publication was right. His correspondence with Gray reveals that he played his role as intermediary between the London and Yorkshire associations very carefully, and was anxious not to appear neglectful of the latter. On 21 February 1780, he wrote of the form of association which had been drawn up by the York Committee during the previous month,[62]

It appears to me now to be advisable to publish the paper of which each member of the Committee had two copies. I speak in this manner, because you say my letters have been opened; but I think you will readily understand my meaning.— Among other reasons for publishing now I will mention this, that in fact the Ministry have got possession of the paper by some means or other.—We shall not publish it here, till it has appeared in your York papers . . . I shall wait your answer by the return of the post, or as soon as possible; & then insert it in all of the Evening [i.e. London] Papers.[63]

A postscript to a circular letter which accompanied the report of the Deputies in 1780 noted: 'It is earnestly requested that no copy of the inclosed papers may be given to endanger their premature appearance in the public prints'.[64] During January 1781, Wyvill twice requested the postponement of an address, until on the 17th he noted, 'I observe our Address has got into the London papers; therefore, I think there is no farther occasion of delay at York, but it may appear in Mr Russells next Courant. I was sorry to see it so soon in the London news'.[65] Similarly, in November 1782, Wyvill wrote that 'seeing that our circular letter is published in the London papers, I think it necessary it should

[61] Wyvill to Gray, [5 Jan. 1783], YCA, Acc. 1663, M25.430.
[62] Wyvill, *Political Papers*, i. 67.
[63] Wyvill to Gray, 21 Feb. 1780, YCA, Acc. 1663, M25.232.
[64] Wyvill, *Political Papers*, i. 441.
[65] Wyvill to Gray, 17 Jan. 1781, YCA, Acc. 1663, M25.352. Russell was in charge of the day-to-day running of the paper for Ward: Christie, *Wilkes, Wyvill and Reform*, 194.

immediately appear in both at York'.[66] In one instance though, an awareness of local particularities meant that Wyvill was not concerned that
those in York receive information at the same time as London, but that
they should not receive it at all. On 17 October 1783, he noted, 'I observe
my answer to the Belfast queries has found its way into the London
papers; by means of some communication from Ireland; & not at all by my
desire or with my knowledge. Possibly, the York Printers might think of
inserting it in their papers; but I wish you to prevent it; as I don't think it
advisable to circulate it in Yorkshire at this moment'.[67]

Almost all the pieces mentioned in Wyvill's letters to Gray can be
traced to at least one, and usually both, of the York papers within a week
or so of their being sent from London. At times of intense reform activity
the speed with which Wyvill and Gray secured the inclusion of items was
even faster. On 26 November 1782, Wyvill wrote to Gray requesting the
immediate publication of the Committee's circular letter in the York
papers.[68] This was published in the *York Courant* just three days later, as
well as in the next edition of the *Chronicle*. A piece sent by Wyvill on 10
December 1782 appeared in the *Chronicle* on the 13th, whilst the 'Country
Vicar's recommendation' which was sent from London on 12 January
1783 made the pages of the *Courant* by the 14th.[69] Newspaper coverage
was valuable enough for Wyvill to spend not only time securing it, but also
committee funds. As was the case with the *Hampshire Chronicle*, the
practice of paying to insert political material in newspapers was not uncommon in York.[70] However, there were clearly regional differences in
practice which should be noted. In 1783, Gamaliel Lloyd wrote to inform
Francis Foljambe that he had followed his instructions and had had copies
of George Saville's resignation address inserted in both Leeds papers.
Lloyd noted the different conditions under which reformist propaganda
was published by the York and Leeds newspapers: 'with the approbation
of Mr Wyvill I made an agreement with the printers of both the papers,
that they should have all the advertisements of the Association, on
condition of their inserting *gratis* such short paragraphs as should be sent
them, and for which the printers of the York papers are paid very
handsomeley'.[71]

---

[66] Wyvill to Gray, 26 Nov. 1782, YCA, Acc. 1663, M25.404.

[67] Wyvill to Gray, 17 Oct. 1783, YCA, Acc. 1663, M25.491.

[68] Wyvill to Gray, 26 Nov. 1782, YCA, Acc. 1663, M25.404.

[69] Wyvill to Gray, 10 Dec. 1782, YCA, Acc. 1663, M25.409; Wyvill to Gray, 12 Jan. 1783,
YCA, Acc. 1663, M25.443.

[70] For example, the writer of the letter signed 'T T' was informed by the editor of the
York Chronicle on 17 Mar. 1780 that it would have to be paid for if it was to be inserted.

[71] Gamaliel Lloyd to Francis Foljambe, [Leeds, Nov. 1783?], NRO, DDFJ/11/1/7/163.

Christie noted Wyvill's hope that the Association would not have to pay to publish material,[72] but it is clear that the reformer's wish was not always granted. Amongst the Association papers held in the York City Archives are bills sent to the York Committee by Ann Ward and William Blanchard, the owners of the two York newspapers.[73] Both refer to the period between December 1779 and March 1780, and include charges for publishing various pieces in the York papers. Ward's bill (excluding fees for arranging the publication of various pieces in the London papers) totalled £17 14s. for this period, whilst Blanchard charged £8 9s. Ward's fee was higher since she was also paid for printing copies of the petition and various circular letters. Many of the items listed in these accounts were undisguised pieces of Committee-sponsored publicity, that is, easily recognizable advertisements for meetings and the resolutions and pro-posals resulting from them. However, of the eight charges listed in Blanchard's bill of 10 December 1779, only three were clear advertise-ments, connected with the general meeting called for the end of the month. Of the other five items listed, two concerned 'paragraphs', and the rest the insertion of letters. Two payments of 7s. and one of 3s. 6d. were made (the price being determined by the number of lines) to insert letters signed 'Attilius', 'E O', and 'One of the People'. All three letters appeared in the *Chronicle*'s issue for 24 December. The pieces signed 'One of the People' and 'Attilius' were both complaints about the waste of public money, the corruption of Parliament, and the present sorry state of the country. 'One of the People', having congratulated Yorkshiremen on the approaching general meeting, asserted that 'it would be endless, and would exercise the patience of a stoic to enumerate the scandalous waste of the public money in obsolete useless places, sinecures, enormous sal-aries for doing little or nothing, pensions, bribes, &c. Such abuses, cer-tainly, demand a speedy reform, or the nation must sink in inevitable ruin and beggary, if obliged to maintain a very expensive war'. The letter from 'E O' contradicted reports in the London press that the York meeting was the invention of the parliamentary Opposition.

The two paragraphs listed in Blanchard's bill are less easy to identify, since the only clue given to their identity is that they were both 'respecting an intended meeting of the Yorkshire Freeholders'. However, it seems very likely that the paragraphs referred to were those carried in the 'York' section of the newspaper on 10 and 17 December. The first assured the public that an advertisement to call a county meeting would appear in the next issue of the *Courant*, and predicted that 'a petition to the House of

[72] Christie, *Wilkes, Wyvill and Reform*, 105.   [73] YCA, Acc. 1663, M32.

Commons will be proposed at the meeting, that the abuses of the Civil List may be inquired into and corrected by Parliament; and that the large sums of money which may be saved by reducing exorbitant salaries, and striking off sinecure places, and unmerited pensions, may be applied to the service of the State, before any new tax be granted for that Honourable House'. This paragraph was later to find its way into the London press.[74] The following week the *Chronicle* published what appeared to be the second of the Committee-sponsored paragraphs. This piece was less concerned with reformist rhetoric and merely urged attendance at the general meeting, 'which is proposed, not with any Party view, but solely on considerations of general utility'.[75]

Ann Ward's bill for the York Committee reveals a similar pattern. Amongst the many charges for undisguised advertisements for the Yorkshire Committee are others for less obviously sponsored publicity.[76] An entry for 7 December 1779 shows that payment was made by the Committee for 'advertising a letter from a Yorkshire Gentleman, recommending a county meeting'. The letter itself hoped that previous pro-reform material in the paper 'may have the desired effect, and rouse the spirit of the gentlemen of this large and lately opulent county'. Further entries in Ward's bill point to subsequent pieces being sponsored by the York Committee. A paragraph on 21 December defended the Committee's reluctance to produce a plan before the general meeting on the 30th, whilst the bill shows a charge of 3s. 6d. being incurred on 28 December 1779 for a 'contradiction of a false report of the committee'. As was the case with the *Chronicle*, the *Courant* was also paid to insert various letters in its pages. Ward's bill lists two payments for letters printed on 25 January and 8 February. The first, a letter from 'A Yorkshire Freeholder', defended and explained the Yorkshire petition and described it optimistically as 'founded . . . on solid legal Principles, and supported by Men of Moderation and Independence, there is great reason to hope that your petition will be well received by every true Lover of his country, and duly attended to by Parliament'. The second letter was written by 'Detector'. It attacked pieces hostile to the reform movement written by Josiah

---

[74] *London Courant*, 17 Dec. 1779.   [75] *York Chronicle*, 17 Dec. 1779.

[76] It appears that Ward was also acting as agent for the York association for advertising in the London press, as total charges of £3 11s. 2d. are listed in respect of 'cash paid for advertising the Heads of the Association for supporting the County Petitions in the following London Papers, by order of Mr Wyvil [*sic*]: In Lloyd's Chronicle . . . General Evening Post . . . Whitehall Evening Post . . . English Chronicle . . . London Chronicle . . . London Evening Post . . . St. James's Chronicle', and in addition, the sum of 19s. 6d. was charged for a similar service via a 'Mr Slack of Newcastle': YCA, Acc. 1663, M32.

Tucker under the pseudonym of 'Cassandra', which had appeared in both London and provincial newspapers.[77]

Wyvill may have been prepared to pay for the publication of material sympathetic to reform in the first months of the movement's life, but it was an attitude which he was to modify in light of the movement's growing importance and newsworthiness. On 25 April 1780, he wrote to Gray,

I observe in Blanchards paper a note, that a Letter signed a Petitioner could not be inserted unless paid for, being in answer to a publication in a former paper that had been inserted on those terms. I would wish you to represent to the Printers the necessity there is for an open press upon such subjects; by which I am persuaded they will find their own interest not hurt, but rather benefited. If you mention this at the next meeting of the Sub-Committee I dare say, they will agree with me, that this matter deserves their attention. It will probably add weight of their authority in making the necessary application to the Printers.[78]

Here Wyvill reflects not only a belief that newspapers could benefit by publishing material which was of particular interest to their readers, but also the ideal of the press providing a public service by informing readers of matters about which they had a right to know. But Wyvill's hopes concerning free publicity in the York press were not always rewarded. An examination of both his letters to Gray after April 1780, and of the contents of the York papers during the same period, reveals a less straight-forward relationship than that to which Wyvill aspired. On several occasions, pieces which Wyvill requested Gray to insert in the York papers do not seem to have been published. There is no sign of the 'verses from an unknown hand' that Wyvill sent on 14 May 1780,[79] nor the 'printed papers' which Wyvill posted from London on 25 September 1784. In the latter case, Wyvill had informed Gray that 'I wish them to be inserted without expense to the Committee. When we begin to move again, I should not think it too much to pay for the insertion of paragraphs or letters as before; in the mean time, the appearance of such articles as I have inclosed, may have a good effect, & I imagine the Printers will have no objection to oblige me'.[80]

On 18 September 1782, Wyvill instructed Gray: 'the inclosed manu-script paper you will get inserted in *both* the York papers next week. If it should be taxed as an advertisement you must pay for it; for I think its

[77] See above, Chap. 3.

[78] Wyvill to Gray, 24 Apr. 1780, YCA, Acc. 1663, M25.280.

[79] Wyvill to Gray, 14 May 1780, YCA, Acc. 1663, M25.286.

[80] Wyvill to Gray, 25 Sept. 1784, YCA, Acc. 1663, M25.515.

insertion at this time material'.[81] On 13 February 1784, Wyvill sent two pieces to Gray for inclusion in the York papers. One of these was an answer to the remaining part of 'a Freeholder's letter', which Wyvill instructed Gary to 'insert as usual'; on the other, concerning Ireland, Wyvill commented that 'I hope the Printers will so far oblige me as to publish them without expense to me, or to the committee'.[82] However, whilst the first piece did appear in one of the York papers,[83] the material which Wyvill wanted printed 'without expense' did not. It would seem that Wyvill resigned himself to making payments to the York papers. On 29 June 1784, he wrote that 'I think Mr Hartleys piece will be very useful to revive the attention of the county to the grand subjèct, & it will have the better effect, as its author is known not to be friendly to the present Administration. I therefore wish it published in the Papers, not withstanding the heaviness of the expense'.[84]

Although Wyvill was forced to resort to payment to publish much reformist material, the relationship between the reformers and the press in York was not a strictly financial one. Wyvill and his followers could guarantee the insertion of pro-reformist propaganda by paying the York papers, but other pieces similar to the paragraphs and letters already mentioned, and not listed on the two bills, also found their way into both newspapers. A letter from 'A Freeholder of Yorkshire' which appeared in the *York Chronicle* of 3 December 1779 proclaimed that

I cannot help expressing my surprise at the inactivity and seeming indifference of our principal gentlemen, at a time when the whole nation is sinking fast into poverty, and when the North in particular is threatened with a double land-tax, which, under the pretence of greater equality, in that tax, will leave not a shilling in this country. And all for what? To kick against the pricks for two years more, and then find our misfortunes without a remedy.

Another letter, from 'An Englishman', which appeared in the *Chronicle* on 10 December was also not listed on Blanchard's bill. Its writer expressed his hope that 'some of the leading men in this county may take the hint given in your paper last week, and promote a general meeting of the Freeholders at this very alarming crisis'. In addition to such apparently free puffs for the Yorkshire reform movement, no mention is made on

---

[81] Wyvill to Gray, 18 Sept. 1782, YCA, Acc. 1663, M25.389; this appears to be a reference to a paragraph stressing the importance of constitutional rule, which appeared in the *York Courant* of 24 Sept. 1782 and the *York Chronicle* of 27 Sept. 1782.
[82] Wyvill to Gray, 13 Feb. 1784, YCA, Acc. 1663, M25.509.
[83] See *York Chronicle*, 5 Mar. 1784.
[84] Wyvill to Gray, 29 June 1784, YCA, Acc. 1663, M25.513.

Ann Ward's bill of the paragraph that appeared in the *York Courant* on 14 December, proclaiming that 'We are informed from good authority that so many answers have already been received, (fully approving the measure) that there is no shadow of doubt but the GENERAL MEETING will be a very respectable one'.

Moreover, whilst it is clear that the York Committee often had to pay newspapers, it is also apparent from Wyvill's letters that at times it did not. Wyvill's letters to Gray were often worded as orders rather than as entreaties to the newspaper publishers, despite the fact that he was after free publicity.[85] This is surprising given that he hoped to rely on the goodwill of the printers rather than the Committee purse, but Wyvill may also have been banking on the commercial value of the material itself to the printer: in other words, that the 'news' he was sending would help sell papers. This was suggested on 14 November 1782, when Wyvill wrote,

As to the Notts meeting, if Russell keeps his word & inserts the Acct of it to the end of Sir G Savill's [*sic*] speech next Tuesday, & the remainder, the week following I shall be very well satisfied; but then it will be upon these conditions; viz, that the acct of the Newcastle meeting with the paragraph annexed be inserted; also, the inclosed Acct of our committee resolutions, & any paragraphs which may be sent by Mr Mason or Myself.[86]

An examination of the *York Courant* on 19 and 26 November shows that Russell kept his word at least as far as the accounts of the Newcastle meeting and York committee proceedings were concerned. Wyvill's letters to Gray reveal that he was also sending material for the York papers which was not directly related to reform, but which he may have supplied as part of a deal with the York papers to secure the publication of reform material. On 14 January 1781, for example, he sent copies of the treaties between America and France to the *Courant*,[87] whilst in the following June he posted an account of the debate on the India Bill to York, which appeared in the *Chronicle*.[88]

Clearly, local political activists such as those in the Yorkshire reform movement could significantly influence the content and political stance of provincial newspapers. In John Carr's complaint to Fitzwilliam in 1784 about the hostility shown by York papers towards the Coalition, he

[85] See letters from Wyvill to Gray, 27 Jan. 1781, 12 Jan. 1783, and 19 Sept. 1783; YCA, Acc. 1663, M25.354, 443, and 489.
[86] Wyvill to Gray, 14 Nov. 1782, YCA, Acc. 1663, M25.401.
[87] Wyvill to Gray, 14 Jan. 1781, YCA, Acc. 1663, M25.350; *York Courant*, 23 Jan. 1781.
[88] Wyvill to Gray, 17 June 1781, YCA, Acc. 1663, M25.366; *York Chronicle*, 22 June 1781.

contrasted the lack of localized propaganda undertaken in Fitzwilliam's cause with that of Associators, such as 'the Revd Mr Mason and the Irishman Burgh who resides here', who was 'his agent, in writing paragraphs in our papers'.[89] However, organized propaganda campaigns could not determine the entire politics of local newspapers, as the preceding discussion has suggested, and as local activists knew only too well: hence Wyvill's request to Gray in 1782 that 'I should be glad to know whether anything has appeared for or against us in the York paper for sometime'.[90]

No doubt the individual political allegiances of newspaper editors had some bearing in terms of what appeared in print. In his study of the Bristol press in the eighteenth century, Jonathan Barry has argued that many printers were committed partisans, and that this affected the papers they produced.[91] However, in York at least, it is less clear that the politics of those who ran newspapers were what determined the political character of their publications. Ann Ward was the owner of the *York Courant*, and took over the paper and a printing business in 1759, upon the death of her husband.[92] Although she appears to have retained control of the business overall, the day-to-day running of the newspaper was undertaken by a manager, David Russell.[93] Little is known of the political affiliation of either, although Davies notes that Ward published a version of Smelt's speech to the York county meeting on 30 December 1779, which was described by Walpole as being 'published by Whigs'.[94] However, in a letter to Rockingham in December 1779, after a disagreement with David Russell, Stephen Croft declared that 'he is a Scott & [it] is & was a Court paper since the present admin. the other Blanchard will be well inclined for Liberty'.[95] Croft's neat distinction between Russell and Blanchard, however, was not borne out by the contents of their respective newspapers, since in terms of politics, there was little to differentiate between the two.

If Russell was indeed a ministerialist, this could not have made him more different from William Blanchard, the owner of the *York Chronicle*. Blanchard had clear political connections and loyalties as a member of the Rockingham Club in York,[96] a political group allied, as its name implied,

[89] Carr to Fitzwilliam, York, 8 Mar. 1784, WWM, F34/59.
[90] Wyvill to Gray, 17 Jan. 1782, YCA, Acc. 1663, M25.375.
[91] Barry, 'The Press and the Politics of Culture in Bristol', 62.
[92] *Victoria County History of Yorkshire: The City of York*, ed. P. M. Tillott (Oxford, 1961), 250.
[93] Christie, *Wilkes, Wyvill and Reform*, 194.
[94] Davies, *A Memoir of the York Press*, 286.
[95] Croft to Rockingham, York, 10 Dec. 1779, WWM, R136/6.
[96] List of members of the Rockingham Club, 1783, WWM, F41/20.

to the Rockinghamite interest in the county. Yet Blanchard's paper showed none of the concern that the Rockingham Whigs displayed over the increasing strength and radical nature of the association movement. However, Blanchard's letter, which appeared in the paper on 21 January 1780, may have been a sign of his personal discomfort:

The Editor of the YORK CHRONICLE, sensible how difficult it is to steer a course so perfectly inoffensive, as not, now and then to incur the censure of, here and there, an *individual*, thinks himself happy in the general *approbation*, and begs leave, to return his warmest thanks to the PUBLIC, for the patronage with which they have favoured the Chronicle, and which they still continue to extend to it. He is exceedingly sorry that he should, in any instance, have incurred the imputation of a fault of which he is not at all conscious. As to the articles which he himself selects for the public entertainment, it has been only his object together with the news of the day, to communicate to them, without regard to its peculiar political character, whatever he found, that might, in any manner, gratify the curiosity, or contribute to the information of his readers. As to the applications that have been made to him from others, his paper, so far as it has been at the time unoccupied, always was, and always will be, open to sensible and decent writers of every principle. He flatters himself, that he is as free from all illiberal sentiments of party as any one who can reproach him with them.

This paragraph may well have been published in response to complaints from local Rockinghamites concerning a piece referred to by Croft in a letter to Rockingham: 'The paragraph yr Lordship sent me from the York paper was not fabrocated in York but taken from the English Chronicle but Blanchard told me he was calld on by some fr[eehol]d[er]s here saying his was a partial paper & that he never published any thing but on one side which would hurt the sale of his paper & gave him this paragraph to put in which he durst not refuse'.[97] This incident does not suggest that Blanchard's personal political affiliations determined the political contents of his paper. On the contrary, Blanchard himself made clear his intention to secure public favour and patronage, rather than seek to please 'an individual' or party, whilst Croft's letter suggests the printer's main concern was to produce a newspaper with as broad an appeal as possible. The implication that newspaper politics were influenced by commercial considerations, rather than by matters of principle or party-political loyalty, is clear.

In 1784, Blanchard was again in conflict with the Rockinghamite interest, although by now it had been formally inherited by Fitzwilliam. The *Courant* of 27 April 1784 reported that Blanchard had argued with the

---

[97] Croft to Rockingham, York, 14 Jan. 1781, WWM, R140/98.

Rockingham Club, and had been forced to apologize over the insertion of an advertisement in the *Chronicle* which had mocked the Club's annual celebratory meeting of 6 April. A paragraph had appeared in Blanchard's paper which asserted that 'the principles on which the said club was instituted, viz those of FREEDOM and INDEPENDENCE [had] been discarded, and the most arbitrary and TYRANNICAL ones instituted in their stead', and advised every 'true Briton' to resign.[98] The Club's demand for an apology was not met with the degree of acquiescence that the *Courant* suggested. Although Blanchard did produce a public apology, he wrote his own rather than use that given him by the Club, and would not reveal the author of the offending paragraph. The *Chronicle* had been openly hostile to the Fox–North coalition, which Fitzwilliam backed, and to those Yorkshire parliamentary representatives who supported it, from its formation. However, it appears that by 1783 the Club itself had split into opposing factions. As Charles Duncombe informed Fitzwilliam, 'the Rockingham Club differs from what it formerly was. It is no more the firm phalanx as in the time of our honourable friend; but splits into different factions, animated with a degree of virulence against each other scarce to be believed'.[99]

In attacking the Coalition in Yorkshire, Blanchard appears to have been following a decidedly popular line, as will be suggested in the next chapter. Given his avowed intention to appeal to the public at large, it would have been unwise to defend the Coalition, particularly since his newspaper seems to have depended for its success on a happy co-existence with the *Courant*. If Blanchard had attempted to campaign against local opinion in the *Chronicle*, this relationship would probably have been transformed into one of outright commercial rivalry based upon political divisions, as was the case elsewhere. Yet unlike other places, where audiences existed to support politically divergent newspapers, the York press appears to have catered for a more homogeneous readership. Russell and Blanchard may well have held very different political beliefs, but what mattered in terms of their papers' politics was not their personal views, but the perceived opinion of their readers and the need to cater for local preoccupations and concerns.

[98] *York Courant*, 9 Apr. 1784.
[99] Duncombe to Fitzwilliam, 11 Sept. 1783, WWM, F135/57. See also F. C. Price, 'The Parliamentary Elections in York City 1754–1790' (University of Manchester MA thesis, 1958), 195–7.

6

PROVINCIAL NEWSPAPERS
AND REFORM

Like London newspapers, the provincial press was commonly believed both to influence public opinion and to act as a conduit for popular sentiment. However, the public which formed the readership of provincial newspapers would have been more limited than in the capital. Outside London, papers were less readily available and were published more infrequently. Although most provincial towns supported coffee-houses and inns where newspapers were easily accessible, this could not be said of rural areas. Moreover, lower levels of literacy, coupled with a generally narrower franchise and lesser degree of popular political participation than in London, would have further acted to limit the size of the audience for the provincial newspaper press. The more restricted readership of newspapers in the provinces was reflected by the papers themselves, which defined the public in a much more limited sense than in the capital. However, despite reaching a smaller and less concentrated audience than London newspapers, the provincial press of the late eighteenth century can still tell historians much about the nature of local public opinion.

The preceding examination of the York press suggested that editors tried to reflect local opinion, particularly in terms of political sentiment, as a strategy to attract readers. As this chapter will show, provincial newspapers differed greatly in terms of their political character. This reflected a diversity of opinion in the provinces which stemmed from the independence of provincial culture and political life. Moreover, these variations occurred not only in the types of opinion which the papers expressed, but also in the way in which they did so. Although all newspapers displayed some sort of identifiable political stance or combination of stances, some papers, like those produced in Derby, Sherborne, and Birmingham, were generally more muted in their politics than their more vocal counterparts in places like York, Leeds, Newcastle, and Canterbury. Because of the relationship between newspapers and their readers, these differences could have reflected the varying intensity of debate in these areas and the levels of feeling which they aroused. However, it must also be allowed that differing levels of interest in political matters, especially controversial ones, might also have reflected a reticence on the part of the editor. As was the case in London, editorial style could have a major impact on newspaper contents. The *Western Flying-Post*, for example, appeared generally less concerned with politics than other papers, and this lack of interest affected its coverage of the reform movement. In contrast, other newspapers were more likely to adopt forceful arguments on one side or the other of major debates. Even allowing for such editorial variations, though, the contents of provincial newspapers suggest significant differences in regional opinion, and in the case of the reform movement, the press provides a unique barometer of the nature of localized sentiment.

The picture of opinion in the provinces presented by a survey of provincial newspapers as a whole implies that historians of the reform movement may have failed to gauge adequately, or to explain, the level of popular support which it attracted. Perhaps this is not surprising, given that studies have tended to rely largely upon the papers and correspondence of the politicians involved (both parliamentary and non-parliamentary), which has meant that the history of the movement has been written in terms of a struggle for control between the radical reformers and the parliamentary Opposition.[1] But this is an approach which has underestimated the role of 'the people'. In existing works on the reform movement, the country gentlemen who backed the petitioning movement in the provinces can appear as an inert mass which could be effectively mobilized at will by the reform agitators, whether by committed extra-parliamentary campaigners like Wyvill and the London radicals, or by the Rockinghamite lords who sought to further their own narrow political ends.[2] Black argues that 'most of the original petitioning counties were recruited by the magnates through their territorial and family connections. Such bodies, though superficially impressive, were a frail foundation for agitation'.[3] Christie acknowledges that the York reformers had the support of a large proportion of the county's freeholders, but claims that the response from the other counties was disappointing. 'Even where favourable resolutions were passed at county meetings,' he argues, 'these had only limited significance. They were products, in the first place, of

[1] In *George III, Lord North and the People*, Herbert Butterfield does use newspaper evidence to give some idea of 'popular opinion' during this period, but his lead has not been followed by subsequent historians of the reform movement. See: N. C. Phillips, 'Edmund Burke and the County Movement, 1779–1780', *EHR* 76 (1961), 254–78; Christie, *Wilkes, Wyvill and Reform*; Black, *The Association*.

[2] Black, *The Association*, 82, 125, and 129; Phillips, 'Edmund Burke and the County Movement', 265–70.

[3] Black, *The Association*, 125.

small groups of enthusiasts who had drawn them up, and, in the second, of relatively small numbers of people who agreed with them sufficiently to turn out for public meetings'.[4]

An examination of provincial newspapers and the popular sentiment which they reflected suggests that historians might have seriously underestimated the degree to which the public supported reform in the early 1780s. The contents of provincial newspapers produced in York, Cambridge, Lewes, Canterbury, and Bath all provide evidence that reform was given popular backing in these regions. However, in places like Oxford, Northampton, Leicester, and Birmingham, this seems not to have been the case. Elsewhere, local newspapers reflect the existence of a heated debate concerning the merits of reform. This was the case in Leeds, which will be discussed in greater detail below, and in Newcastle and Bristol. In all three instances, newspapers produced in each town reflected bitter local political divisions in the late eighteenth century which local historians have already noted. In Newcastle, a strong radical and Dissenting interest has been identified amongst Newcastle freemen who sought to challenge the power of the city's corporation.[5] The corporation's merchant oligarchy was also the subject of criticism in Leeds, where a rich Dissenting elite was excluded from political power,[6] whilst in Bristol, local politics also appear to have been polarized.[7] Similar splits in opinion are evident in the single newspapers produced in Gloucester and Hereford. In both, a 'neutrality' concerning reform, which involved publishing arguments both for and against it, suggest that each paper was forced to maintain a precarious balance in its representation of opposing local camps. In the case of Gloucester, the chairman of the town's reform

---

[4] Christie, *Wilkes, Wyvill and Reform*, 105–6 and 113–14. Frank O'Gorman has recently challenged Christie's assertions about the levels of support for radical reform outside Yorkshire and London. He claims that this was growing steadily, even though it did not influence the 1780 elections: *Voters, Patrons, and Parties*, 304–5.

[5] H. T. Dickinson, *Radical Politics in the North-East of England in the Later Eighteenth Century* (Durham, 1979); T. R. Knox, 'Popular Politics and Provincial Radicalism: Newcastle upon Tyne, 1769–1785', *Albion*, 11 (1979), 224–41, and ' "Peace for Ages to Come": The Newcastle Elections of 1780 and 1784', *Durham University Journal*, 84 (1992), 3–19; J. E. Bradley, *Religion, Revolution and English Radicalism* (Cambridge, 1990); Wilson, *The Sense of the People*, chap. 7; O'Gorman, *Voters, Patrons, and Parties*, 302–4. See also [J. Murray], *The Contest* (Newcastle upon Tyne, 1774).

[6] R. G. Wilson, *Gentlemen Merchants: The Merchant Community in Leeds, 1700–1830* (Manchester, 1971); R. G. Wilson, 'Georgian Leeds', and R. J. Morris, 'Middle-Class Culture, 1700–1914', in D. Fraser (ed.), *A History of Modern Leeds*, (Manchester, 1980); R. Sweet, *The Writing of Urban History in Eighteenth-Century England* (Oxford 1997).

[7] *History of Parliament*, i. 287–9; O'Gorman, *Voters, Patrons, and Parties*, 302–4.

committee, Sir George Onesiphorous Paul, admitted in a letter to Wyvill in October 1782 that the county had always been split politically, and that it was 'next to impossible to obtain unanimous concurrence on any political truth, however obvious to sense and reason'.[8]

Evidence to reinforce the argument linking the politics of provincial newspapers to the nature of local public opinion in the 1780s is, once again, most abundant in the case of Yorkshire. One major source is the York Committee's surviving correspondence, which chronicles the rise and fall of reform interest in the county. From December 1779 to January 1780, the committee received over 150 letters from Yorkshiremen offering their support for the campaign.[9] Many wished to be added to the lists of names which formed part of the Committee advertisements. In typical examples, a Mr Barlow from Allerton wrote that 'I *heartily* approve of the plan', Christopher Rawdon from York informed the Committee that he should 'esteem himself happy to have his name announced to the Public as one who feels for the Disgrace & Distress of his Country', and William Waines proclaimed that 'you have my hearty assent, to every thing, that may promote the good of my country'.[10] Letters from men like Robert Harper, who opposed holding a county meeting, were rare.[11]

But the degree of enthusiasm for reform which the Committee's correspondence suggests did not last. Not only did the volume of letters tail off after 1780, but from 1784, a significant proportion of writers appeared to have lost faith in the cause. On 12 April 1784, Thomas Weddell wrote from Waddow that 'if the association still subsists, I desire, you will strike my name out of the list'.[12] George Osbaldeston, who had also supported reform in the past, informed the Committee in March 1785 that 'as my sentiments are no longer agreable to a reform in Parliament I have to desire you would take the proper steps to erase my name from the Association'.[13] The Revd Thomas Zouch, a resident of Wycliffe, provides a

---

[8] Wyvill, *Political Papers*, iv. 236–43. See also O'Gorman, *Voters, Patrons, and Parties*, 304.

[9] YCA, Acc. 1663, M25.1–178.

[10] Barlow to the York Committee, Allerton, 11 Dec. 1779, YCA, Acc. 1663, M25.5; Rawdon to the York Committee, York, 13 Dec. 1779, YCA, Acc. 1663, M25.34; Waines to the York Committee, 14 Dec. 1779, YCA, Acc. 1663, M25.59.

[11] Harper to the York Committee, Heath, 18 Dec. 1779, YCA, Acc. 1663, M25.103.

[12] Weddell to the York Committee, Waddow, 12 Apr. 1784, YCA, Acc. 1663, M32.23. See also J. Mitchell to the York Committee, Thornhill, 26 Apr. 1784; Robert Lumb to the York Committee, Wakefield, 11 Mar. 1784; William Buck to the York Committee, Halifax, 5 May 1784; Thomas Willis and W. Gawthorp to the York Committee, Sedbergh, 22 Aug. 1784; A. Swainston to the York Committee, 2 Apr. 1784, all in YCA, Acc. 1663, M32.23.

[13] Osbaldeston to the York Committee, Welbeck Street, 12 Mar. 1785, YCA, Acc. 1663, M32.33. Cf. Osbaldeston to the York Committee, 21 Dec. 1779, YCA, Acc. 1663, M25.135.

good example of shifting attitudes. In December 1779, he had proclaimed that 'as an independent & uninfluenced man, I beg leave to intimate that I consider a county meeting to be highly necessary to this critical juncture of public distress. I shall be happy to contribute every thing within the sphere of my abilities to promote such measures as may tend to ward off the ruin with which this once great empire is now threatend'.[14] In 1786 he wrote requesting that 'his name be crossed out of the association book as he will pay no more of any expenses whatsoever'.[15] This trend of withdrawing from the Association was clearly a cause of some concern to the York Committee in these later years, and formed the subject of letters which appeared in both York papers in April 1784.[16]

The York Committee's correspondence reinforces the pattern of changing support found in the York newspapers and described in the previous chapter. Initial excitement concerning reform was intense, but eventually this turned to apathy. These changes are also borne out by other records and by local observers. In 1780, the signatories to the Yorkshire petition included some 8,000 names.[17] In January of that year, William Hall wrote from Scarborough to his employer, Sir Charles Hotham Thompson, that 'since you left Yorkshire, frugality has been dictated to the county in a most violent manner, and by great numbers who wear intire [*sic*] strangers to any such thing'.[18] In sharp contrast, four years later in 1784, Henry Zouch wrote to Fitzwilliam from Yorkshire, 'that spirit for a parliamentary reform which hath prevailed for the last three years seems to be very much abated in this country'.[19] In November, Francis Edmunds of Sheffield informed Samuel Shore that 'the people of the county are wearied with petitions'.[20] Christopher Wyvill was forced to agree in the following month when he informed Lord Stanhope that 'there is undoubtedly a general languor upon the subject in Yorkshire as well as in other parts of the Kingdom'.[21]

Not only did support for reform decline in Yorkshire as the decade progressed, but there is also evidence that at least one significant pocket of resistance had always existed in the county. Although opinion in York and

[14] T. Zouch to the York Committee, Wycliff, 19 Dec. 1779, YCA, Acc. 1663, M25.107.
[15] T. Zouch to the York Committee, [20 May 1786], YCA, Acc. 1663, M32.23.
[16] See, for example, *York Chronicle*, 16 Apr. 1784; *York Courant*, 20 Apr. 1784.
[17] York Central Reference Library, Y328.42.
[18] Hall to Thompson, Scarborough, 28 Jan. 1780, Brynmor Jones Library, Hotham Papers, DDHO/4/21.
[19] H. Zouch to Fitzwilliam, Sandal, 3 Jan. 1784, WWM, F34/30.
[20] Edmunds to Shore, 26 Nov. 1784, Sheffield City Archives, Worsbrough Muniments, WM220.
[21] Wyvill to Lord Stanhope, St. James's, 8 Dec. 1784, Bradford Archives, Spencer Stanhope MSS, Sp. St. 11/5/6/16.

throughout much of Yorkshire appears to have been supportive of the reform movement during the early 1780s, this was not the case in parts of the West Riding where local sentiment seems to have been decidedly mixed. When Edward Elmshall supplied Sir George Savile with a report of his visits to Wakefield and Halifax in April 1780, he was not optimistic about the Association's prospects there. Elmshall was told at Wakefield that 'about Pontefract & that country, they were generally averse to it', whilst at Halifax he was informed that 'a very considerable Majority' from the town was 'warmly agt. signing the association' and that 'at Leeds, Bradford and Huddersfield, & considerable towns all round these places, all were unanimously against the Association'.[22] However, the York re-formers also appear to have found many supporters in this area. William Walker, Obadiah Dawson, and Milnes Raynor were amongst over forty men from Leeds alone who wrote to the York Committee between December 1779 and January 1780 promising their support.[23] Writers from the West Riding more generally constituted a significant proportion of the Committee's correspondents during this period. Of course, as has been noted, the local papers for this part of the county, the *Leeds Mercury* and the *Leeds Intelligencer*, never showed the degree of unanimity towards reform that the two York papers did. Indeed whilst the *Mercury* always supported the cause, the rival *Intelligencer* appeared particularly hostile. As Gamaliel Lloyd noted to Francis Foljambe in 1784, the *Intelligencer* was 'very inimical' to the Association.[24] In Yorkshire then, newspaper politics appear to have reflected very closely the nature of local sentiment, so that whilst the York press largely catered for a politically homogeneous public, the Leeds papers served one which was politically divided.

In addition to the York Committee correspondence, an equally striking picture of the nature of Yorkshire opinion emerges from correspondence relating to Fitzwilliam's declining influence in the county, which was closely linked to popular feeling concerning Pitt and the Coalition. It has already been noted that both York newspapers assumed a Pittite stance between 1783 and 1784, directly opposing the desires of the Fitzwilliam camp. Again, this line appears to have been adopted in response to local opinion. In February 1784, the Revd Henry Wood wrote to his brother, Sir Francis Wood, from York,

[22] Elmshall to Savile, Thornhill, 1 May 1780, NRO, Papers of John Hewett, DDFJ 11/1/7/24.

[23] YCA, Acc. 1663, M25.

[24] Lloyd to Foljambe, [Nov.? 1784], Foljambe, DDFJ/11/1/7/163.

A meeting has been advertiz'd for the 25th for people to declare their political sentiments. . . . The majority I think will support the present ministers The meeting will occasion rancor and animosity, and tend to no good end. . . . I think that Lord Fitzwilliam will hurt his future consequence by interfering at this time Six parts out of seven of the county are in their hearts against the Opposition The populous parts especially, and he will run a risque of overturning his interest at York, should he thwart the inclinations of the many and powerful who are determined supporters of the present ministers. . . . Ld F[itzwilli]ams character is respected and may be of use to him, nay will be so, if he proceeds with caution at his setting out, but I do believe if he opposes the sense of the county at this time, he will lose the consequence he would otherwise have, nay will create an opposition to all his future views.[25]

Wood's unhappiness about the 'sense of the county' was repeated by many of the earl's correspondents. Stephen Croft warned Fitzwilliam that 'the cry against Mr Fox is most astonishing I see it strong in the light you state is that *the people* are really against themselves'.[26] Another correspondent echoed Croft's sentiments, and noted ruefully 'how blind ye people are now disposed to be to their true interest' so that 'many who were talking treason last year, are at this time ye K——'s dearest friends'.[27] Peregrine Wentworth wrote of a visit to York that

The York paper which I got yesterday morning informed me of the nonsense, and mischief that was carried forward in this town, which induced me to order my horses and to set [out] immediately to be satisfied. I am sorry to acquaint your Lordship, that I am far from being satisfied in the matter I could wish, as I see such I may almost say an universal propensity in the People to be very awkward and untoward. . . . I see such a determined set of people in the towns, in favor of Mr Pitt, that I cannot help being very much alarmed. . . . I have been informed since I came here of a requisition to the [High Sheriff] to call a county meeting [which] many have signed, & if such a meeting is called, from the temper of the People at present, I fear it would be attended with bad consequences, as they will certainly ask [for] an address, which (if possible) will make things worse.[28]

Fitzwilliam's request that individuals outside York relay news to him of the tenor of local opinion led to further disappointments. Sir William Mordaunt Milner informed the earl that although he was opposed to Pitt himself, and would attend the meeting at York to say so, 'I believe very many of my friends will be against me, their idea being supporting Mr Pitt

---

[25] Henry to Francis Wood, York, [Feb.?] 1784, Borthwick Institute of Historical Research, Hinckleton Papers, A2.2/2.

[26] Croft to Fitzwilliam, York, 6 Mar. 1784, WWM, F34/53.

[27] J. Fountayne to Fitzwilliam, York, 28 Feb. 1784, WWM, F34/45.

[28] Wentworth to Fitzwilliam, Wakefield, 11 Feb. 1784, WWM, F34/34.

is supporting the cause of our Association'.[29] From Wentworth, the Revd
Henry Hunter wrote that 'Since the receipt of your Lordship's letter, I
have conversed with most of the neighbouring Gentlemen upon the object
of the approaching county meeting. They are almost unanimous in approbation of the support given by the King to Mr Pitt. . . . Several of the
neighbours intend to be at York, most of whom, I fear, think differently
from your Lordship'.[30] George Osbaldeston reported that 'the contest at
Scarbro' is very warm . . . the popular opinion in favor of Pitt',[31] whilst
Henry Wood informed Fitzwilliam, via his brother, that the news from
Halifax was also unfavourable, adding that 'the same sentiments seem to
have been adopted by almost every consequential man I have met with
either in Leeds or Wakefield'.[32] After the election, and given hindsight,
the weight of popular opinion made the Coalition cause seem even more
hopeless. William Weddell, one of the Coalition candidates at York, confided to his wife that 'Our returns did not answer ye expectations of ye
Gentlemen & ye popular clamour is so great, & such a senseless noise of
Pitt & Fox, & King & I know not what,—that it has had a wonderful effect
amongst [the] lower people. Our time was not long enough to set them
right'.[33] Godfrey Wentworth wrote to Fitzwilliam that 'It is certainly
rather mortifying to have been defeated by Dr. Wyvil [*sic*] & his Associated', but concluded that 'considering the present infatuation of *all ranks*
of people, it was, as certainly most prudent not to persist in a losing
game'.[34]

Political battles in Yorkshire produced a level of contemporary correspondence about the nature of local public opinion which could not be
found elsewhere. However, some important evidence of other regional
sentiment does exist. For example, the Duke of Manchester informed
Rockingham in 1780 that a Cambridge reform meeting was so numerous
that 'it was impossible to assemble all the people' in one hall, and that the

[29] Milner to Fitzwilliam, [Crikhill?], 28 Feb. 1784, WWM, F34/46.
[30] Hunter to Fitzwilliam, Wentworth, 5 Mar. 1784, WWM, F34/52.
[31] Osbaldeston to Fitzwilliam, [Hutton Bushel?], 14 Mar. 1784, WWM, F34/75.
[32] Henry to Francis Wood, Hemsworth, 15 Mar. 1784, WWM, F34/77.
[33] William Weddell to his wife, Newby, 9 Apr. 1784, Leeds Record Office, Ramsden
Collection, 2c/50.
[34] Wentworth to Fitzwilliam, Hickleton, 14 Apr. 1784, WWM, F34/125. The Yorkshire
election also caused much activity in London, where rival election committees fought to
influence Yorkshire voters resident in the capital. Events in London did not differ much
from those in Yorkshire, and it appears that the Yorkshire Coalition candidates did not
receive the degree of support offered to those who backed Pitt: PRO, Chancery Masters
Exhibits, *Disney* v. *Wilkinson*, Papers of John Reynolds, C1/11/202. I am grateful to
Christopher Briggs for drawing these documents to my attention.

local MPs who spoke against reform were given a hostile hearing by a crowd universally in favour of petitioning.[35] This picture of Cambridge politics was certainly echoed in the *Cambridge Chronicle*, which showed itself consistently opposed to the North Administration and a keen supporter of reform. The same level of enthusiasm was not evident in the *Western Flying-Post*, produced in Sherborne. Although generally pro-reform, the paper showed little sustained interest in the issue. In September 1780, Anthony Chapman wrote to George Savile:

I am sorry to say I fear the spirit of Liberty & independance in our country is not yet sufficiently roused to adopt at present measures to procure those desirable ends, however, I propose [?] some of our principal gentry on the subject, as it would be the hight of impudence to make any attempt without being previously satisfied of their concurring for by the bye our county has always been noted for high principles, has not been stirred for near thirty years, & therefore sunk into such a torpid & inactive state that it was with great difficulty we prevailed on some of our gentlemen to join in calling a county meeting, & were obliged to hold out the most moderate measures to induce them to concur.[36]

In Kent, both the *Canterbury Journal* and the *Kentish Gazette* showed themselves to be consistent supporters of reform. In April 1780, a Mr Hill, supposedly writing on behalf of Lord Mahon, confirmed the levels of local support for reform which the newspapers indicated when he informed the York Committee that 'I have the *greatest* hopes of Kent. The Gentlemen, Clergy & Freeholders who have signed *our* petition in Kent are 3,120, besides copies not yet received. The counter-petition (or rather, the protest) is signed by only 1830 several of whom are, as I hear, not Freeholders; & a great many of them, who signed ours, & have wrote after their names, *having signed the counter-petition by mistake*'.[37]

The unique insight into local opinion provided by provincial newspapers forces us to reassess not only the regional pattern of support given to the reform movement, but also the way in which the campaign was popularly perceived. Unlike many twentieth-century historians, provincial newspapers did not depict reform activity as the preserve of an elite group of politicians. Although their involvement was certainly not ignored, far greater stress was placed upon the popular nature of the reform movement, suggesting the importance which the public themselves

[35] Manchester to Rockingham, Kimbolton Castle, [26 Mar. 1780], WWM, R1/1885.

[36] Chapman to Savile, [London?], 25 Feb. 1780, Gloucester Record Office, Papers of Granville Sharpe, D3549/13/1/C26.

[37] J. Hill [on behalf of Lord Mahon?] to the York Committee, London, 14 Apr. 1780, YCA, Acc. 1663, M25.263.

placed upon the actions and opinions of the wider political nation. This was true both for those papers hostile to the reformers, which denied that they either represented the people or had popular support, and those which backed reform, and legitimated the movement in terms of its utility and popularity. Indeed, despite the political diversity over reform apparent in the provincial press as a whole, much of the political language used and the beliefs which underpinned it were remarkably similar. Provincial newspapers of all political persuasions turned the spotlight upon the wider political nation and sought to legitimate their own political views by claiming them to be the 'sense of the people'.

In common with the reformist press in London, its provincial counterpart was quick to adopt an ideology of popular sovereignty which placed the impetus for reform with the people rather than with politicians. Initially however, much emphasis was placed in the provinces on the need for leadership from members of local elites. A Lincolnshire resident in favour of reform predicted that unless a county meeting was 'well headed by people of the first Rank and Property we small ones can do little, however salutary and reasonable these measures may be'.[38] In response to the York Committee's call to attend the county meeting, Samuel Beilby replied that '[I] do entirely approve of the proposed meeting: but, as I am a Freeholder of very little importance in the county, I apprehend that my personal attendance at York on the 30th will be unneccessary'.[39] In November 1779, Wyvill wrote to Sir George Savile that 'It is not proposed to publish the above advertisement unless the signatures of twenty gentlemen of character, & weight of properties in this county or more, should be obtained'.[40] Such sentiments were echoed in provincial newspapers. 'A Freeholder of Yorkshire', writing in the *York Chronicle* in December 1779, asserted that

We who are in lower stations naturally look up to our superiors for assistance, in times of public danger and distress. On this occasion, if gentlemen of rank and property would stand forth, and endeavour in a legal way to obtain some change in the present destructive measures, or some relief from the difficulties and distress which are now so severly felt in this country, they would certainly find themselves supported by the middling class of people to a great majority.[41]

---

[38] A. Bouchertt, Senr. to John Hewett, Willingham [Lincs.], 19 Feb. 1780, Foljambe, DDFJ/11/1/5/23–4.

[39] Beilby to the York Committee, Ferriby, nr Hull, 14 Dec. 1779, YCA, Acc. 1663, M25.43.

[40] Wyvill to Savile, 27 Nov. 1779, Foljambe, DDFG/11/1/7/4.

[41] *York Chronicle*, 3 Dec. 1779. See also the *Leeds Mercury*, 7 Dec. 1779.

An address to 'the freeholders of the county of Suffolk' from 'a Suffolk freeholder' which appeared in the *Ipswich Journal* on 5 February 1780 assured readers that 'it is not the want of inclination in many of large property and distinguished rank' which had prevented a county meeting being called, but that 'the earnest wish of the author of this address, is, that some gentlemen (however few in numbers) will propose a time and place of meeting'.

However, appeals for support in provincial newspapers rapidly changed tack, removing the focus from local elites, and favouring instead the activities of a broader public. 'An Old Englishman' in the *Bristol Gazette* claimed that 'The spirit that is diffusing itself through all the kingdom gives a hope, to every true lover of his country, of the revival of our ancient national virtue. Nothing short of the general exertion of the people can restrain all the craving, all devouring appetites, of the race of locusts, the idle unnecessary placemen, the worthless pensioners, and the unprincipled contractors'.[42] According to the *Glocester Journal*, 'nothing but the determined resolutions of the people, the temperate and firm decisions of Englishmen, united in one plan, and pressing to one point, can save them. Thus united, thus exerting themselves, no Prince however obstinate, no Parliament however venal, can oppose or resist them'.[43] With parliamentary corruption so rife, the *Bath Chronicle* was incredulous that 'the nation should have been *deceived* by the *arts* and *interests*' of MPs for so long, and noted that 'it is hoped the people at large will now begin to think, and judge, and act for themselves'.[44] The *York Courant* acknowledged the battles waged in Parliament concerning reform, but concluded that 'it is now in the power of the People to defeat the purposes of their Constitutional Enemies, if they will stand up firm in this hour of which they may truely call their own'.[45]

Appeals to 'the people' became increasingly common in 1780. After it became apparent that the government was ignoring the first round of county petitions, the *York Chronicle* commented that 'what the people at large will do, is not so certain, the matter now lies upon them'.[46] The *Leeds Mercury* praised the county meetings because they 'raised a spirit in the people at large highly laudable and becoming at this perilous situation of public affairs',[47] and later noted that 'it is yet some comfort that history affords no example in which the people, when under oppression, did not

---

[42] *Bristol Gazette*, 3 Feb. 1780.
[44] *Bath Chronicle*, 6 Jan. 1780.
[46] *York Chronicle*, 25 Feb. 1780.
[47] *Leeds Mercury*, 1 Feb. 1780.
[43] *Glocester Journal*, 7 Feb. 1780.
[45] *York Courant*, 12 Sept. 1780.

at length stand forth in their own cause, and in which the cause of the people did not therefore ultimately triumph'.[48] By 1783, Wyvill was also appealing over the heads of the local elites. He arranged for a paragraph to be published in the newspapers which stated, 'If a substantial reformation of parliament should be obtained, it will be chiefly owing to the virtuous exertions of the people; fortunately, genuine patriotism, or a disinterested zeal for the public welfare is a virtue more frequently to be found, we believe, in the middle classes of men than in the highest'.[49]

But despite the appeals to popular sovereignty, reformist newspapers in the provinces did not display the same radical commitment of those in London. Radical arguments did appear: in the *Cambridge Chronicle* on 15 April 1780 for example, 'Alfred' described the rights of Englishmen's Anglo-Saxon ancestors, and posed a series of rhetorical questions to readers, including asking whether all taxpayers should not be able to vote, and if annual parliaments were not preferable to septennial.[50] However, such ideas were expressed infrequently in provincial newspapers. When a correspondent in the *Western Flying-Post* suggested that parliamentary reform, by combating corruption, would be 'one great step towards recovering from destruction the almost expiring liberties of Britons',[51] he was referring to rights established by the Revolution Settlement, rather than those which supposedly pre-dated the Norman Conquest. The Country ideology which influenced the press in London, in combination with more radical ideas, appeared in a less diluted form in provincial newspapers. A more moderate approach to constitutional reform is evident in the widespread support given to the Yorkshire reformers' platform, which advocated far less sweeping changes than did radical reformers in the capital. Indeed, early on in the reform movement's life, Wyvill had written of his hope that 'there is still sufficient vigour & public spirit left in this kingdom, *to form a country party, able to cope with the Crown, & save the constitution*'.[52] In keeping with the more moderate ideas of Wyvill and his followers, the *Kentish Gazette* concluded in March 1780 that Wyvill's proposals for more equal representation, abolishing rotten boroughs, and adding one hundred knights of the shire to Parliament would 'fully secure the independence of parliament, and strike at the very root of corruption'.[53]

[48] *Leeds Mercury*, 13 Mar. 1781.
[49] Wyvill to William Gray, YCA, Acc. 1663, M25.479, enclosed in a letter dated 21 Mar. 1783, YCA, Acc. 1663, M25.478.
[50] The same letter appeared in the *Ipswich Journal* of 17 Mar. 1780.
[51] *Western Flying-Post*, 14 Feb. 1780.
[52] Wyvill to George Savile, Burton Hall, 18 Dec. 1779, Foljambe, DDFJ/11/1/7/6.
[53] *Kentish Gazette*, 22 Mar. 1780.

The attitude of the reformist press in the provinces towards 'high' politics was also very different to that of their London counterparts, despite their shared emphasis on popular sovereignty. There was a good deal of hostility shown by provincial newspapers towards attempts by parliamentarians to involve themselves in local reform activity, but this was not usually apparent where national politics were concerned. Certainly, provincial newspapers did not display the type of generalized cynicism toward politicians' motives found in the capital. Only non-allegiance to 'party' politics at local level was seen as particularly important. 'A Freeholder', who wrote in the *Kentish Gazette*, was keen to stress that factional politics should have nothing to do with the county meeting at Maidstone: 'Whig and Tory, High-Church and Low-Church may in this instance join in one *last pull* for their country'.[54] This attitude was repeated elsewhere.[55] The *Bath Chronicle* of 3 February 1780 noted that 'Protests from the counties of Hertford, Huntingdon, Sussex and Surry' were due to the fact that 'the spirit of party blazes high in several counties'.[56] However, despite the professed dislike of party at local level, national politics were seen as something different, and perhaps more distant, so that papers such as the *Bath Chronicle* described the reform effort as one which 'honest Whigs in parliament' would properly promote as 'the friends of the people'.[57]

Concern that the stability of the country was under threat led those provincial newspapers opposed to reform to appeal to the public to defend the nation's peace. The *Chelmsford Chronicle* of 21 January 1780, whilst admitting the need for lower public spending, was nervous about the results of the county meetings:

it is to be hoped the good sense, sound patriotism, and judgement of the yeomanry of the people of England, will direct them properly, in the present almost general call for county-meetings; if faction and party once lead them into error on these public occasions, they may too late repent the situation of this happy country, and remember, with remorse and horror, how such practices led the nation into the calamities of civil war, a little more than a century ago, and even in our own times to rebellion in America.

Other papers contained much more explicit claims that the reformers would destroy the constitution as well as threatening disorder.[58] Both the

---

[54] Ibid. 19 Jan. 1780.   [55] See *Chelmsford Chronicle*, 21 Jan. 1780.
[56] See also *Bath Journal*, 14 Feb. 1780.
[57] *Bath Chronicle*, 8 Mar. 1781. See also *Cambridge Chronicle*, 10 Mar. 1780 and 23 Nov. 1782; *Sussex Weekly Advertiser*, 10 Apr. 1780.
[58] *Hereford Journal*, 30 Mar. 1780; *Jackson's Oxford Journal*, 5 Feb. 1780; *Felix Farley's Bristol Journal*, 29 Jan. 1780; *Glocester Journal*, 31 Jan. 1780.

Leeds Intelligencer and the *Newcastle Courant* published a paragraph which stated that

Appeals to the people from their representatives in parliament have always been accounted dangerous . . . Such a proceeding must always imply, that the people and their representatives have different interests; or, in other words, that the former have only delegated but a part of their power to the latter. But this is an idea entirely subversive of the principles of the constitution, and would, if well founded, be productive of the greatest confusion and mischief, by rendering the most deliberate and solemn decisions of the senate precarious and uncertain . . .[59]

Like many London papers, provincial newspapers which were hostile to reform asserted that the movement was the result of an Opposition plot and factional intrigue.[60] As the *Newcastle Courant* put it, the reform movement stemmed from 'dangerous and selfish views'.[61] The *Leeds Intelligencer* reported that much of the attendance at a county meeting at Carlisle 'may be attributed to the letters and solicitations of some persons of high rank, and in avowed opposition to the present Administration', and that the Yorkshire movement was the result of 'the attempts of the Opposition to raise dissentions, and perhaps insurrections, in the kingdom'.[62] In such dangerous circumstances, it was hoped that the good sense of the public would save the day. A writer styling himself 'A Freeholder of the County of Northumberland' wrote a letter to the *Newcastle Courant* in which he voiced his hope that the county's freeholders would be able to resist 'the wanton and tyrannical attempts of a posse of factious men'.[63] The *Leicester and Nottingham Journal* prayed that 'the good sense, sound patriotism, and judgement of the yeomanry of the people of England' would prevent them from becoming involved in county meetings infected by faction and party.[64]

In common with the London press, then, provincial newspapers on either side of the reform debate placed great emphasis on the role of the people and of public opinion in current political debates. As the *Newcastle Courant* of 29 January 1780 argued, politicians could not 'go on a safer and more constitutional bottom, than to defend and enforce the opinions of

---

[59] *Newcastle Courant*, 29 Jan. 1780; *Leeds Intelligencer*, 1 Feb. 1780.
[60] See, for example, *Leeds Intelligencer*, 25 Jan. 1780, 17 Apr. 1781; *Newcastle Courant*, 4 Mar. and 1 Apr. 1780; *Glocester Journal*, 3 Apr. 1780; *Leicester Journal*, 22 Jan. 1780; *Reading Mercury*, 21 Feb. 1780.
[61] *Newcastle Courant*, 29 Jan. 1780.
[62] *Leeds Intelligencer*, 8 Feb. 1780.
[63] *Newcastle Courant*, 4 Mar. 1780.
[64] *Leicester and Nottingham Journal*, 22 Jan. 1780.

the public at large'.[65] Indeed, it was this thinking which lay behind the anti-reform press's tendency to blame reform agitation on politicians and thus deny its popular basis.[66] However, faced with the question of who 'the people' were, the provincial press differed significantly from its London counterpart. For provincial newspapers of whatever political persuasion there was no ambiguity about the relationship between individual rights and property ownership. For them, the identity of the people was based, to a large degree, firmly and explicitly upon wealth and proprietorship. This was, of course, in marked contrast to the views of the London radicals, and provided a much narrower definition of the wider political nation even than that given by the anti-reformist press in the capital. In February 1780, the *Bath Journal* published a paragraph which listed the counties petitioning Parliament for economic reform, or intending to do so, and commented that

These thirty six counties pay upwards of 7 8ths of the land tax, and possess more property ten times over than the other silent counties, and one hundred times more than all the other Protestors in England. If the sentiments of such a decisive majority may not be deemed the voice of the People, but the clamour of a mob, it would be worth the Minister's while to define what he really means by the *voice of the people*.[67]

Such statements, which conferred political rights by virtue of property ownership and material contribution to the state, were constantly reiterated by the rest of the provincial press. An advertisement placed in the *Northampton Mercury* which publicized the Hertfordshire meeting was addressed to 'the nobility, gentry, clergy, freeholders, land-owners, landholders, and every description of men of the county of Northampton, paying taxes for the support of government'.[68] A letter to the printer of the *York Chronicle* on 10 December 1779 suggested that simply by gathering the county's freeholders together, one would be able to ascertain 'the general sense of the people'. A paragraph in the *Northampton Mercury* on 17 January 1783 advised that those who were not freeholders, and therefore unable to support the petition 'with his hand', should do so simply 'with his heart'.

---

[65] See also *Reading Mercury*, 31 Jan. 1780.

[66] *Leeds Intelligencer*, 18 Jan., 1 and 8 Feb. 1780; *Glocester Journal*, 21 Feb. 1780; *Northampton Mercury*, 7 Feb. 1780.

[67] *Bath Journal*, 28 Feb. 1780. This paragraph also appeared in the *Leeds Mercury* on 29 Feb. 1780, and in the *York Chronicle* on 3 Mar. 1780. It has been traced to the London paper, the *Gazetteer*, 2 Feb. 1780, where it was probably first printed.

[68] *Northampton Mercury*, 24 Jan. 1780.

This focus on social status was also evident in a description of Christopher Wyvill which appeared in 1779, when he was largely unknown outside Yorkshire. The portrait of Wyvill which appeared in papers in Bath and Canterbury noted that 'the Rev. Mr. Wyvil [*sic*] from Yorkshire' was 'a gentleman of ancient family, and large estate, and who first, without any party views, suggested the Yorkshire meeting'.[69] Another paragraph in the *Hereford Journal* commented that 'the Rev. Christopher Wyvil [*sic*], who is now at the head of the County Associations, and who formerly distinguished himself at the Feathers-Tavern, is a near relation of the late Sir Marmaduke Wyvil, whose sister he married, and with her he has got a fine estate at Constable Burton in Yorkshire, of about 4,000 l. per annum'.[70] Other members of the York Committee were also championed on a similar basis. A paragraph defending the pedigree of the York petitioners, which the *Bristol Gazette* took from the *London Courant*, was also printed by other provincial papers. In response to attacks in the capital's ministerial press, it was claimed that 'Notwithstanding what has been advanced, by some ministerial hirelings, that the meeting at York consisted of low, indifferent people, the fact is, that the committee there appointed, and the persons there thanked, are proprietors of more landed property in this country, than all the other members of the House of Commons put together'.[71]

In common with the advertisements calling county meetings, which usually asked 'nobility, gentlemen and clergy' to attend, many of the letters which appeared in newspapers on the subject of reform were particularly addressed to, or purported to be from, individuals in certain social groups. In this context, 'gentleman', 'tax-payer', and 'freeholder' were the most frequently used, with 'freeholder' being by far the most common.[72] Although all denoted a degree of wealth, such modes of address were deliberately vague, and were not used in order to define an audience with any degree of rigour. In the case of freeholders, their

[69] *Bath Chronicle*, 23 Mar. 1780, and *Canterbury Journal*, 21 Mar. 1780.

[70] *Hereford Journal*, 30 Mar. 1780.

[71] *Bristol Gazette*, 13 Jan. 1780. The paragraph had originally appeared in the *London Courant*, 8 Jan. 1780, and was also printed in the *York Chronicle* of 14 Jan., the *Cambridge Chronicle* of 15 Jan., and the *Leeds Mercury* of 18 Jan.

[72] For example, see letters in: *Ipswich Journal*, 5 and 12 Feb. 1780; *Leeds Mercury*, 7 Dec. 1779, 18 Jan. 1780, 31 Dec. 1782; *Newcastle Courant*, 4 Mar. 1781, 24 Mar. 1782; *Glocester Journal*, 18 Jan. and 7 Feb. 1780; *York Chronicle*, 7 and 14 Jan. 1780, 12 and 17 Mar. 1780, 3 Jan. 1783; *Bristol Gazette*, 3 and 17 Feb. 1780; *Reading Mercury*, 31 Jan. 1780; *Western Flying-Post*, 8 and 15 Mar. and 5 Apr. 1784; *York Courant*, 7 Dec. 1779; *Bath Chronicle*, 10 Feb. 1780; *Kentish Gazette*, 12, 22, and 26 Jan., 9 and 16 Feb., and 1 Mar. 1780.

numbers in a county could be huge, since the property qualification was low. Many such men would not have been viewed by those of more superior social standing in their community as particularly respectable, and certainly not as gentlemen. However, freeholders were important in terms of local politics, not least because they could vote, and also, crucially in ideological terms, because they were property owners.

The popular basis of the reform movement was something which reform activists were eager to prove, and although the definition of 'popular' did not embrace the population as a whole, it did encompass all freeholders. In January 1780, Wyvill wrote to Sir George Savile about the necessity of getting as many freeholders as possible to sign the petition: 'if after having applyed to the Freeholders, we present our petition without having obtained a majority of them, it may be said by our adversaries, that notwithstanding the numerous & very respectable meeting on the 30th of December, the measure then adopted was not agreeable to the general sense of the County; the major part of the electors having declined to sign the petition'.[73] J. Stovin had written to the York Committee expressing similar sentiments: 'I apprehend', he said, that 'numbers are absolutely necessary to give due weight to the petition'.[74] In the following month, Stephen Croft wrote to Rockingham about the number of signatures obtained, and stated that 'no Roman Catholicks but one & no marks upwards of 8,500 must be thot. respectable & a majority of the county'.[75] Freeholders were actively encouraged to support the reform cause. A writer to the *Ipswich Journal* who discussed a forthcoming meeting at Stowmarket wrote of his hope that 'every freeholder of this county, who has any regard for his money, and has courage or opportunity to defend his privileges, will exert himself upon this occasion with that coolness and firmness, which becomes Englishmen'.[76] Similarly, the *York Chronicle* urged freeholders to 'come forward to your own rescue', since 'your liberty, your property, your all is at stake'.[77]

In addition to the importance of freeholders as property owners and voters, 'freeholder' was used as a rhetorical tool to conjure up images of the ancient constitution in which landed property determined power and

---

[73] Wyvill to Savile, Burton Hall, 17 Jan. 1780, Foljambe, DDFJ/11/1/7/10.

[74] Stovin to the York Committee, Whitgift Hall, nr Thorne, 20 Jan. 1780, YCA, Acc. 1663, M25.206.

[75] Croft to Rockingham, York, 6 Feb. 1780, WWM, R140/58.

[76] *Ipswich Journal*, 4 Mar. 1780.

[77] *York Chronicle*, 19 Mar. 1784.

freeholders possessed a 'legendary integrity'.[78] Despite the importance
that property ownership was thought to have in conferring political rights
and in distinguishing 'the people' and the 'sense of the county', it is clear
that other characteristics were also perceived to be important. The constant refrain of reformers and anti-reformers alike was that support
needed to be 'respectable'. *Aris's Birmingham Gazette*, like most other
reformist provincial papers, was at pains to assure readers that county
meetings were 'very respectable'.[79] In a typical description, the *Northampton Mercury* portrayed a meeting in Winchester as 'the most respectable
and numerous known in Hampshire for many years'.[80] The stress placed
by newspapers on respectability was also shown by political activists. In
December 1779, Rockingham wrote to Stephen Croft in York and noted,
'I think it very important that the meeting should be very numerous and
very respectable'.[81] Croft replied the following week that 'you have
Blanchards paper wch is dated for tomorrow in which you will see what I
hope you will esteem a very *numerous* & very *respectable* list of indept
gentlemen'.[82]

In part, to be respectable meant to be propertied, but this was not the
full meaning of the term: thus Wyvill was concerned to get support from
gentlemen of both 'respectable character, & weight of property'.[83] Respectability also conveyed a moral meaning, linked to one's ability to act in
the public interest. Hence Miles Smith's letter to the York Committee in
which he wrote that 'I think it my duty to attend a meeting promoted by
so respectable a body of Freeholders; and wish the result to it may prove
a real service to the public good'.[84] Political independence was deemed an
important part of respectable behaviour, and as Frank O'Gorman has
noted, eighteenth-century voters 'revelled in the rhetoric of popular independence, perceiving themselves as independent agents with powers of
judgement and a conscience'.[85] So, for example, the *York Chronicle* championed those Yorkshire gentlemen who supported reform as 'honest and
independent men'.[86] A letter from 'Cato' in the *Newcastle Chronicle*

---

[78] Langford, *Public Life and the Propertied Englishman*, 272.
[79] See, for example, *Aris's Birmingham Gazette*, 10 Jan. 1780.
[80] *Hereford Journal*, 13 Jan. 1780. See also *Sussex Weekly Advertiser*, 17 and 24 Jan. 1780;
Jackson's Oxford Journal, 22 Jan. 1780.
[81] Rockingham to Croft, 12 Dec. 1779, WWM, R1/1869.
[82] Croft to Rockingham, York, 16 Dec. 1779, WWM, R136/11.
[83] Wyvill to Rockingham, Burton Hall, 26 Nov. 1779, WWM, R140/27.
[84] Smith to the York Committee, Sunderlandwick, 12 Dec. 1779, YCA, Acc. 1663,
M25.18.
[85] O'Gorman, *Voters, Patrons, and Parties*, 245.   [86] *York Chronicle*, 29 Dec. 1780.

proudly asserted that he would sign the local petition along with 'the free, independent, unplaced, unpensioned, uninfluenced landlords of the county'.[87] When Samuel Shore wrote to William Bagshaw from Wakefield in 1782, he noted that

There was a full and respectable appearance at York on the fourth.—About sixty gentlemen attended and I was much pleased to see the usual spirit of independence pervaded the meeting. The resolutions were unanimously passed after being fully and properly discussed . . . I only here give you a faint idea of the substance of the resolutions, and hope such a temperate and steady line of conduct will be generally approved of. It will at least shew that we are no party men and that we adhere firmly to our principles whoever may be in power.[88]

Political independence and the ability to act in the public good were virtues which were made easier by the ownership of property, since a degree of wealth was thought to allow individuals to act unhindered by other political and social obligations. The 'respectability' which such behaviour conferred was portrayed by the press as a prerequisite to taking one's legitimate place in the public arena of political action, as one of 'the people'.

By examining both correspondence and newspaper contents from the 1780s, this chapter has tested the theory that the politics of provincial newspapers reflected local public opinion. It has also demonstrated the great diversity of regional opinion in relation to reform, and has indicated levels of popular support for the campaign which other historians appear to have overlooked. Moreover, it has emerged that despite political differences, provincial newspapers shared a common set of beliefs about not only the importance of public opinion and 'the people' in the nation's political affairs, but also who 'the people' were. It is clear that the public was portrayed as a much narrower constituency by the provincial press than by papers in the capital. Although newspapers in both London and the provinces championed 'the people' and the role of public opinion, the press clearly defined these terms in different ways. Indeed, there is a strong sense that the manner in which newspapers described the public owed much to an identification of their readership. In London, this was particularly large and socially diverse, whilst in the provinces, readers appear to have been relatively less numerous and represented a more limited section of society. The implication of this in terms of the relationship between newspapers and public opinion in late eighteenth-century

---

[87] *Newcastle Chronicle*, 12 Feb. 1780.
[88] Shore to Bagshaw, Wakefield, 6 Apr. 1782, Sheffield City Archives, Oakes Deeds.

England is not just that the press reflected popular sentiment according to its perception of who 'the public' was, but that newspapers also acted in some way to construct the identity of the public themselves, through their varying definitions of 'the people'.

CONCLUSION

For many contemporaries in late eighteenth-century England, the influence which the press exerted over politics and public opinion was a blessing which both prevented politicians from misusing their power and gave the people a voice. Others felt that newspapers had a more sinister character, capable of misleading the public and creating unrest and dissent. Commentators' views may have diverged sharply on such issues, but most eighteenth-century Englishmen and women were united in their belief that the press held a particularly powerful position in society. This is something which historians have certainly not ignored, but a failure to understand the processes by which newspaper politics were fashioned has led them to portray newspapers as either propaganda sheets or randomly constructed and characterless publications. By stressing the commercial concerns of newspaper editors and proprietors, and by exploring the links between newspapers and their readers, this book has challenged the existing historiography of the press, and emphasized the role of public opinion in determining newspaper contents. In doing so, it both rehabilitates the reputation of eighteenth-century English newspapers and sheds new light on an historical source which is increasingly used by those engaged in research into popular politics and the role of 'the public' in Hanoverian England.

Of course, such interests are not unique to British historians. In recent years, the emergence of a public sphere and the influence of public opinion have become the subjects of much debate amongst historians of eighteenth-century continental Europe. The work of Jürgen Habermas on the development of a 'bourgeois public sphere' has provided many with a theoretical basis from which to explore the political culture of the *ancien régime*. For Habermas, the political public sphere was part of a specific stage in early capitalist commercial relations. It was directly linked to the growth of a self-conscious bourgeoisie and the emergence of a 'reasoning public' which could be critical of administration and sought to influence public power. The formation of this new public was dependent upon new networks of communications, not just because factors like a press and a reading public ensured the exchange of information and ideas, but in the larger sense of a new institutional context for political action. Habermas argues, therefore, that the political public sphere issued directly from the public literary sphere based in salons, coffee-houses, and periodical literature.[1]

One can identify social developments which appear to fit into Habermas's model in most countries in eighteenth-century Europe, but historians should be wary of accepting his vision of the emergence of the public sphere as a generalized European concept. Having revised the accepted view of the press in late eighteenth-century England and examined its role and influence in English society, it is apparent that the nature of the newspaper press here, and of the 'public sphere' in general, make many of Habermas's assertions concerning pan-European developments appear shaky. This becomes evident when one compares the situation in England with that depicted by recent historical work on France. In the new 'cultural history' of the French Revolution, where the emergence of the public sphere is linked to the collapse of *ancien régime* society, the character of the public and of public opinion are described in ways which make them appear starkly different to their English counterparts.[2]

Associated with such differences are the disparities between the print culture of each country. In the case of newspapers, the press in pre-Revolutionary France was dwarfed by comparison with that of England. Even if we take into account the French-language papers distributed in France but printed abroad, the number of newspapers available to the French people and the size of the newspaper-reading public in that country was far smaller than was the case across the Channel.[3] The implication for the nature of the public in both countries is significant. The picture of the salon-based social elite which emerges in the French case contrasts forcibly with the far more socially diverse and numerically large body found in England. There is also an obvious difference in the content of the periodical literature of each country which supposedly encouraged the politicization of the public sphere. It appears that before the Revolution at least, French newspapers were devoted almost entirely to reporting events 'without bias'. Even those papers published outside France, and thus

---

[1] Jürgen Habermas, *The Structural Transformation of the Public Sphere*, trans. Thomas Burger (Cambridge, Mass., 1989). See also Geoff Eley, 'Re-thinking the Political: Social History and Political Culture in 18th and 19th Century Britain', *Archiv für Sozialgeschichte*, 21 (1981), 427–57.

[2] Jack R. Censer and Jeremy D. Popkin (eds.), *Press and Politics in Pre-Revolutionary France* (Berkeley, 1987); Robert Darnton and Daniel Roche (eds.), *The Revolution in Print: The Press in France, 1775–1800* (Berkeley, 1989).

[3] *Ancien régime* France had only one daily newspaper, whilst Popkin asserts that 'the diverse and colourful array of newspapers created by revolutionary journalists and publishers never became a genuine mass medium': Jeremy D. Popkin, 'Journals: The Face of the News', in Darnton and Roche, *The Revolution in Print*, 141–64, p. 141.

beyond the reach of its strict censorship laws, seem to have avoided assuming a political stance, let alone presuming to represent the views of its readers and of public opinion.[4] It has been argued that even as the political culture of *ancien régime* France was transformed by increasingly intense political battles, there was considerable hostility towards any inclination to follow the perceived English example of politics, with its open disputes and factional divisions. Under such circumstances, public opinion seems to have been conceived of in France with a primarily social meaning, as a collective judgement in matters of morality, reputation, and taste, within an idealized vision of a progressive politics of rational consensus, grounded in enlightened public opinion.[5]

This attempt to 'depoliticize' public opinion appears in stark contrast with the situation in England, where the press defined public opinion largely and overtly in political terms. The situation in France certainly changed after 1789, but even then there is a sense that the French press, lacking a tradition of the kind of links that had been forged between English newspapers and their readers, still held a very different position in political life than was the case in England. It was for this reason that foreign visitors were constantly struck by the novel character of the newspaper press in England. Although (in common with many English observers) they might not have approved of its predilection for scandal and its disrespectful attitude towards those in positions of authority, they could not help but notice how much freer the press was, and how its liberty and influence gave it a prominence in English society to which they were clearly unaccustomed.[6]

[4] Jeremy D. Popkin, 'The *Gazette de Leyde* and French Politics under Louis XVI', in Censer and Popkin, *Press and Politics in Pre-Revolutionary France*, 75–132, and *News and Politics in the Age of Revolution: Jean Luzac's Gazette de Leyde* (Berkeley, 1989).

[5] Keith Michael Baker, 'Politics and Public Opinion under the Old Regime', in Censer and Popkin, *Press and Politics in Pre-Revolutionary France*, 204–46, and *Inventing the French Revolution* (Cambridge, 1990). See also Mona Ozouf, 'L'Opinion publique', in Keith Michael Baker (ed.), *The Political Culture of the Old Regime* (Oxford, 1987), 419–34; François Furet, *Interpreting the French Revolution*, trans. Elborg Forster (Cambridge, 1981); Daniel Gordon, 'Philosophy, Sociology, and Gender in the Enlightenment Conception of Public Opinion', *French Historical Studies*, 17 (1992), 882–911; Dena Goodman, 'Public Sphere and Private Life: Toward a Synthesis of Current Historiographical Approaches to the Old Regime', *History and Theory*, 31 (1992), 1–20.

[6] See, for example, Lolme, *The Constitution of England*; Goede, *The Stranger in England*; Archenholz, *A Picture of England*.

BIBLIOGRAPHY

MANUSCRIPT SOURCES

Borthwick Institute of Historical Research, York
  Hinkleton Papers, A2.2/2
Bradford Record Office, Bradford
  Spencer Stanhope Papers, Sp. St. 11
British Library, London
  European Magazine Minutes, Add. MS 38728
  Hardwicke Papers, Add. MS 35594
  Henry Sampson Woodfall Papers, Add. MS 27780
  John Almon Papers, Add. MS 20733
  Liverpool Papers, Add. MS 38212
  London Packet Minutes, Add. MSS 38728-9
  Public Advertiser Accounts, Add. MS 38169
  Whitefoord Papers, Add. MSS 36593-5
British Museum, London
  Department of Prints and Drawings, Cartoons and Political Satires
Brynmor Jones Library, Kingston upon Hull
  Hotham Papers, DDHO/4
Castle Howard Archives, Castle Howard, Yorkshire
  Frederick Howard, 5th Earl of Carlisle Papers, J14/1
  George Selwyn Papers
Centre for Kentish Studies, Maidstone
  Pratt MS, C173
Essex Record Office, Chelmsford
  Chelmsford Chronicle Minute Book, Acc. 5197, D/F 66/1
  Sir Robert Smyth Papers, D/DFg/Z1
Gloucester Record Office, Gloucester
  Gloucester Committee Proceedings, D1356
  Granville Sharp Papers, D3549/13/1
Hampshire Record Office, Winchester
  Banbury/Knollys Papers, IM44/67
Humberside County Record Office, Beverley
  Grimston Papers, DDGR 42/29
Leeds Record Office, Leeds
  Harewood Papers
  Ramsden Collection
Lincolnshire Archive Office, Lincoln
  Diary of Matthew Flinders

North Yorkshire Record Office, Northallerton
   Scrope Papers, ZPT/5
   Wyvill Papers, ZFW/7/2
Nottinghamshire Record Office, Nottingham
   Foljambe of Osberton MS, DDFJ/11/1
Public Record Office, London
   Audit Office, General Account of Stamp Duties, AO3/949–80
   Chatham Papers, 30/8, 145/2
   Lawsuits:
      Disney v. *Wilkinson*, John Reynold Papers, C. 1/11/202
      Vint v. *Watkins*, Books and Correspondence of the *Gazetteer*, C. 104/67–8
      Wilkes v. *Collins*, Exhibits: *Hampshire Chronicle* Account Book, E. 140/90–1
   Wills:
      Alexander Chalmers, PROB. 11/676
      William Parker, PROB. 11/567
      James Perry, PROB. 11/683
      Henry Sampson Woodfall, PROB. 11/879
      William Woodfall, PROB. 11/744
Sheffield City Archives, Sheffield
   Oakes Deeds
   Wentworth Woodhouse Muniments, Burke Papers, BK. 1/1557
   Wentworth Woodhouse Muniments, Fitzwilliam Papers, F. 34–5
   Wentworth Woodhouse Muniments, Rockingham Papers, R. 1, R. 136–59
   Worsbrough Papers, WM 200–21
Shropshire Records and Research Unit, Shrewsbury
   Salopian Journal, Article of Agreement, D. 2713
   Salopian Journal, Minutes and Accounts, MS 1923
York Central Reference Library, York
   Lists of Petitioners, Y324.42 and Y328.42
York City Archives, York
   Dr. White's Diary, Acc. 163
   York Association Papers, Acc. 1663, M/25, M/32, M/83, and M/90

PRINTED SOURCES

Newspapers and periodicals

Aris's Birmingham Gazette
Bath Chronicle
Bath Journal
Berrow's Worcester Journal
Bristol Gazette, and Public Advertiser
British Chronicle or, Pugh's Hereford Journal
Bury Post, and Universal Advertiser

Cambridge Chronicle and Journal
Canterbury Journal
Chelmsford Chronicle
Creswell and Burbage's Nottingham Journal
Cumberland Paquet
Drewry's Derby Mercury
European Magazine
Felix Farley's Bristol Journal
Gazetteer
General Advertiser
General Evening Post
Gentleman's Magazine
Glocester Journal
Hampshire Chronicle
Harrison's Derby and Nottingham Journal, or, Midland Advertiser
Ipswich Journal
Jackson's Oxford Journal
Jopson's Coventry Mercury
Kentish Gazette
Kentish Weekly Post
Leeds Intelligencer
Leeds Mercury
Leicester and Nottingham Journal
Lloyd's Evening Post
London Courant
London Evening Post
Maidstone Journal and Kentish Advertiser
Monthly Miscellany
Morning Chronicle
Morning Herald
Morning Post
Newcastle Chronicle
Newcastle Courant
Northampton Mercury
Public Advertiser
Reading Mercury, and Oxford Gazette
Shrewsbury Chronicle
St. James's Chronicle
Sussex Weekly Advertiser: or, Lewes Journal
Town and Country Magazine
Western Flying-Post; or, Sherborne and Yeovil Mercury and General Advertiser
Whitehall Evening Post
York Chronicle
York Courant

Other primary printed sources

[ALMON, JOHN], *A Letter to the Right Honourable George Grenville in Defence of J. Wilkes* (London, 1763).

——*A Letter to the Right Honourable Charles Jenkinson* (London, 1781).

——*An Address to the Interior Cabinet* (London, 1782).

—— *The Revolution in MDCCLXXXII Impartially Considered* (London, 1782).

——*Memoirs of a Late Eminent Bookseller* (London, 1790).

—— *Biographical, Literary, and Political Anecdotes, of Several of the Most Eminent Persons of the Present Age* (London, 1797).

ARCHENHOLZ, JOHANN WILHELM VON, *A Picture of England* (Dublin, 1791).

BENJAFIELD, JOHN, *Statement of Facts* (Bury St Edmunds, [1813]).

BOND, DONALD F. (ed.), *The Spectator*, 5 vols. (Oxford, 1965).

BOYD, HUGH, *The Miscellaneous Works of Hugh Boyd, the Author of the Letters of Junius*, ed. Lawrence Dundas Campbell, 2 vols. (London, 1800).

BURKE, EDMUND, *The Works of the Right Honourable Edmund Burke*, 8 vols. (London, 1854–71).

—— *The Correspondence of Edmund Burke*, ed. T. W. Copeland *et al.*, 10 vols. (Cambridge, 1958–78).

—— *The Writings and Speeches of Edmund Burke*. Vol. II: *Party, Parliament, and the American Crisis, 1766–1774*, ed. Paul Langford (Oxford, 1981).

CARTWRIGHT, JOHN (ed.), *The Life and Correspondence of Major Cartwright*, ed. F. D. Cartwright, 2 vols. (London, 1826).

COTTON, HENRY, *Fasti Ecclesiæ Hibernicæ*, 4 vols. (Dublin, 1845–50).

The Correspondence of King George the Third, ed. Sir John Fortescue, 6 vols. (London, 1927–8).

The Later Correspondence of George III, ed. A. Aspinall, 5 vols. (Cambridge, 1962).

GOEDE, CHRISTIAN AUGUST GOTTLIEB, *The Stranger in England: or, Travels in Great Britain*, 3 vols. (London, 1807).

GOODRICKE, HENRY, *Observations on Dr. Price's Theory and Principles of Civil Liberty and Government, Preceded By a Letter . . . On the Pretensions of the American Colonies in Respect of Right and Equity* (York, 1776).

HARTLEY, DAVID, *An Address to the Committee of the County of York, on the State of Public Affairs*, 2nd edn. (London, 1781).

Historical Manuscripts Commission, *The Manuscripts of J. B. Fortescue, Esq, Preserved at Dropmore*, 9 vols. (London, 1892).

—— *Report on the Manuscripts of the Marquess of Lothian Preserved at Blickling Hall, Norfolk* (London, 1905).

Irish Manuscripts Commission, *Correspondence of Emily, Duchess of Leinster*, ed. Brian Fitzgerald, 3 vols. (Dublin, 1953).

JACKSON, WILLIAM, *A Collection of the Constitutions of the Thirteen United States of North America* (London, 1783).

—— *Thoughts on the Causes of the Delay in the Westminster Scrutiny* (London, 1784).

JEBB, JOHN, *The Works Theological, Medical, Political, and Miscellaneous of John Jebb . . . With Memoirs of the Life of the Author*, ed. John Disney, 3 vols. (London, 1787).

JERDAN, WILLIAM, *The Autobiography of William Jerdan*, 4 vols. (London, 1832).

KNOX, VICESIMUS, *The Works of Vicesimus Knox*, 7 vols. (London, 1824).

LOLME, J. L. DE, *The Constitution of England, or an Account of the English Government* (London, 1784).

Low-Life: or One Half of the World Knows Not How the Other Half Live, 3rd edn. (London, 1764).

MILES, WILLIAM AUGUSTUS, *The Correspondence of William Augustus Miles on the French Revolution 1789–1817*, ed. Charles Popham Miles, 2 vols. (London, 1890).

[MURRAY, J.], *The Contest* (Newcastle upon Tyne, 1774).

O'BEIRNE, THOMAS LEWIS, *A Candid and Impartial Narrative of the Transactions of the Fleet Under the Command of Lord Howe* (London, 1779).

—— *Considerations on the Late Disturbances* (London, 1780).

—— *Considerations on the Principles of Naval Discipline and Courts-Martial, in Which the Doctrines of the House of Commons and the Conduct of the Naval Courts-Martial on Admiral Keppel and Sir Hugh Palliser are Compared* (London, 1781).

—— *The Proposed System of Trade With Ireland Explained* (London, 1785).

The Parliamentary History of England, From the Earliest Period to the Year 1803, 36 vols. (London, 1806–20).

ROBINSON, JOHN, *The Parliamentary Papers of John Robinson, 1774–1784*, ed. W. T. Laprade, Camden 3rd ser., vol. xxxiii (London, 1922).

SAUSSURE, CÉSAR DE, *A Foreign View of England in the Reigns of George I and George II* (London, 1902).

SAVAGE, JAMES, *An Account of the London Daily Newspapers, and the Manner in Which They Are Conducted* (London, 1811).

SCOTT, JOHN, *A Short Review of Transactions in Bengal During the Last Ten Years* (London, 1782).

—— *A Letter to . . . Edmund Burke, in Reply to the Insinuations in the Ninth Report of the Select Committee, Which Affect the Character of Mr Hastings* (London, 1783).

—— *A Letter to the Right Honourable Charles James Fox* (London, 1783).

—— *The Conduct of His Majesty's Late Ministers Considered* (London, 1784).

—— *A Reply to Mr Burke's Speech of the First of December, 1783, On Mr Fox's East-India Bill* (London, 1784).

—— *Major Scott's Charge Against . . . Edmund Burke* (London, 1789).

—— *A Letter to . . . Edmund Burke, in Reply to His 'Reflections on the Revolution in France', &c* (London, 1790).

SMELT, LEONARD, *An Account of Some Particulars Relative to the Meeting Held at York* (London, 1780).

Society for Constitutional Information, *Tracts Published and Distributed Gratis By the Society for Constitutional Information, With a Design to Convey to the Minds of the People a Knowledge of Their Rights; Principally Those of Representation* (London, 1783).

STEPHEN, JAMES, *The Memoirs of James Stephen. Written by Himself For the Use of His Children*, ed. Merle M. Bevington (London, 1954).

TAYLOR, JOHN, *Records of My Life*, 2 vols. (London, 1832).

TRUSLER, JOHN, *The London Advisor and Guide* (London, 1786).

TURNER, THOMAS, *The Diary of a Georgian Shopkeeper* (Oxford, 1979).

WALPOLE, HORACE, *Horace Walpole's Correspondence*, ed. W. S. Lewis, 48 vols. (London, 1937–83).

[WEST, W.], *Fifty Years' Recollections of an Old Bookseller* (Cork, 1835).

WHITEFOORD, CHARLES, and WHITEFOORD, CALEB, *The Whitefoord Papers. Being the correspondence of Colonel Charles Whitefoord and Caleb Whitefoord from 1739 to 1810*, ed. W. A. S. Hewins (Oxford, 1898).

WILKES, JOHN, *Correspondence of the Late John Wilkes, With His Friends, Printed from the Original Manuscripts, In Which Are Introduced Memoirs of His Life*, ed. John Almon, 5 vols. (London, 1805).

WOODFORDE, JAMES, *The Diary of a Country Parson, 1758–1802* (Oxford, 1978).

WYVILL, CHRISTOPHER, *Political Papers, Chiefly Representing the Attempt . . . to Effect a Reformation of the Parliament of Great Britain*, 5 vols. (York, 1794–1802).

Secondary sources

1720. 1901. History of the Northampton Mercury (Northampton, 1901).

ANDREW, DONNA T., 'Popular Culture and Public Debate: London 1780', *Historical Journal*, 39 (1996), 405–23.

ANDREWS, ALEXANDER, *The History of British Journalism, from the Foundation of the Newspaper Press in England, to the Repeal of the Stamp Act in 1855, with Sketches of Press Celebrities*, 2 vols. (London, 1859).

ASPINALL, A., 'The Social Status of Journalists at the Beginning of the Nineteenth Century', *The Review of English Studies*, 21 (1945), 216–32.

—— 'Statistical Accounts of the London Newspapers in the Eighteenth Century', *EHR* 62 (1948), 210–32.

—— *Politics and the Press: c. 1780–1850* (London, 1949).

AUSTIN, R., 'Robert Raikes, the Elder, & the "Gloucestershire Journal"', *The Library*, 3rd ser., 6 (1915), 1–24.

BAKER, KEITH MICHAEL, *Inventing the French Revolution* (Cambridge, 1990).

BARRY, J., 'The Press and the Politics of Culture in Bristol, 1660–1775', in J. Black and J. Gregory (eds.), *Culture, Politics and Society in Britain, 1660–1800* (Manchester, 1991), 49–81.

BECKETT, ARTHUR, 'The First Sussex Newspaper', *The Sussex County Magazine*, 15 (Aug. 1941), 247–54.

BLACK, EUGENE CHARLTON, *The Association: British Extra-parliamentary Political Organization, 1769–1793* (Cambridge, Mass., 1963).

BLACK, JEREMY, 'Flying a Kite: The Political Impact of the Eighteenth-Century British Press', *Journal of Newspaper and Periodical History*, 1 (1984), 12–19.

—— *The English Press in the Eighteenth Century* (Beckenham, 1987).

BORSAY, PETER, *The English Urban Renaissance: Culture and Society in the Provincial Town 1660–1770* (Oxford, 1989).

BOURNE, H. R. FOX, *English Newspapers: Chapters in the History of Journalism*, 2 vols. (London, 1887).

BRADLEY, J. E., *Religion, Revolution and English Radicalism* (Cambridge, 1990).

BREWER, JOHN, *Party, Ideology and Popular Politics at the Accession of George III* (Cambridge, 1976).

—— *Sinews of Power: War, Money and the English State, 1688–1783* (London, 1989).

BROOKE, RICHARD, *Liverpool as it Was During the Last Quarter of the Eighteenth Century: 1775 to 1800* (Liverpool, 1853).

BROOKS, COLIN, 'John Reeves and his Correspondents: A Contribution to the Study of British Loyalism, 1792–1793', in L. Domergue and G. Lamoine (eds.), *Après 89: La Révolution modèle ou repoussoir* (Toulouse, 1991), 49–76.

BRUSHFIELD, T. N., *The Life and Bibliography of Andrew Brice, Author and Journalist; With Some Remarks On the Early History of the Exeter Newspaper Press* ([Exeter?], 1888).

BURTON, K. G., *The Early Newspaper Press in Berkshire (1723–1855)* (Reading, 1954).

BUTTERFIELD, HERBERT, *George III, Lord North and the People: 1779–1780* (London, 1949).

CANNON, JOHN, *Parliamentary Reform 1640–1832* (Cambridge, 1973).

CENSER, JACK R., and POPKIN, JEREMY D. (eds.), *Press and Politics in Pre-Revolutionary France* (Berkeley, 1987).

CHRISTIE, IAN R., *Wilkes, Wyvill and Reform: The Parliamentary Reform Movement in British Politics, 1760–1785* (London, 1962).

—— 'British Newspapers in the Later Georgian Age', in Ian R. Christie, *Myth and Reality in Late Eighteenth-Century British Politics and Other Papers* (London, 1970), 311–33.

CLARE, D., 'The Growth and Importance of the Newspaper Press in Manchester, Liverpool, Sheffield and Leeds', *Transactions of the Lancashire and Cheshire Antiquarian Society*, 123 (1963), 101–23.

CLARKE, PETER (ed.), *The Transformation of English Provincial Towns 1660–1800* (London, 1984).

CLARKE, W. J., *Early Nottingham Printers and Printing*, 2nd edn. (Nottingham, 1953).

COLERIDGE, HARTLEY, *The Worthies of Yorkshire and Lancashire* (London, 1836).

COLLEY, LINDA, *In Defiance of Oligarchy: The Tory Party, 1714–1760* (Cambridge, 1982).

—— *Britons: Forging the Nation 1707–1827* (New Haven and London, 1992).

CRANE, R. S., and KAYE, F. B., 'A Census of British Newspapers and Periodicals, 1620–1800', *Studies in Philology*, 24 (1927), 1–205.

CRANFIELD, G. A., *A Handlist of English Provincial Newspapers and Periodicals 1700–1760*, Cambridge Bibliographical Society Monographs, 2 (Cambridge, 1952).

—— 'A Handlist of English Provincial Newspapers and Periodicals, 1700–1760: Additions and Corrections', *Transactions of the Cambridge Bibliographical Society*, 2 (1956), 269–74.

—— *The Development of the Provincial Newspaper, 1700–1760* (Cambridge, 1962).

CRESSY, D., *Literacy and the Social Order* (London, 1975).

CROLY, GEORGE, *The Personal History of His Late Majesty George the Fourth*, 2nd edn. (London, 1841).

DARNTON, ROBERT, and ROCHE, DANIEL (eds.), *The Revolution in Print: The Press in France, 1775–1800* (Berkeley, 1989).

DAVIES, R., *A Memoir of the York Press* (London, 1868).

DICKINSON, H. T., *Liberty and Property: Political Ideology in Eighteenth-Century Britain* (London, 1977).

—— *Radical Politics in the North-East of England in the Later Eighteenth Century* (Durham, 1979).

—— *The Politics of the People in Eighteenth-Century Britain* (Basingstoke, 1995).

DYMOND, ROBERT, 'Trewman's Exeter Flying Post', *The Western Antiquary*, 5 (1886), 163–6.

EARLE, PETER, *The Making of the English Middle Class: Business, Society and Family Life in London, 1660–1730* (London, 1989).

EHRMAN, JOHN, *The Younger Pitt: The Years of Acclaim* (London, 1969).

ELEY, GEOFF, 'Re-thinking the Political: Social History and Political Culture in 18th and 19th Century Britain', *Archiv für Sozialgeschichte*, 21 (1981), 427–57.

ELLIS, AYTOUN, *The Penny Universities* (London, 1956).

FEATHER, JOHN, *The Provincial Book Trade in Eighteenth-Century England* (Cambridge, 1985).

FERDINAND, C. Y., 'Local Distribution Networks in Eighteenth-Century England', in R. Myers and M. Harris (eds.), *Spreading the Word: The Distribution Networks of Print 1550–1850* (Winchester, 1990), 131–49.

—— *Benjamin Collins and the Provincial Newspaper Trade in the Eighteenth Century* (Oxford, 1997).

FRASER, D., 'The Press in Leicester c. 1790–1850', *Transactions of the Leicestershire Archaeological and Historical Society*, 42 (1966–7), 53–75.

—— (ed.), *A History of Modern Leeds* (Manchester, 1980).

FURET, FRANÇOIS, *Interpreting the French Revolution*, trans. Elborg Forster (Cambridge, 1981).

GIBB, MILDRED A., and BECKWITH, FRANK, *The Yorkshire Post, Two Centuries* (Leeds, 1954).

GOODMAN, DENA, 'Public Sphere and Private Life: Toward a Synthesis of Current Historiographical Approaches to the Old Regime', *History and Theory*, 31 (1992), 1–20.

GOODRICKE, CHARLES ALFRED (ed.), *History of the Goodricke Family* (London, 1885).

GORDON, DANIEL, 'Philosophy, Sociology, and Gender in the Enlightenment Conception of Public Opinion', *French Historical Studies*, 17 (1992), 882–911.

GRANT, JAMES, *The Newspaper Press: Its Origin, Progress, and Present Position*, 3 vols. (London, 1871–2).

GREGORY, A., *Robert Raikes: Journalist and Philanthropist* (London, 1877).

GUNN, J. A. W., *Beyond Liberty and Property: The Process of Self-Recognition in Eighteenth-Century Political Thought* (Kingston, Ont., 1983).

HABERMAS, JÜRGEN, *The Structural Transformation of the Public Sphere*, trans. Thomas Burger (Cambridge, Mass., 1989).

HADLEY, W. W., *The Bi-centenary Record of the Northampton Mercury* (Northampton, 1920).

HAIG, ROBERT L., *The Gazetteer, 1735–1797: A Study in the Eighteenth-Century English Newspaper* (Carbondale, Ill., 1960).

HAMMOND, N. G. L., and SCULLFORD, H. H. (eds.), *The Oxford Classical Dictionary*, 2nd edn. (Oxford, 1970).

HANDOVER, P. M., *A History of the London Gazette* (London, 1965).

HANSON, LAURENCE, *Government and the Press, 1695–1763* (Oxford, 1936).

HARRIS, BOB, *A Patriot Press: National Politics and the London Press in the 1740s* (Oxford, 1993).

——*Politics and the Rise of the Press: Britain and France, 1620–1800* (London, 1996).

HARRIS, MICHAEL, *London Newspapers in the Age of Walpole: A Study in the Origins of the Modern English Press* (London, 1987).

——and LEE, ALAN (eds.), *The Press in English Society from the Seventeenth to the Nineteenth Centuries* (London, 1986).

HARRIS, TIM, *London Crowds in the Reign of Charles II: Propaganda and Politics from the Restoration until the Exclusion Crisis* (Cambridge, 1987).

HELLMUTH, ECKHART, '"The Palladium of All Other English Liberties": Reflections on the Liberty of the Press in England during the 1760s and 1770s', in Eckhart Hellmuth (ed.), *The Transformation of Political Culture: England and Germany in the Late Eighteenth Century* (Oxford, 1990), 467–501.

HERD, HAROLD, *The March of Journalism: The Story of the British Press from 1622 to the Present Day* (London, 1952).

HICKS, P. S., *Neo-classical History and English Culture: From Clarendon to Hume* (New York, 1996).

HILL, JOSEPH, *The Book Makers of Old Birmingham* (Birmingham, 1907).

HINDLE, WILFRID, *The Morning Post, 1772–1937: Portrait of a Newspaper* (London, 1937).

HODGSON, J., THE YOUNGER, 'Thomas Slack of Newcastle, Printer, 1723–1784,

Founder of the "Newcastle Chronicle"', *Archaeologia Aeliana*, 3rd ser., 17 (1920), 145–52.

HOLMES, G., 'The Sacheverell Riots: The Crowd and the Church in Early Eighteenth-Century London', *Past and Present*, 72 (1976), 55–85.

HOPPIT, JULIAN, *Risk and Failure in English Business 1700–1800* (Cambridge, 1987).

HOUSTON, R., *Scottish Literacy and Scottish Identity: Illiteracy and Society in Scotland and Northern England 1600–1800* (Cambridge, 1985).

HOWATSON, M. C. (ed.), *The Oxford Companion to Classical Literature*, 2nd edn. (Oxford, 1989).

HUNT, F. KNIGHT, *The Fourth Estate: Contributions towards a History of Newspapers, and the Liberty of the Press* (London, 1850).

KNOX, T. R., 'Popular Politics and Provincial Radicalism: Newcastle upon Tyne, 1769–1785', *Albion*, 11 (1979), 224–41.

——'"Peace for Ages to Come": The Newcastle Elections of 1780 and 1784', *Durham University Journal*, 84 (1992), 3–19.

LANGFORD, PAUL, *A Polite and Commercial People* (Oxford, 1989).

——*Public Life and the Propertied Englishman, 1689–1798* (Oxford, 1991).

LAW, C. M., 'Some Notes on the Urban Population in the Eighteenth Century', *Local Historian*, 10 (1972), 13–26.

LILLYWHITE, BRYANT, *London Coffee Houses* (London, 1963).

LLOYD, LLEWELYN C., 'The Book Trade in Shropshire', *Shropshire Archaeological Society Transactions*, 98 (1935–6), 65–142 and 145–200.

LOONEY, J. JEFFERSON, 'Cultural Life in the Provinces: Leeds and York, 1720–1820', in A. L. Beir, David Cannadine, and James M. Rosenheim (eds.), *The First Modern Society: Essays in English History in Honour of Lawrence Stone* (Cambridge, 1989), 483–510.

LUTNICK, SOLOMON, *The American Revolution and the British Press: 1775–1783* (New York, 1967).

MCKENDRICK, N., BREWER, J., and PLUMB, J. H., *The Birth of a Consumer Society: The Commercialization of Eighteenth-Century England* (London, 1992).

MACKENZIE, E., *A Descriptive and Historical Account of the Town and County of Newcastle upon Tyne* (Newcastle upon Tyne, 1827).

MAXTED, IAN, *The London Book Trades 1775–1800* (Folkestone, 1977).

MITCHELL, B. R., *British Historical Statistics* (Cambridge, 1988).

MITCHELL, L. G., *Charles James Fox* (Oxford, 1992).

MONEY, JOHN, *Experience and Identity: Birmingham and the West Midlands, 1760–1800* (Manchester, 1977).

MORGAN, F. C., 'Hereford Printers and Booksellers', *Transactions of the Woolhope Naturalists' Field Club, Herefordshire* (1941), 106–27.

MUDDIMAN, J. G., *A Tercentenary Handlist of English and Welsh Newspapers, Magazines and Reviews* (London, 1920).

NAMIER, SIR LEWIS, and BROOKE, JOHN, *The History of Parliament: The House of Commons, 1754–1790*, 3 vols. (London, 1964).

NEWMAN, AUBREY (ed.), *The Parliamentary Lists of the Early Eighteenth Century: Their Compilation and Use* (Leicester, 1973).

NICHOLS, JOHN, *Literary Anecdotes of the Eighteenth Century*, 9 vols. (London, 1812–15).

NUTTALL, D., 'A History of Printing in Chester', *Journal of the Chester Archaeological Society*, 54 (1967), 37–95.

O'GORMAN, FRANK, *Voters, Patrons, and Parties: The Unreformed Electoral System of Hanoverian England 1734–1832* (Oxford, 1989).

OZOUF, MONA, 'L'Opinion publique', in Keith Michael Baker (ed.), *The Political Culture of the Old Regime* (Oxford, 1987), 419–34.

PEBODY, CHARLES, *English Journalism, and the Men Who Have Made It* (London, 1882).

PETERS, MARIE, *Pitt and Popularity: The Patriot Minister and London Opinion during the Seven Years' War* (Oxford, 1980).

——'Historians and the Eighteenth-Century English Press: A Review of Possibilities and Problems', *Australian Journal of Politics and History*, 34 (1988), 37–50.

PHILLIPS, N. C., 'Edmund Burke and the County Movement, 1779–1780', *EHR* 76 (1961), 254–78.

POCOCK, J. G. A., *Virtue, Commerce and Society* (Cambridge, 1976).

POPKIN, JEREMY D., *News and Politics in the Age of Revolution: Jean Luzac's Gazette de Leyde* (Berkeley, 1989).

PORRITT, EDWARD, 'The Government and the Newspaper Press in England', *Political Science Quarterly*, 12 (1897), 666–83.

RAVEN, JAMES, *Judging New Wealth: Popular Publishing and Responses to Commerce, 1750–1800* (Oxford, 1992).

——SMALL, HELEN, and TADMOR, NAOMI (eds.), *The Practice and Representation of Reading in England* (Cambridge, 1996).

READ, DONALD, 'North of England Newspapers (c.1700–c.1900) and their Value to Historians', *Proceedings of the Leeds Philosophical and Literary Society*, 8 (1957), 200–15.

——*Press and the People, 1790–1850: Opinion in Three English Cities* (London, 1961).

REID, CHRISTOPHER, *Edmund Burke and the Practice of Political Writing* (Dublin, 1985).

ROGERS, DEBORAH D., *Bookseller as Rogue: John Almon and the Politics of Eighteenth-Century Publishing* (New York, 1986).

ROGERS, NICHOLAS, *Whigs and Cities: Popular Politics in the Age of Walpole and Pitt* (Oxford, 1989).

RUDÉ, GEORGE, *Wilkes and Liberty: A Social Study of 1763 to 1774* (Oxford, 1962).

——*Hanoverian London, 1714–1808* (London, 1971).

RULE, JOHN, *Albion's People: English Society, 1714–1815* (London, 1992).

SAUNDERS, BAILY (ed.), *The Life and Letters of James Macpherson* (London, 1894).

SCHOFIELD, R. S., 'Dimensions of Illiteracy, 1750–1850', *Explorations in Economic History*, 10 (1973), 437–54.

SCHWARZ, L. D., *London Life in the Age of Industrialisation: Entrepreneurs, Labour Force and Living Conditions, 1700–1850* (Cambridge, 1992).

SCHWEIZER, K., and KLEIN, R., 'The French Revolution and the Developments in the London Daily Press to 1793', *Publishing History*, 18 (1985), 85–97.

SHEAHAN, JAMES JOSEPH, *General and Concise History and Description of the Town and Port of Kingston-Upon-Hull* (London, 1864).

SICHEL, WALTER, *Sheridan*, 2 vols. (London, 1909).

SIEBERT, FREDERICK, *Freedom of the Press in England, 1476–1776: The Rise and Fall of Government Control* (Urbana, Ill., 1965).

SMITH, R. J., *The Gothic Bequest: Medieval Institutions in British Thought, 1688–1863* (Cambridge, 1987).

SPUFFORD, MARGARET, 'First Steps in Literacy: The Reading and Writing Experiences of the Humblest Seventeenth-Century Spiritual Autobiographies', *Social History*, 4 (1979), 407–35.

STEINBERG, S. H., *Five Hundred Years of Printing* (London, 1959).

STEPHEN, SIR LESLIE, and LEE, SIR SIDNEY (eds.), *Dictionary of National Biography*, 22 vols. (Oxford, 1917 onwards).

STYLES, JOHN, 'Print and Policing: Crime Advertising in Eighteenth-Century Provincial England', in Douglas Hay and Francis Snyder (eds.), *Policing and Prosecution in Britain 1750–1850* (Oxford, 1989), 55–111.

THOMAS, P. D. G., 'The Beginning of Parliamentary Reporting in Newspapers, 1768–1774', *EHR* 74 (1959), 623–36.

THOMPSON, E. P., 'Eighteenth-Century English Society: Class Struggle without Class?', *Social History*, 3 (1978), 133–65.

TIMPERLEY, C. H., *A Dictionary of Printers and Printing* (London, 1839).

Victoria County History of Warwick. Vol. VII: The City of Coventry and the Borough of Warwick, ed. W. B. Stephens (Oxford, 1969).

Victoria County History of Yorkshire: The City of York, ed. P. M. Tillott (Oxford, 1961).

WAHRMAN, DROR, 'Virtual Representation: Parliamentary Reporting and Languages of Class in the 1790s', *Past and Present*, 136 (1992), 83–113.

WATSON, G. (ed.), *The New Cambridge Bibliography of English Literature* (Cambridge, 1971).

WATSON, S. F., 'Some Materials for a History of Printing and Publishing in Ipswich', *Proceedings of the Suffolk Institute of Archaeology and Natural History*, 24 (1949), 182–227.

WELFORD, R., 'Early Newcastle Typography, 1639–1800', *Archaeologia Aeliana*, 3rd ser., 3 (1907), 1–134.

WERKMEISTER, LUCYLE, *The London Daily Press: 1772–1792* (Lincoln, Nebr., 1963).

WICKWAR, WILLIAM, *The Struggle for the Freedom of the Press* (London, 1928).

WILES, R. M., 'Further Additions and Corrections to G. A. Cranfield's *Handlist of English Provincial Newspapers and Periodicals 1700–1760*', *Transactions of the Cambridge Bibliographical Society*, 2 (1958), 385–9.

—— *Freshest Advices: Early Provincial Newspapers in England* (Columbus, Ohio, 1965).

WILSON, KATHLEEN, *The Sense of the People: Politics, Culture and Imperialism in England, 1715–1785* (Cambridge, 1995).

WILSON, R. G., *Gentlemen Merchants: The Merchant Community in Leeds, 1700–1830* (Manchester, 1971).

WRIGLEY, E. A., and SCHOFIELD, R. S., *The Population of England, 1541–1871* (London, 1981).

Unpublished theses

ANDREW, J. D., 'The Derbyshire Newspaper Press, 1720–1855' (University of Reading MA thesis, 1954).

ASQUITH, IVON, 'James Perry and the *Morning Chronicle*, 1790–1821' (University of London Ph.D. thesis, 1973).

AUSTEN, BRIAN, 'British Mail-Coach Services 1784–1850' (University of London Ph.D. thesis, 1979).

BROWN, SUSAN E., 'Politics, Commerce and Social Policy in the City of London, 1782–1802' (University of Oxford D.Phil. thesis, 1992).

CLARE, D., 'The Growth and Importance of the Newspaper Press in Manchester, Liverpool, Sheffield and Leeds between 1780 and 1800' (University of Manchester MA thesis, 1960).

GALLOP, D. F., 'Chapters in the History of the Provincial Newspaper Press, 1700–1855' (University of Reading MA thesis, 1952).

HUMPHRIES, PETER L., 'Kentish Politics and Public Opinion 1768–1832' (University of Oxford D.Phil. thesis, 1981).

LOONEY, J. J., 'Advertising and Society in England, 1720–1820: A Statistical Analysis of Yorkshire Newspaper Advertisements' (Princeton University Ph.D. thesis, 1983).

PRICE, F. C., 'The Parliamentary Elections in York City 1754–1790' (University of Manchester MA thesis, 1958).

SWEET, R., *The Writing of Urban History in Eighteenth-Century England* (Oxford 1997).

TRIFFITT, JOHN M., 'Politics and the Urban Community: Parliamentary Boroughs in the South West of England 1710–1730' (University of Oxford D.Phil. thesis, 1985).

INDEX